Colin Gunton,
Tim Keller, and the
Trinitarian Challenge
to Individualism

Colin Gunton, Tim Keller, and the Trinitarian Challenge to Individualism

Towards Reframing Faith and Work Theology

Steve Pearson

☙PICKWICK *Publications* · Eugene, Oregon

COLIN GUNTON, TIM KELLER, AND THE TRINITARIAN CHALLENGE TO INDIVIDUALISM
Towards Reframing Faith and Work Theology

Copyright © 2025 Steve Pearson. All rights reserved. Except for brief quotations in critical publications or reviews, no part of this book may be reproduced in any manner without prior written permission from the publisher. Write: Permissions, Wipf and Stock Publishers, 199 W. 8th Ave., Suite 3, Eugene, OR 97401.

Pickwick Publications
An Imprint of Wipf and Stock Publishers
199 W. 8th Ave., Suite 3
Eugene, OR 97401

www.wipfandstock.com

PAPERBACK ISBN: 979-8-3852-2226-1
HARDCOVER ISBN: 979-8-3852-2227-8
EBOOK ISBN: 979-8-3852-2228-5

Cataloguing-in-Publication data:

Names: Pearson, Steve, author.

Title: Colin Gunton, Tim Keller, and the trinitarian challenge to individualism : Towards reframing faith and work theology / Steve Pearson.

Description: Eugene, OR : Pickwick Publications, 2025 | **Includes bibliographical references.**

Identifiers: ISBN 979-8-3852-2226-1 (paperback) | ISBN 979-8-3852-2227-8 (hardcover) | ISBN 979-8-3852-2228-5 (ebook)

Subjects: LCSH: Gunton, Colin E. | Keller, Timothy, 1950–2023. | Theology. | Trinitarians. | Work—Religious aspects—Christianity.

Classification: BT738.5 .P43 2025 (paperback) | BT738.5 (ebook)

VERSION NUMBER 08/01/25

Contents

List of Figures | vii
List of Tables | viii
Acknowledgments | ix
Introduction | xi

1 The Problem of Identity in a Market Economy | 1
2 Gunton's Theology of Identity: *Perichoresis* and the *Imago Dei* | 17
3 Gunton's Biography of Individualism: Tracing the Path from Augustine to Adidas | 68
4 Limitations and Blind Spots in Faith and Work Theology | 130
5 Tim Keller's Cartesian Conversion | 208
6 Theology and Identity in a Market Economy | 249
7 Concluding Reflections, Lessons, and Future Directions | 272

Bibliography | 285

List of Figures

Figure 01: Gunton's Construction View of Individualism Versus Predominant Subtraction Theories | 73

Figure 02: Illustration of Gunton's Position Relative to the Broader Trinitarian Renaissance | 74

Figure 03: Miller's Graphic Depiction of the Integration Box | 148

Figure 04: Radar Chart as an Alternative to Miller's Circles and Square Graphic | 159

List of Tables

Table 1: Gunton's Three Main Complaints Against Augustine | 88

Table 2: Parallel Page References for Augustine and Irenaeus in *The One, the Three, and the Many* | 99

Table 3: Van Duzer's Application of Niebuhr's Typologies | 175

Table 4: Keller's Summary of Theology Shift | 246

Acknowledgments

THEOLOGICAL THINKING AND WRITING are an investment in the mission of the Church. This project has deepened my appreciation for those who have published their thoughts. I acknowledge the privilege of reflecting on their contribution.

I wish to express gratitude to Professor Dion Forster for his guidance, encouragement, and friendship, to Reverend Ian Cowley for decades of mentorship, and to Lee-Anne Roux for invaluable help in editing and proofreading. Finally, I acknowledge the ongoing support of my wife, Mandy, and our three children, Jenna, Zoë, and Lydia.

Introduction

IDENTITY STANDS AS ONE of the most pressing concepts in our society today, shaping our personal and communal realities in profound ways. Among the forces shaping modern identity, the market economy emerges as arguably the most influential. From a theological perspective, identity is central to Christian life, touching on core doctrinal truths. However, while identity in Christianity and the market economy bear similarities, their underlying definitions often diverge significantly. This book argues that theology has largely failed to critically engage with these differences, hindered by a lack of awareness around the doctrines implicit in the market economy. One underlying issue is theology's susceptibility to individualism, which obstructs a clear view of the challenges posed by modern identity. Compounding this is an insufficient connection between identity and the doctrine of God, weakening theological engagement overall.

The aim of this book is to illuminate these overlooked threats and to advocate for a theological re-prioritization within the market economy. The dominant frameworks of ethics and evangelism, widely utilized in this discourse, are often over-relied upon and rooted in an uncritical adoption of individualistic perspectives. This study, therefore, spans two diverse yet interconnected fields: contemporary discussions on faith and work, and the systematic theology of identity. These fields are brought into conversation through two principal thinkers, Colin Gunton and Tim Keller. Keller, a key voice in the faith and work movement, is critically examined here through the lens of Gunton's theology of identity, alongside contemporary social criticism. Where Keller's insights fall short—an unfortunately frequent occurrence—other leading scholars in faith and work are drawn in to strengthen the discussion.

Colin Gunton, a prominent scholar in the Trinitarian movement, is noted for his critical analysis of individualism and his constructive use of *perichoresis* in rethinking modern identity. He sees individualism not as a mere cultural trend but as deeply rooted in a theological construct with origins in Augustine's thought. Gunton advocates for a relational ontology, aiming to address the limitations he perceives in Barth's foundationalism and muted pneumatology, shifting from an *analogia entis* to an *analogia relationis*. Gunton's insights into individualism and his departure from classical theological frameworks provide valuable depth in addressing the contemporary identity crisis, particularly through the doctrine of atonement.

While some of Gunton's theological conclusions are contested, his application of *perichoresis* presents a compelling framework for prioritizing identity as a theological foundation. Among Gunton's contributions, this book argues that the concept of mediation should take a central role, finding its expression in worship, vulnerability, and trust. In so doing, this work seeks to offer a renewed theological approach to identity within the realities of the market economy, grounded in relational and communal understanding.

Chapter 1 introduces the core themes of the book, setting the stage for an exploration of identity within the context of the market economy and its theological implications. The chapter begins by explaining the relevance and importance of the topic, laying out why this conversation matters for contemporary Christian theology. It provides a brief overview of how the concept of identity is shaped by the forces of modernity, particularly within the marketplace. Key figures whose scholarly contributions will guide the discussion—such as Colin Gunton and Timothy Keller—are introduced, giving readers a sense of the theological and intellectual landscape.

This outline of this book's structure offers a roadmap for how the argument will unfold across the subsequent chapters. It also helps orient the reader to the questions driving this book endeavor, particularly how Gunton's theology of identity engages with Keller's approach to faith and work in the modern economy. The final part of this chapter reflects on my personal motivations for pursuing this book, offering insight into the deeper questions and concerns that inspired the project.

Chapter 2 explores the two key aspects of Colin Gunton's contribution to the theology of identity. While Gunton is widely recognized for his constructive Trinitarian theology, this chapter explores how that theology interacts with his equally important critique of individualism—a central theme in this book. This chapter offers an overview of Gunton's theological development, laying the groundwork for chapter 3, which will focus on Gunton's engagement with Augustine and his critique of Western theology.

The chapter traces Gunton's journey from his early academic work, particularly his doctoral thesis on foundationalism, to his role as a leading British theologian. A central focus is on Gunton's shift from the concept of *analogia entis* (the analogy of being) to *analogia relationis* (the analogy of relationship), which shaped his understanding of identity. The doctrine of *perichoresis*, the relational dynamic of the Trinity, becomes key to his theological approach. The chapter also highlights the influences that shaped Gunton's thought, including his challenges to Barth's theology and his appreciation for figures like Coleridge, the Cappadocians, and Irenaeus.

While Augustine is a pivotal figure in Gunton's critique of individualism, his work is only touched upon briefly in this chapter, as a more in-depth examination of Augustine will follow in chapter 3. Here, the focus is on setting the stage for that later discussion by balancing an appreciative review of Gunton's work with the critical responses it has attracted. One of the key questions raised in this chapter is whether Gunton overreaches in his attempt to build a relational ontology. Does his strong emphasis on relationality lead to any significant theological omissions?

Though the chapter does not provide a definitive answer, it lays an essential foundation for the deeper exploration in the next chapter. The groundwork established here will help the reader better understand the stakes involved in Gunton's theological approach, particularly how his views on relational ontology set the stage for his critique of Augustine and the broader theological crisis of individualism in Western thought.

Chapter 3 investigates Gunton's bold and controversial claim that Augustine is the father of modern individualism. Gunton's treatment of Augustine has sparked significant debate and criticism, and this chapter enters the discussion with measured expectations. Nevertheless, it insists that even if Gunton's conclusions are only partially correct, his argument still represents a crucial contribution to theological engagement with the market economy. This chapter situates Gunton's critique within the larger debate over whether individualism is a product construction or subtraction. This is an important preamble to Gunton's views as they draw attention to the subversive claims of his "reversal." Individualism is the offspring of bad theology and not the emancipation from it.

The chapter traces the evolution of Gunton's views on Augustine, noting that his critique intensified as his Trinitarian theology matured. By exploring both Gunton's critics and supporters, this section provides a balanced perspective on his Augustinian critique, while also reinforcing the importance of reading Gunton's thoughts in the context of his broader project on the contemporary theological crisis. To absolve Augustine without addressing Gunton's charge that individualism remains entrenched in modern theology would, according to Gunton, miss the point entirely. His critics, despite their valid insights, fail to fully engage with the heart of his critique.

The chapter also draws parallels between Gunton's ideas and those of Charles Taylor, highlighting the shared recognition of a theological legacy of individualism that demands deeper engagement. Gunton's assertion that Western theology has become overly focused on "mediating grace to the individual" leads to the troubling conclusion that Christianity itself has become a personal identity attribute, shaped by the market's demands. This chapter, in dialogue with the critique of individualism, prepares the ground for the discussions in chapters 4 and 5, where the hypothesis about individualism' *perichoresis* and identity.

Chapter 4 opens with an exploration of David Miller's account of the history of the Faith and Work movement, establishing a solid foundation for understanding the four main genres that have emerged within this movement. Miller's typology is used as a framework to assess the contributions of key thinkers such as Miroslav Volf, Jeff Van Duzer, and Richard Higginson. These engagements serve as preparatory groundwork for the more detailed examination of Timothy Keller's theology in chapter 5.

While the focus on ethics and evangelism within the Faith and Work movement is relatively easy to validate, the absence of a more nuanced and critical engagement with the complexities of modern identity and economics calls for a broader exploration. Chapter 4 expands the conversation beyond the theological academy by incorporating perspectives on the market economy from secular sources. This wider engagement highlights a critical gap in theological responses: the lack of complexity and depth in addressing the forces shaping modern identity.

The chapter argues that this absence of engagement with deeper, more systemic issues in theology is a manifestation of the individualism that draws ethical concerns into a narrow, personal orbit. The result is a theology that remains focused on individual moral responsibility while failing to challenge the broader market structures that influence identity formation. By identifying this gap, chapter 4 sets the stage for the critique of Keller in chapter 5, which will explore how his theology both reflects and struggles with these same limitations.

Chapter 5 builds upon the insights from chapter 4 by offering a detailed and critical engagement with Timothy Keller's theology, specifically through an analysis of *Every Good Endeavor*. A broader introduction to Keller situates his work within the context of his ministry and theological contributions, providing a foundation for a critical reading of his approach to faith, work, and identity. This chapter cross-references Keller's work with his other writings and sermons to ensure a thorough understanding of his theological framework.

However, under closer scrutiny, Keller's theology reveals significant shortcomings. The chapter dedicates substantial attention to Keller's missed opportunities to engage more critically with macroeconomic forces and identity-shaping structures. Keller, despite having the theological resources to offer a more critical perspective, falls short in addressing these broader issues. This failure echoes Charles Taylor's concept of "curious blindness," where one fails to fully grasp or confront the deeper implications of one's own position. The chapter concludes by aligning Keller's limitations with Gunton's description of a deeper theological crisis, reinforcing the need for more profound engagement with modernity.

Additionally, the chapter examines Keller's references to the Trinity—both explicit and implicit—and their influence on his understanding of identity. Despite Keller's opposition to individualism, his theology remains entrenched in the very individualism he seeks to critique. This paradox underscores the larger argument of the chapter: that Keller's approach, while influential, is ultimately shaped by the very cultural forces it aims to resist.

Chapter 6 brings together the key threads of the book, addressing the central question of how Gunton's theology can provide resources for a more robust theology of faith and work. It argues that the current theological response to the market economy, particularly regarding identity, is insufficient. The chapter highlights how the market economy has a more profound influence on the formation of identity than theology currently does, exposing the urgent need for a more effective theological engagement.

This chapter revisits the complexities of causality and individualism, drawing on the insights of both Gunton and Taylor to argue that theology has played a significant role in shaping modern individualism. Gunton's claim that individualism is the offspring of flawed theology—rather than its antidote—becomes central to the argument. The chapter asserts that individualism, as it manifests in today's culture, is fundamentally at odds with its own promises of freedom and autonomy, and theology must be the first to address this contradiction.

However, the chapter also acknowledges the limitations of Gunton's constructive theology. While his ideas provide a valuable foundation for rethinking identity and relationality, they also exhibit some of the same weaknesses found in Augustine and Keller's theologies. Gunton's work alone cannot serve as a stand-alone solution but must be integrated into a broader, multidisciplinary response that addresses the complexities of modern identity in relation to the market economy. By recognizing these limitations, the chapter advocates for a more moderate approach that incorporates theological insights within a wider framework of critical engagement.

Chapter 7 serves as a conclusion, directly addressing the questions posed in the beginning of the book. It reflects on how the inquiry evolved over its course, leading to shifts in emphasis and a re-balancing of priorities as new insights emerged. This chapter revisits these questions, aligning their answers with the discussions and findings presented in the preceding chapters, particularly the synthesis provided in chapter 6.

In weaving these elements together, chapter 7 identifies the key issues that have surfaced as critical to the engagement of theology with the market economy and identity. The chapter moves beyond a simple recap, motivating for a conclusion that underscores the book's contributions to an under-explored and under-resourced field.

1

The Problem of Identity in a Market Economy

INTRODUCTION

CHRISTIAN DOCTRINE EXTENDS BEYOND personal belief, playing a crucial role in addressing the disconnect—sometimes even alienation—between faith and daily life.[1] The focus of this book is on the concept of identity, a subject that resonates deeply with every Christian and lies at the heart of Christian doctrine. The central issue examined concerns the Christian doctrine of human identity and how it is significantly undermined by the market economy.[2] By exploring identity formation and linking it to the doctrine of God, it is argued that Reformed[3] theology offers vital resources for engaging with the market economy.

---

1. Agang, "Work."

2. The intent here is to provide a broad definition of the market. This book does not engage in macroeconomics or offer a detailed description of market economy types. Instead, it focuses on the challenges to Christian identity arising from participation in economies that are largely governed by the laws of supply and demand. The use of "global" acknowledges the interrelation between market economies across national borders and the similarities this creates between these economies. Specifically, Christians living in London or New York will have similar experiences within the economy.

3. The diversity of theology requires careful use and explanation of terminology. Ford's adaptation of Frei's typology in *Modern Theologians* provides valuable clarity in delineating the focus area for this book. Ford's Type 2 "insists that Christian identity is

Drawing on Colin Gunton's critique of individualism as a foundation, this book examines the legitimacy of individualism in modern society. Gunton's concept of *perichoresis*—the interrelationship within the Trinity—offers a theological foundation for understanding human identity in connection to the doctrine of God. For Gunton, the predominant theological heritage of the West leaves it impotent in discerning the contemporary theological crisis and, consequently, unable to offer an adequate response.

Interrogating Gunton's claims involves exploring individualism alongside the implicit and explicit use of *perichoresis* in the works of Timothy Keller—a prominent figure in the Faith and Work field.[4] By critically examining Keller and others, this analysis argues that Faith and Work theology is not adequately equipped to bridge the disconnect Christians often experience between their faith and everyday life.[5] This weakness arises from a lack of critical depth and an insufficient grounding of identity in the doctrine of God.

---

primary and that all other reality needs to be construed in relation to it, but also that Christianity itself needs continually to be rethought and that theology must engage seriously with the modern world in its quest for understanding" (p. 2). This definition captures the essential components of the primacy of Christian identity and the necessity of rethinking theology to engage with the modern world. Both points apply to the selected authors and will be supported through the research itself.

To explain how "Reformed" is understood in this book, Fergusson and Nimmo's *Cambridge Companion to Reformed Theology* provides valuable insight. They caution against narrowly defining "Reformed" solely through the legacy of Calvin. Instead, they describe it as an "identifiable set of theological instincts, a doctrine of impulses—a certain Christian sensibility" (pp. 4–5) Central to this sensibility is the "regular preaching of the Word of God . . . accompanied by a commitment to adult education" (p. 4). Nimmo and Fergusson further emphasize a defining characteristic of Reformed theology: the integration of systematic theology, practical theology, and ethics. They observe that "the commitment both to the unity of Scripture and to a programme of individual and social sanctification ensured that these disciplines were often closely intertwined" (p. 5).

4. This book uses the term "faith and work" to describe the resources available for Christians seeking to critically examine the relationship between their faith and their work in the market economy. In this context, it is acceptable to substitute "work" with "market economy." The first reason for choosing "work" is that it aligns with the terminology used by the Center for Faith and Work, founded by Timothy Keller in New York. The literature review will demonstrate that this movement currently lacks a universal descriptor, and that the use of "faith and work" is suitable for this project. The second reason for selecting "work" is that it is, in many ways, a subset of the term "market economy," specifically referring to individuals engaged in the economy for their livelihood.

5. Agang, "Work," 4.

An argument of this scope demands a broad approach, one that systematically engages with the doctrine of God while also addressing theology's interaction with the market economy. It must span from an in-depth analysis of Augustine's dualism to the theological frameworks of Miller and the Faith and Work movement, and further, into Rosa's theory of dynamic stabilization. This wide-ranging perspective is essential for addressing the central issue. To manage this expansive reach, the focus will be placed on identity formation within the market economy. Though this represents only one aspect of the broader market economy, the argument will assert its critical significance.

The placement of this discussion within systematic theology may seem obvious, given the centrality of the doctrine of God. However, the complexity of modern identity challenges the traditional confines of theological specialization. The findings will demonstrate that understanding identity extends beyond the scope of a single discipline like systematics, and beyond the insights of any one theologian, including Gunton. What is needed is a more collaborative, interdisciplinary approach to fully grasp the nuances of identity in today's context.

The rest of this chapter will offer a broader overview of the topic, underscoring its significance and relevance. This work seeks to bring a fresh perspective to a pressing theological issue. The following sections will outline the main research question and sub-questions, detailing the key considerations that informed their development, and will conclude with a summary to close the chapter.

The Pressing Need for Engagement of the Global Market Economy by Reformed Theology

One of the primary reasons for Christian engagement with the global market economy is its immense influence. If influence were the sole criterion for prioritizing engagement, then the market economy should arguably be at the forefront of Reformed theology's concerns. As Van Duzer notes, "The twenty-first century is destined to be the century of global business. More than any other institution, business is likely to shape the face of our world. The sheer magnitude of resources controlled by companies makes it almost certain that business will dwarf the influence of other traditional institutions."[6] Influence is an aspirational commodity for Reformed the-

---

6. Van Duzer, *Why Business Matters*, 20.

ology, so the notion that the mission of the market might overshadow the *missio Dei* presents an unsettling challenge that requires a thoughtful response—a response that must face the possibility that Reformed theology itself has come under the influence of the market economy.

Van Duzer asserts, "For Christians interested in advancing God's agenda of peace, justice and reconciliation, focus on business and its role in society is critical."[7] For Christian leaders and academics, engaging with the market economy becomes essential. Regardless of personal preferences, the market economy profoundly shapes the daily realities of Christians who turn to universities and church leadership for guidance and resources. In this book, the term "faith and work" refers to those works that have embraced the challenge of critical engagement with these issues. While the primary focus is on identity as a subset of the market economy's influence, there will also be continuous engagement with the broader Faith and Work literature.

Despite the undeniable influence of the market economy, one might expect to find a wealth of critical and diverse resources in the Faith and Work field. However, an initial review of the literature suggests otherwise. Contributions from Reformed theology, in particular, are surprisingly scarce. This gap between expectation and reality is echoed by Volf, who notes, "Amazingly little theological reflection has taken place in the past about an activity that takes up so much of our time. The number of pages theologians have devoted to the question of transubstantiation—which does or does not take place on Sunday—for instance, would, I suspect, far exceed the number of pages devoted to work that fills our lives Monday through Saturday."[8]

Not only are contributions to the Faith and Work field limited in quantity, but they are also narrow in scope. Chapters 4 and 5 will argue that most resources within this literature focus primarily on ethics and missiology.[9] In preparatory research for his own contribution to this subject, Van Duzer comments, "We found a number of useful resources about personal ethics in the workplace but little or no work on building

---

7. Van Duzer, *Why Business Matters*, 21.

8. Volf, *Work in the Spirit*, 69.

9. Unfortunately, some distorted theologies play a significant role in this field. Higginson (*Faith, Hope and the Global Economy*, 24) identifies these as: "prosperity theology," "anti-capitalist theology," and other related forms advocating a "sacred-secular divide." Prosperity theology is an example where the ultimate purposes of the market economy and the church have become blurred. While these distorted theologies will be briefly addressed in the literature review, they largely fall outside the scope of this book.

the underlying theological framework for the discipline as a whole."[10] It is precisely in this area—the development of a robust theological framework—that this work aims to contribute.

We can frame this conclusion in market terms: the vast influence of the market economy creates a strong demand for critical Reformed Christian engagement, a demand that is currently undersupplied. Although contributions to the field are growing, they are predominantly focused on ethics and missiology. What is urgently needed are resources that equip Christians with deeper theological foundations, rather than offering primarily missiological approaches and ethical conclusions.

Identity in the Shifting Landscape of the Global Market Economy

There are many potential points at which to critically engage the market economy, but this work focuses on its impact on identity. The motivation for this choice stems from the significance of identity itself. As noted earlier, "It is a concept that touches every Christian as well as engaging the core of Christian doctrine." The following paragraphs will outline the central challenges related to this topic. These include the overwhelming array of choices involved in identity formation, the fact that these choices are often made with less rationality than we tend to assume, and the frequent absence of a "fixed horizon" to guide decision-making. Additionally, the ever-changing nature of the market introduces new and evolving options for participants, further complicating the process.

Navigating Identity Formation in a World of Limitless Choices

When it comes to choices, identity is increasingly seen as an individual construct rather than an ideological given. The challenge in making these choices lies in the absence of a solid framework to guide decision-making. Taylor describes this dilemma as a "lack of frame or horizon within which things can take on a stable significance, within which some life possibilities can be seen as good or meaningful, others as bad or trivial. The meaning of all these possibilities is unfixed, labile, or undetermined."[11] This work argues that for many Christians, the global market economy

---

10. Van Duzer, *Why Business Matters*, 15.
11. Taylor, *Sources of the Self*, 28.

serves as one of the most influential sources of identity formation. These possibilities come with various labels—corporate culture, company vision and values, financial growth, consumerism, materialism, and brand loyalty. Some of these influences may complement Christian identity, while others may create conflict. Without adequate theological resources, Christians may unknowingly make choices that conflict with or even erode their Christian identity.

The Hidden Forces Shaping Identity: Beyond Rational Choice

Current research is adding more complexity to this challenge by revealing that the identity choices we make are far less rational than we might assume.[12] Smith argues, "Because our hearts are oriented primarily by desire, by what we love, and because those desires are shaped and moulded by the habit-forming practices in which we participate, it is the rituals and practices of the mall—the liturgies of mall and market—that shape our imaginations and how we orient ourselves to the world."[13] This growing complexity increases the pressure on how we resource these challenges, requiring far more than just an ideological response.

Smith highlights a crucial observation regarding the disconnect between the high influence of the market on identity formation and the lack of critical resources to address it. He states, "Christians fail to articulate strategies of resistance because they fail to see a threat. Because they fail to see these cultural institutions and practices as formative—fail to see them as liturgies rather than just neutral, benign 'things we do'—they also fail to recognize what's at stake in them."[14] This theme will be revisited throughout this work. The core issue suggests that not only is there ignorance about the nature of this influence, but that insufficient Christian doctrine may actually contribute to the very forces we seek to challenge. It is ignorance, rather than apathy, that limits our ability to develop a meaningful and critical response.

---

12. While the current research is gaining popularity, the concepts presented are not new. Their origins can be traced back to key resources, such as Polanyi's *Personal Knowledge*. Contemporary researchers are building on these foundations to gain a better understanding of identity formation in modern society.

13. Smith, *Desiring the Kingdom*, 25.

14. Smith, *Desiring the Kingdom*, 126.

Navigating Identity amid Constant Change

The final component of complexity is that many identity choices are dynamic in nature. Chapter 5 will explore Ferry's influence on Timothy Keller and his argument that the natural product cycle relies on redundancy and supersession, creating both technological dependency and an obligation to keep up. Ferry views the market economy as placing "all human activities in a state of perpetual and unending competition."[15] He traces the market economy back to its ideological roots, asserting, "In accordance with Nietzsche's wishes, the idols are all dead; no ideal, in effect, animates or disturbs the course of things, only the imperative of change for the sake of change."[16] While Ferry may overstate the impact of constant change, his point remains valid: the forces of the market are inherently dynamic. The challenges we face today may not be the same as those we will confront tomorrow.

The challenge of constant change should not be underestimated, especially when responding from a Reformed perspective. Reformed theology emerged from a retrospective and defensive context. While the twentieth century has equipped it with more self-critical tools, there remains significant potential for Reformed theology to evolve as a proactive contributor of critical resources.

Introducing Colin Gunton and Timothy Keller

The preceding paragraphs have outlined the critical challenge of identity, emphasizing the significance of the Faith and Work field and the urgent need for theological resources to address human identity. Chapters 4 and 5 will argue that the contributions from the Faith and Work movement are disproportionately small compared to the magnitude of the identity

---

15. Ferry, *Brief History of Thought*, 207.

16. Ferry, *Brief History of Thought*, 207. An additional quote from Ferry (*Brief History of Thought*) is useful. He needs to unpack the irony of Nietzsche's iconoclastic intent, which has created a new form of prisoner. The very change that was intended to liberate has seemingly become a new, iterative prison. "There is a paradox here, of course. On the surface, nothing could seem further removed from the technical world—with its democratic mandate, insipid and collectivist, at the opposite pole to any notion of a 'grand style'—than the aristocratic and poetic formations of Nietzsche. However, by smashing all our idols with his hammer, and delivering us—in the guide of clear-sightedness—bound and gagged to the world of whatever is the case, Nietzsche's thought serves however unintentionally the incessant flux, the hither and thither of modern capitalism" (Ferry, *Brief History of Thought*, 217).

crisis. While identity is a well-researched topic in other areas, its exploration in faith and work literature remains notably light.[17]

The beginning of the chapter highlighted the difficulty of framing a theological problem that resonates deeply within the Faith and Work context, while also allowing for focused and in-depth research. This challenge is addressed through a critical examination of two theologians from different contexts and periods—Timothy Keller, a North American Presbyterian, and Colin Gunton, a British United Reformed scholar. Despite their differing backgrounds, both Keller and Gunton share a common critique of the market and its underlying ideologies. Their concerns center on how these forces can undermine our Christian identity, rooted in being created in the image of God. Both theologians fit into Ford's "Type 2 categorization."[18]

The key difference between Keller and Gunton lies in the depth of their critical engagement and the theological response they offer, particularly concerning the doctrine of God and its connection to identity. As a result, their positions diverge significantly, especially when examining their articulation of *ordo salutis* (the order of salvation). Colin Gunton's Trinitarian theology provides a framework that could have enriched Keller and Alsdorf's book, *Every Good Endeavor: Connecting Your Work to God's Work*.[19] Despite the overlap in their writings, Gunton's central focus on the Trinity is notably absent from Keller's. This omission limits Keller's contribution to the broader theological foundations of the discipline.

Gunton's critique of individualism and his constructive Trinitarian theology, missing in Keller's work, is the gap this book aims to address. However, this endeavor proceeds cautiously, recognizing the relatively selective or limited adoption of Gunton's theology. If Gunton's critiques and constructs sparked a revolution within Reformed theology at the close of the twentieth century, the question remains: what became of that revolution, and why has its influence waned?[20]

---

17. An important question for the reader is why this book does not narrow its focus to identity within the market economy. While there is significant research on the relationship between a market economy and human identity, very little exists within a Christian apologetic framework designed to provide Christians with theological resources. This is only part of the research problem, and the response is better motivated when framed within a broader contextual response to the market economy.

18. Ford, *Modern Theologians*, 2.

19. Keller and Alsdorf, *Every Good Endeavor*.

20. There is a play on the title of Gunton's popular work on Trinitarian theology, *The*

Colin Gunton and *Perichoresis*: A Lens for Human Identity in Modernity

The challenges of modernity made the twentieth century a highly active period for systematic theologians. These challenges centered on modernity's rise to academic prominence at the beginning of the century and its *supposed* collapse toward the end of the century.[21] At the height of its prominence, the central theological debate revolved around the credibility of divine revelation in the face of modernity's emphasis on reason. By the 1980s and 1990s, modernity appeared to be losing ground, as critical reasoning began to turn inward. The focus of debate shifted to the oppressive nature of metanarratives, with many postmodern thinkers viewing homogenization as the antithesis of human freedom.

The late Colin Gunton emerged as a key voice in response to these challenges, particularly during the early 1990s when he became a leading thinker in the "trinitarian revolution."[22] Among his many works, *The One, the Three, and the Many* stands out for its more apologetic tone, directly engaging with the criticisms of homogenization levied against Christianity, particularly Reformed theology. Gunton goes further, turning the critique back on secular culture, accusing it of perpetuating the very tendencies it claims to resist. As he argues, "The much vaunted pluralism of modern secular cultures conceals an underlying tendency to deny plurality and individuality. Modern individualism breeds homogeneity."[23]

Gunton's work is undeniably ambitious, tackling the doctrine of God, offering critiques of Augustine, and still positioning itself firmly within the Reformed tradition. The book maintains a delicate balance: it acknowledges the criticisms modern culture levels against Christianity while simultaneously highlighting modernity's failure to live up to its own core ideals. Gunton goes further, accusing modern culture not only of failing to deliver on its promises of freedom but of replacing it with totalitarianism.[24] For Gunton, the stakes in this debate are significant.

Promise of Trinitarian Theology. In this book, he coins the term "trinitarian revolution" (Gunton, *Promise of Trinitarian Theology*, 128).

21. The use of the word "supposed" is intentional. Part of my later argument regarding the connection between Gunton and Keller is that the modernity project is alive and well in the world of advanced capitalism. This will be both addressed and substantiated in the development of the argument.

22. Gunton, *Promise*.

23. Gunton, *One*, 30.

24. Gunton, *One*, 13.

He reframes the discussion through a redactive critique that effectively rewrites the historical narrative of individualism.

At the heart of Gunton's argument lies the doctrine of God. He asserts, "Modern relativism and scepticism are, then, in part the outcome of the failure of the doctrine of God, and particularly of a doctrine of God as creator."[25] To address this, Gunton turns to the doctrine of the Trinity as the foundation for his relational theology. He argues, "The doctrine of the Trinity replaces a logical conception of the relation between God and the world with a personal one, and accordingly allows us to say two things of utmost importance: that God and the world are ontologically distinct realities; but that distinctiveness, far from being the denial of relations, is its ground."[26]

In his articulation of the Trinity, Gunton builds on Barth's work but aims to move beyond what he views as Barth's limitations. Central to Gunton's argument is the concept of *perichoresis*, which he employs to shift from a logical to a relational understanding of the Trinity. He explains, "The central point about the concept is that it enables theology to preserve both the one and the many in dynamic interrelations. It implies that the three persons of the Trinity exist only in reciprocal eternal relatedness. God is not God apart from the way in which Father, Son and Spirit in eternity give to and receive from each other what they essentially are."[27] This relational view marks a significant departure from the predominant doctrines of God in Western theology. By asserting that the persons of the Trinity exist "only in reciprocal eternal relatedness," Gunton challenges traditional understandings of God's 'substance' or 'being,' engaging critically with Augustine and other theologians on this foundational issue.

The doctrine of the being of God is foundational to theology, with any alteration in this doctrine having far-reaching consequences for

---

25. Gunton, *One*, 123.

26. Gunton, *Promise*, 71. Gunton's primary focus in *The One, the Three, and the Many* is his response to the culture of modernity, leading to a relatively brief treatment of *perichoresis*. For a more detailed engagement with this concept, we must turn to his other works, particularly *The Promise of Trinitarian Theology*, which provides a more comprehensive exploration. The significance of *perichoresis* does not lie in its novelty; relational theology was already well established, with figures like the Cappadocians and Athanasius championing it. Gunton also draws on a range of contemporary theologians to support his emphasis on relationality. What makes *perichoresis* particularly important in this context is its direct challenge to Augustine and the traditional Western doctrine of God, marking a significant theological shift.

27. Gunton, *One*, 164.

other beliefs and doctrines. Gunton highlights this when he critiques Augustine: "In Augustine we are near the beginning of the era in which the church is conceived essentially as an institution mediating grace to the individual rather than of the community formed on the analogy of the Trinity's interpersonal relationships."[28] This quote captures the purpose of this book. If we accept Gunton's critique of individualism and his application of *perichoresis*, along with its implications for the church's soteriological role, then we must ask: has the church moved beyond its role as a mediator of grace to individuals?

Gunton recognizes the significant challenges in reforming our doctrine of God and, by extension, our understanding of relationships and identity. He notes, "Modernity has grave difficulties in construing the relation of people to each other, as we have seen. It has grave difficulties in accepting a perichoretic rather than a mechanistic view of the universe. But these difficulties are nothing compared with its problems in coming to terms with the relationship of the one to the other; the personal to the impersonal."[29] This work argues that the ideals of modernity—particularly homogenization and individualism—remain embedded within the market economy, and that these are precisely the challenges the Faith and Work movement must confront. The question arises: Has Gunton found a solid foundation in the doctrine of *perichoresis*, or has he overreached? Furthermore, in the two decades since the publication of *The One, the Three, and the Many*, has relational theology helped Christian theology formulate a better response?

Introduction to Timothy Keller and the Center for Faith and Work in New York

In exploring the influence of Trinitarian theology within the contemporary Faith and Work movement, this work will engage primarily with

---

28. Gunton, *Promise*, 51. The theme of the "individualisation" of redemption recurs frequently in Gunton's work. In *The Triune Creator*, he draws on Feuerbach's critical assessment of Christianity, highlighting the narrow focus on personal salvation: "Nature, the world, has no value, no interest, for Christians. The Christian thinks only of himself and the salvation of his soul" (Feuerbach, *Essence of Christianity*, 287). Gunton echoes this critique, emphasizing that redemption is not merely about individual souls but encompasses the entirety of creation: "Redemption means the completion of the whole project of creation, not the saving of a few souls from hell" (Gunton, *Actuality of the Atonement*, 171).

29. Gunton, *One*, 173.

Timothy Keller and Katherine Alsdorf's *Every Good Endeavor*, published in 2012, two decades after Gunton's Bampton lectures.[30] While it may be unrealistic to expect Keller to explicitly reference *perichoresis*, the doctrine has undeniably shaped the broader shift toward relational theology. Its influence is discernible in both Keller's theological arguments and the priorities he emphasizes for engagement. This book endeavor thus asks: does Keller's work indicate that Reformed theology has made progress in moving beyond the traditional role of simply mediating grace to the individual?

The selection of Timothy Keller for this book is highly strategic. His academic rigor, combined with a strong foundation in apologetics, has played a crucial role in shaping his ministry and theological approach. This background was instrumental in his establishment of the Center for Faith and Work in New York City, widely regarded as a global hub of the market economy. As a key ministry of his church, the Center has become a focal point for exploring the intersection of "faith" and "work." Through numerous publications and initiatives, Keller has significantly contributed to the dialogue on how Christian beliefs interact with contemporary culture. What we see in Keller is an important combination of substance and influence.

Unlike Gunton, Keller is not writing for an academic audience. His target readers are well-educated Christians within his congregation who are actively engaged in the market economy. *Every Good Endeavor*, Keller's key contribution to the Faith and Work dialogue, reflects this practical focus. At the time of writing, the book ranks as the fourth most purchased in the "Christian Business and Professional Growth" category on Amazon.[31]

Several notable contenders beyond Keller could have been selected, many of whom are explored in the literature review of this book. The decision to focus on Keller for deeper engagement was influenced by how he addresses the theme of individualism. My decision to focus on Keller for deeper engagement was primarily driven by his treatment of individualism, which I believed offered more avenues for exploration.[32]

30. Keller and Alsdorf, *Every Good Endeavor*.

31. "Amazon Best Sellers."

32. Chapter 5 will reveal that this initial decision was ultimately incorrect. Engaging with Keller proved to be disappointing from the perspective of critique. However, this shortcoming opened the door to unexpected insights, particularly concerning the underlying drive of ethical dominance in the Faith and Work movement. These revelations led to a shift in understanding that will be further explored in chapters 5 and 6.

For instance, Higginson's *Faith, Hope and the Global Economy: A Power for Good* presents a significant academic contribution, targeting a similar audience as Keller.[33] However, as part of a series, it potentially lacks a holistic perspective on the topic. Additionally, Higginson's background as a lecturer in Christian ethics shapes the book with a clear ethical bias. This emphasis, while valuable, results in less comprehensive engagement with modernity—an area that is central to the aims of this book.

Van Duzer was another strong contender, having transitioned from a lawyer to the dean of the School of Business and Economics at Seattle Pacific University. However, his focus as a professor of business law and ethics places the bulk of his contributions within the "ethics" school, which limits their relevance for this book. His book, *Why Business Matters to God*,[34] leans heavily on Niebuhr's typologies, which, while influential, feel outdated given the advances in discussions on culture and worldviews since their introduction in the 1950s.

Miller's work, while valuable, was more suitable as a complementary source, offering a historical overview of the Faith and Work movement rather than being central to the study. Additionally, Volf was chosen for supplementary engagement. Though an influential theologian, Volf's work was not selected as the primary dialogue partner due to its reliance on Niebuhr's framework and its more focused approach, which engages with a specific angle rather than a general view.

In selecting Keller, it is important to acknowledge that his book *Every Good Endeavor* is co-authored by Katherine Leary Alsdorf, which complicates the task of pinpointing Keller's specific stance on systematic theological issues. Co-authorship can sometimes blur the views of the primary author, raising questions about which parts of the book's doctrinal content can be directly attributed to Keller. Fortunately, this challenge is mitigated by the fact that co-authoring is rare for Keller. As a prolific communicator, he has authored numerous books and delivered presentations on faith and work at various seminars. These resources provide ample material to substantiate Keller's position with clarity.[35]

---

33. Higginson, *Faith, Hope and the Global Economy*.
34. Van Duzer, *Why Business Matters*.
35. When citing *Every Good Endeavor*, reference will be made to Keller, not Keller and Alsdorf, as the views being cited are those of Keller.

The Structure of Keller's Argument

While Gunton's starting point was the philosophical sentiment of modernity, Keller's focus is on the production of modernity itself. In the introduction to *Every Good Endeavor*, Keller acknowledges that much of the contemporary Christian literature on faith and work is rooted in missiological perspectives. From the outset, he seeks to chart a different course by first developing a theology of work as a platform for a Christian response. This approach is significant, requiring the "deconstruction" of many of the *a priori* theological assumptions underpinning this theology.

Like Gunton, Keller devotes significant attention to the culture of modernity. Drawing on the insights of French academic Luc Ferry, Keller acknowledges the market economy's soteriological claims and highlights the dangers of synchronicity, which he categorizes as idolatry. However, while Keller focuses heavily on the market economy's promotion of radical individualism, he offers little to no engagement with the threat of homogenization—a central concern for Gunton. The link between individualism and homogenization, which Gunton sees as interconnected, is not immediately apparent to Keller.

Keller summarizes his views as follows:

> Christians should be aware of this revolutionary understanding of the purpose of their work in the world. We are not to choose jobs and conduct our work to fulfil ourselves and accrue power, for being called by God to do something is empowering enough. We are to see work as a way of service to God and neighbour, and so we should both choose and conduct our work in accordance with that purpose.[36]

Here is where the contrast between the two theologians begins to emerge. Gunton's soteriological focus is introspective, urging Christians to critically examine their own paradigms and theological assumptions. In contrast, Keller's focus is external, projecting a soteriological framework onto the capitalist economy. This is where Keller misses a significant opportunity. For Keller, the soteriological purpose of God in restoring his image remains largely logical rather than relational. From a *perichoretic* perspective, Keller seems to follow the Augustinian path, where love is something people do, rather than something that defines who they are. This approach

---

36. Keller and Alsdorf, *Every Good Endeavor*, 57.

limits Keller's vision to a repurposed theology of ethics rather than offering a new relational understanding of God and human identity.

This is evident in the following quote: "To be a Christian in business, then, means much more than just being honest or not sleeping with your co-workers. It means more than personal evangelism or holding Bible study at the office. Rather, it means thinking out the implications of the gospel worldview and God's purpose for your whole work life—and for the whole of the organization to be under your influence."[37] Paraphrased, Keller is telling Christians to "try harder."

Gunton's theology of createdness within the soteriological framework carries profound implications for both our theology of grace and our theology of diversity. His vision suggests a reformation that would reshape these doctrines, yet there remains insufficient evidence that Gunton's proposed reforms have been fully realized in contemporary theological discourse. Keller, on the other hand, misses an important opportunity to provide a clearer soteriological critique of individualism and the discrimination prevalent in the workplace. Furthermore, he fails to emphasize the formative nature of soteriology over its transactional implications.

EXPLORING QUESTIONS DRIVING THIS RESEARCH

Gunton's call to the Reformed tradition centers on building Christian identity through a relational doctrine of God and an understanding of humanity as created in God's image. This relational perspective offers a framework for addressing contemporary issues, including how the church engages with the pervasive influence of the market economy. The central question of this book, therefore, seeks to explore how Gunton's theological insights might enrich and challenge the Reformed tradition's approach to the market economy, particularly as seen in the theology of Timothy Keller. Thus, the primary question this investigation seeks to address is: What contribution might Gunton's link between identity and the doctrine of God make to contemporary Reformed theology's engagement with the market economy as exemplified in the theology of Timothy Keller?

This core question seeks to investigate whether Gunton's relational ontology, particularly his use of *perichoresis*, can provide a more robust

---

37. Keller and Alsdorf, *Every Good Endeavor*, 168.

theological response to the challenges posed by the market economy than Keller's approach currently offers.

To go deeper into this inquiry, several subsidiary questions are explored: What relational ontological resources do we find in Gunton's use of *perichoresis* and his understanding of identity as being created in the image of God? How is this validated within the Reformed tradition, and where might Gunton have overreached or excluded key elements in his interpretation? To what extent can Christian traditions be held responsible for the radical individualism evident in today's global market economy, and what is the link between theological legacies such as Augustine's influence and modern economic structures like those of Adidas?

Furthermore, Gunton critiques many Reformed theologians for focusing on "mediating grace to the individual," suggesting that an inadequate understanding of the Trinity leads to a limited view of salvation. This book asks how Keller's theology demonstrates this conclusion and whether Gunton's critique holds. Finally, how might Gunton's use of *perichoresis*—and its link to human identity—reshape Keller's priorities to better equip Christians for more critical engagement with the market economy?

This investigation sets the foundation for exploring how Gunton's relational understanding of God could offer new insights into Christian engagement with the economic forces of modern life. By using Keller as a case study, the research assesses whether Gunton's theological innovations present a more comprehensive alternative to the individualistic tendencies often found in Christian responses to market dynamics.

CONCLUSION

The aim of this introductory chapter has been to provide an overview and context for the research problem while persuading the reader of the importance of connecting identity and the market economy. Given the magnitude of the issues at stake, the number of theologians engaging with this relationship is small, and their contributions often fall short of addressing the complexity of the task. Before diving deeper into this engagement in chapter 4, it is crucial to first examine Gunton's theology and the resources he offers, as they provide a foundation for exploring how identity, theology, and the market economy intersect. This review will establish the groundwork for the subsequent analysis of contemporary responses.

2

Gunton's Theology of Identity
Perichoresis and the *Imago Dei*

INTRODUCTION

THIS CHAPTER EXPLORES THE relational ontological insights of Colin Gunton's theology, focusing particularly on his use of *perichoresis* and the concept of human identity as grounded in the *imago Dei* (image of God). It seeks to examine how these ideas align with and find validation within the Reformed tradition while critically engaging with potential limitations in Gunton's interpretation, especially where his framework may overreach or exclude key elements.

The inquiry is twofold: first, to uncover the contributions of Gunton's relational framework to a richer understanding of identity; and second, to critically evaluate the constraints and blind spots in his approach. Through this process, the chapter aims to highlight both the enduring and the areas where Gunton's work may fall short in addressing the complexities of identity within theological discourse.

At the heart of this exploration lies the concept of "relational ontological resources." These insights are evaluated not merely for their theoretical merit but for their relevance to the broader aim of this book: offering a critical theological reflection on identity in the context of today's market-driven world.

Engaging with these questions is no small task. Nearly two decades after Gunton's untimely passing, his work on the Trinity and identity continues to inspire but also invites significant critique. Many, like Nausner,[1] contend that Gunton's ambitious Trinitarian framework does not fulfill its promise. He argues that "Gunton is not capable of delivering on his promise to show how everything looks different from a trinitarian perspective."[2] Other critics have voiced similar doubts, questioning whether Gunton's ideas possess the lasting power to reshape theological reflection in a meaningful way.

Yet, identity remains in deeper crisis than ever, and the Reformed theological response has been slow to address these complexities. This chapter, therefore, revisits Gunton with a different question in mind: might his insights contain underappreciated resources that could aid us in this era of identity flux? If such resources exist, what are they, and how might we justify their validity?

The sections that follow explore these questions, assessing both the strengths and limitations of Gunton's thought, with an eye toward their relevance for contemporary theological discourse on identity.

Gunton and *Perichoresis*

For Gunton, *perichoresis* is just the tip of the iceberg, offering a glimpse into his deeper theological vision. As a concept, *perichoresis* itself is straightforward and could be treated briefly. However, its true value in this discussion lies in its placement within Gunton's broader theological response to the perceived limitations of his theological landscape. Understanding *perichoresis* within Gunton's context and the journey he undertook to arrive at this concept is, arguably, as important—if not more—than the term itself. This chapter, therefore, prepares readers to explore the formative journey that shaped Gunton's theological framework and to reflect on how this journey was distinct, almost countercultural, especially in light of his departures from Augustine and, to a lesser extent, Barth. While some now share his views, these shifts were radical in his time.

This chapter anticipates a substantial engagement with epistemology and ontology, inviting the discipline of semantics into a close examination of the term "person." Rooted in the framework of Reformed theology, this exploration will naturally engage more extensively with

---

1. Nausner, *Failure of a Laudable Project*.
2. Nausner, *Failure of a Laudable Project*, 420.

Barth, whose influence on Gunton is profound, though ultimately transformed. Gunton's theological journey marks a significant shift, illustrated by his development of *analogia relationis* as a progression from Barth's *analogia fidei*.

Nausner's critique underscores the importance of a rigorous, critical engagement with Gunton's theology in this chapter.[3] Given the research question's focus on the potential for Gunton's "over-reaching," the analysis will present and argue through several clearly defined points, ensuring transparency and thoroughness in examining his theological framework. Readers should note that this critique will unfold iteratively: while critical insights will be addressed within relevant sections, their interwoven nature requires that they be revisited and synthesized before presenting the chapter's final conclusions.

This iterative approach not only clarifies the complexities in Gunton's thought but also invites readers to assess my perspective. By openly engaging with the intersections between my theological background and the critical examination of Gunton's resources, the chapter aims to bring a self-reflective dimension into the discourse. This reflective layer allows the reader to judge whether my theological formation has influenced, positively or otherwise, the capacity to objectively seek resources that speak meaningfully to questions of identity and relationality within the context of the market economy.

An Ambitious Question

Addressing this question within a single chapter is undeniably ambitious. It tackles the convergence of multiple significant theological and anthropological disciplines, each rich with complex debates and varied perspectives that demand careful reflection. As the chapter engages with these disciplines, it will quickly become clear that their interwoven nature defies simple compartmentalization or neat boundaries. Each area unfolds into the others, resisting any attempt at curtailment.

The ambition of this chapter's question extends beyond its scope to the very nature of the topic itself. As Cunningham aptly expresses, "We thus need to hold together three strands that are always threatening to unravel: the character of God's inner life, the nature of God's relationship with the world, and God's role as the ultimate source of our knowledge of

---

3. Nausner, *Failure of a Laudable Project*.

God."[4] Cunningham highlights a circularity inherent in studying divine identity—a dynamic not only central to the Reformed tradition but also woven throughout this chapter's engagement with the classical theological tradition.

Scope and Limitations

In light of both the inherent circularity and the convergence of multiple disciplines, a few comments on scope and limitations are necessary to set realistic expectations for the reader. The doctrine of God stands as the cornerstone of the theological framework, interconnected with all other areas within systematic theology. Exploring this doctrine within the boundaries of this project demands a balance of depth and efficiency. Complex topics, such as the term "person" as it relates to divine identity, have been and will continue to be subjects of entire studies. This book aims to contribute by applying these doctrines rather than expanding their qualifications. Put simply, while it is essential to demonstrate an awareness of the theological landscape, an equal need for conciseness is required.

This need for limitation—though it may sound somewhat evasive—is particularly relevant when engaging with theologians or theological frameworks that have influenced Gunton. Some selective commentary is necessary, but only to the extent that it enhances our appreciation or critique of Gunton's contributions. The aim of this chapter is to strike a careful balance, examining the influence of others without getting sidetracked by fully supporting or critiquing these secondary positions. Barth serves as a fitting example. The focus here is not on Barth's theology per se, but on the movement between Barth's stance and Gunton's, and, more specifically, on the pathway Gunton forged to develop *perichoresis* as a lens for understanding ontology and identity.

In this book, Barth and other figures play a supporting role, as the primary focus remains on Gunton and his potential contributions to theological reflections on identity within the market economy. To aid readability, footnotes will serve as bridges to supplementary material, allowing for reference to relevant tributaries without requiring detailed engagement within the main text. This approach keeps the chapter

---

4. Cunningham, *These Three Are One*, 57. To this point, Cunningham (*These Three Are One*, 59) also adds, "The idea of an 'internally self-differentiated being' is a difficult one; in the created order there are no perfect analogies to describe it."

streamlined, ensuring that only essential content is foregrounded to build toward the chapter's conclusions.

Trinitarian Theology: Theological Recovery from a "Different Angle"

Ford, in his introduction to *The Modern Theologians: An Introduction to Christian Theology since 1918*, writes, "Most theologians discussed in these volumes are engaged in a recovery of Christianity in the face of unprecedently devastating, sophisticated and widely disseminated dismissals of both Christianity and theology."[5] Perhaps these dismissals have become so pervasive that we are now almost numb to their "unprecedently devastating" nature. Ford's perspective as a commentator on contemporary theologians serves as a valuable reminder of what is truly at stake, setting forth key criteria for what we should expect in a modern theologian. To meaningfully engage with the critiques against Christianity, theologians must demonstrate three qualities: an acute awareness of the key issues; an ability to receive these and understand their implications for theology; and a deep commitment to respond.

Gunton's keen awareness of a cultural environment steeped in dismissals of faith is clear from the opening line of his first book. He begins *Becoming and Being* with the statement: "The decline of belief in God in the Western World has been documented and analysed in many ways. . . . This study is written in the belief that the situation is by no means as simple as it is sometimes made to appear, and that much light can be thrown by looking at it from a different angle."[6] When Gunton penned these words, this "different angle" lacked a defined name. However, through the foundational work of Gunton and his contemporaries, the term "Trinitarian theology" has since emerged to describe this approach.

In this study, Gunton is engaged as a key representative of the so-called "Trinitarian Revolution"—a term with a far more dramatic ring than "Trinitarian Recovery," yet reflective of the movement's true aim. This "Trinitarian" emphasis arose in response to what many, including Gunton, perceived as a widespread neglect of the Trinity within Western theology. Rahner famously observed that "despite their orthodox confession of the Trinity, Christians are, in their practical life, almost mere

---

5. Ford, *Modern Theologians*, 6.
6. Gunton, *Becoming and Being*, 1.

'monotheists.' We must be willing to admit that, should the doctrine of the Trinity have to be dropped as false, the major part of the religious literature could well remain virtually unchanged."[7] Heron makes a similar point, noting that this neglect has often led to "a good deal of theology and piety to the concentration of attention on a vaguely unitarian God, loosely identified with the Father, and to increasing difficulties in connecting that up in any coherent way with either the Trinity or the incarnation."[8] What these theologians share is the conviction that understanding God as Trinity is essential to the recovery of theology.[9] Gunton's work represents a view that the doctrine of *perichoresis* is central to this task.

What Is the Hypothesis?

Before delving into Gunton's work, it's helpful to follow the advice of Stephen Covey in *The 7 Habits of Highly Effective People*, where he encourages readers to "Begin with the end in mind."[10] In its simplest terms, the hypothesis here is that Gunton's contribution rests in a mediated relational ontology—one that not only accommodates the particular but requires it, rooted as it is within the Trinity itself.

7. Rahner, *Trinity*, 10–11. This is the first reference to Rahner, and one which may be unexpected in a book that has stipulated a focus on Reformed theology. There are two important points to be made here: 1) much of the debate on the doctrine of God precedes the delineation of theological tradition; and 2) Rahner is an important ally of Gunton, one whom Gunton, for whatever reason, failed to leverage despite their overlapping discontent with the handling of the Trinity that began with Augustine. This point will be elaborated further later in the chapter.

8. Heron, *Century of Protestant Theology*, 93.

9. Alan Torrance is another key contributor to Trinitarian theology. His quote below captures the determination to recenter theology on the doctrine of the Trinity.

> The communion of the Trinity as such constitutes the *arche* and *telos* of all that is. . . . Nothing less, therefore, than the most fundamental ontological and cosmological issues are at stake here in the debate concerning the mutuality and communion which characterise the Triunity. Lack of clarity here has ramifications for the whole of theology—not least the nature-grace debate and the doctrine of creation, reconciliation and the covenant as these are irreducibly bound up with the doctrine of God. (Torrance, *Persons in Communion*, 258–59)

Although he uses strong words here, he is essentially reminding us that everything is at stake with the doctrine of God. Gunton would agree. Despite his reputation for not always being the most structured theologian, we see a consistency in always bringing the debate to the doctrine of God and then weaving its ramifications into the study at hand, be it ontology, Christology, creation, or revelation.

10. Covey, *Seven Habits*, 102.

However, there are obstacles within Gunton's theology, some of which are substantial enough to hinder the straightforward adoption of his ideas as he presented them. The task of this chapter is to critically examine these obstacles and determine whether they ultimately disqualify his framework. By the chapter's end, the question will be whether sufficient resources remain to support a meaningful engagement between Reformed theology and the challenges posed by the market economy.

INTRODUCTORY COMMENTS ON GUNTON'S FORMATION

To fully grasp the content of Gunton's theology, an overview of his formative influences is essential. This approach is particularly fitting for Gunton, who took a distinctly redactive view of theological history. He strongly believed in the power of key historical figures to shape the course of theology through their interpretations of Scripture and core doctrines. In the spirit of Gunton's own method, this chapter seeks to identify the events and influences that may have directed his theology along specific paths. What aspects, both included and omitted, have played a role in shaping Gunton's theological vision? By tracing these factors, we can better understand the underpinnings of his contributions to contemporary theology.

Key Milestones

Gunton was born in 1941 in Nottingham, England, and identified himself as a "dissenter"—a description that has historical resonance in Nottingham, known for its tradition of nonconformity. This label is a fitting starting point for understanding a Reformed theologian with Presbyterian leanings working within an Anglican-dominated context.[11] While North American readers may be tempted to downplay the influence of ecclesial affiliations in the twentieth century, history repeatedly demonstrates that any formal alignment of church with state authority, as is the case with the Anglican Church, creates a theological hegemony. For Gunton, even

---

11. Gunton's role as a dissenter is affirmed by his colleagues. Webster attributes part of this orientation to the influence of Barth. "Barth helped Gunton—already a nonconformist in the Oxford Anglican establishment—to swim against the stream" (Webster, "Gunton and Barth," 15).

as a prominent English academic, this alignment placed him in a unique position as something of an outsider in his own theological landscape.

Gunton completed his BA in classics at Oxford University, followed by an MA in theology the next year. In 1967, he embarked on his doctoral studies under the supervision of Robert Jenson, a prominent figure in Trinitarian theology. His doctoral journey spanned three supervisors and concluded in 1973, focusing on the doctrine of God in the writings of Charles Hartshorne and Karl Barth. This study laid a crucial foundation for Gunton's later theological contributions, shaping the contours of his distinctive approach to the doctrine of God.

In 1969, while still pursuing his PhD, Gunton joined the faculty at King's College, London, where he would remain until his death in 2003. His tenure at King's marked significant milestones: he became the college's first lecturer in systematic theology in 1980, was appointed professor in 1984 at the age of forty-three, and took on the role of chair of Christian doctrine in 1985. In 1999 he became one of the founding editors of the *International Journal of Systematic Theology*.[12] Although his long career at King's might seem unusual, it would be a mistake to view it as either isolating or limiting. For Gunton, King's served as a vibrant hub for both local and international theological engagement.[13]

A notable aspect of his career is the interplay between academics and ministry. Ordained in 1972 within the United Reformed Church, he went on to serve as Associate Minister at Brentwood United Reformed Church from 1975 until his passing in 2003. To Gunton, these two roles—academic and ministerial—were inextricable. Yet, in practice, his scholarship often took center stage, with less of the concrete, actionable focus seen in thinkers like Bonhoeffer or Niebuhr.

Throughout his career, he published numerous works, some of which have become influential texts in their fields. A shift in focus is evident in his later publications, which increasingly explore the practical

---

12. Holmes, "In Memoriam."

13. 1) Gunton placed a high value on the contribution of his colleagues at King's both personally and professionally. We see this in the frequent referencing of their writings in his own. Sure, this could be a kind of "professional courtesy," but unlikely as there is little evidence of this sentimentality in Gunton's writing. It's his short dedication in *The Triune Creator* in 1998 that is the most telling. His simple use of *"gratitude and affection"* points to a valued partnership. 2) King's valued his contribution, and he was able to progress his careers through seniority and increased responsibilities. 3) King's was a useful platform from which to reach other audiences. We can see this through a geographically and ecclesiologically wide lecture base from which he was able to publish.

implications of Trinitarian theology. From 1991 onward, three themes emerge as central, repeatedly examined and refined in his work:

1. The Trinity and divine identity
2. Persons and mediation
3. Modernity and its Greek/Augustinian heritage

Gunton's foundation in the classics significantly shapes his themes, grounding his critique of historical theological heritage and sharpening his understanding of contemporary context. His strong philosophical background allows him to bring a unique and vital emphasis to these discussions. However, as this chapter argues, his classical training, while a strength, at times became a limitation. It inclined him to view many contemporary issues through a philosophical lens, sometimes overlooking the impact of political, economic, and technological forces. Had he pursued Oxford's PPE instead of classics, we might have seen a theologian more attuned to these dimensions. Additionally, unlike some of his peers, he delayed writing a comprehensive systematic theology, leaving the manuscript—though well-developed—unpublished at his sudden passing at age sixty-two.

The One, the Three, and the Many

This chapter will draw primarily on Gunton's work, *The One, the Three, and the Many*. While Gunton frequently employs concepts like *perichoresis* and relational ontology, this book stands out as his most comprehensive theological response, weaving together his core themes into a cohesive vision that surpasses the scope of his other writings. Typically, Gunton engages theological tradition with an introspective, receptive stance rather than a focus on apologetics. However, here we see a mature Gunton, uncharacteristically setting aside his British reserve to deliver a balanced critique to all sides. This work arguably marks his most substantial contribution to contemporary theological discourse and offers an ideal entry point for engaging his broader corpus. Reflecting Ford's observation of theology's defensive posture, this book represents a formidable and essential defense.

The title is significant. Its simplicity is rare for Gunton and provides a valuable summary of his project as well as talks to the resources he intends to deliver. He summarizes it as follows:

> Antiquity and modernity are remarkably alike in having a defective understanding and practice of what I call relationality. Both eras, in the main streams of their thought, play the one against the many, or the many against the one, in such a way that the rights of both are often lost. Both eras have difficulty in giving due weight to particularity, both in developing a truly relational account of what it is to be, in large part because they are in thrall to a doctrine that the one, but not the many, is of transcendent status.[14]

In this context, Gunton introduces an alternative doctrine of God—and, by extension, of creation—that allows the one and the three to coexist. Far from being mutually exclusive, he argues, particularity and unity can and must harmonize. He writes, "My contrasting positive point is that a renewed doctrine of creation is possible on the basis of a doctrine of God which in some way writes plurality into the being of things."[15] This embedding of plurality into humanity lies at the core of his theological vision.

This chapter will further contend that Gunton's theology evolves significantly over his career. *The One, the Three, and the Many* lacks some of the restraint and emphasis on mediation seen in his later works; for instance, figures like Irenaeus have yet to play a central role. Nonetheless, a focus on relationality and particularity emerges here, themes that remain vital throughout Gunton's subsequent writings.

Wider Context

Mention has been made of the Anglican dominance of Gunton's English context. While this is important, greater significance must be placed on the broader theological and philosophical context of the time.

Philosophical/Theological Context

Gunton was born in 1941, the same year Bultmann published his influential essay "New Testament and Mythology."[16] This essay marked the theological landscape that Gunton would navigate, one defined by a Kantian/

---

14. Gunton, *One*, 6.
15. Gunton, *One*, 151.
16. Bultmann, *New Testament and Mythology*.

Cartesian divide between two theological camps. On the so-called "liberal" side, rationalism and metaphysical skepticism were on the rise, leading to significant theological revision. On the other side, Reformed theology found itself in a defensive and somewhat fragmented stance, lacking what Kotter would describe as a "guiding coalition" to unify its response."[17]

Here, Barth was instrumental in revitalizing Reformed theology, bringing it back into the conversation with both credibility and urgency. With his expertise, he effectively contributed to galvanizing a Reformed response, using a Kantian framework to establish conditions under which metaphysics could regain its footing. Heron fittingly describes this as a "reversal."[18] Thus, in Barth and Bultmann, we find representatives of the two dominant theological streams that shaped European theology throughout much of the twentieth century.

In this milieu, Gunton emerged as a strong advocate for the Barthian stream, yet he was far from a mere follower. Despite a deep respect for Barth, Gunton concluded early on that Barth had ultimately been unable to escape the limitations of classical theology's broken paradigms. Gunton's engagement with Barth remained evident and consistent throughout his career; however, while Barth was not his solution to Reformed theology, he became the critical benchmark from which Gunton sought to advance the conversation. Given that Barth was the subject of Gunton's PhD and that his first supervisor, Robert W. Jenson, was a Barthian scholar, Barth's impact on Gunton's early work is hard to overstate. The two theologians also approached theology from very different contexts: Barth's critical thinking developed in the shadow of Nazism, clearly shaping many of his emphases. One wonders whether some of

---

17. Kotter, *Leading Change*. Kotter refutes the necessity for a key individual in driving change. What is essential, in his view, is the guiding coalition. Specifically, this refers to a group of people who are critical to the early stages of re-engineering a strategy. He identifies four key attributes of these individuals: 1. they must be key players, i.e., they hold power in their positions; 2. they need expertise; 3. they require credibility, i.e., recognition of this expertise by others; and 4. they must have leaders capable of driving the change process (Kotter, *Leading Change*, 57).

18. By the term "reversal," Heron (*Century of Protestant Theology*, 97) proposes that Barth's agenda was in reversing the questions posed by the Enlightenment and not in answering them. "Where others were most sharply conscious of the crisis posed for theology by the development of modern culture and the change in our self-awareness, he saw the real crisis as lying in the inability of theology to do justice to its object, and called it to look in the opposite direction from that it had been taking" (*Century of Protestant Theology*, 97).

their theological disagreements might have softened had they both found themselves on the faculty at King's in the early 1990s.

Philosophical/Political Context

Adding to this theological backdrop, the Second World War dealt a severe blow to the modernity project, turning rationality inward and setting the stage for the reflexivity of modernity. This shift eventually led to the postmodern debates of the late 1980s and early 1990s, marked by a rejection of metanarratives.[19] Transcendental truths were sidelined, and epistemology took center stage. This was the dominant context in which *The One, the Three, and the Many* emerged. Gunton used this book to underscore the impossibility of the modernity project while simultaneously proposing a more promising alternative. While he doesn't state it directly, Gunton likely found the metanarrative debate too steeped in Platonic influence to hold his interest.

Bringing Identity to Center Stage

As the century closed, another paradigm shift took place, moving from a focus on truth to one of identity—a shift well suited to Gunton's deepening interest in personhood and particularity. This transition broadened the conversation on the Trinity and its relation to identity, drawing contributions from theologians across denominations and continents, including Torrance, Zizioulas, LaCugna, Rahner, Boff, Moltmann, and others.

Gunton's formative years also coincided with the Third Industrial Revolution (3IR), which fundamentally transformed human life through digital systems. A defining feature of this era (intensified now as we move into the Fourth Industrial Revolution [4IR]) is convergence: the erosion of post-Enlightenment disciplinary barriers.

This study identifies a significant blind spot in Gunton's approach. For instance, he was a contemporary of David Harvey, who was born six years earlier and completed his doctoral studies at Cambridge. Harvey's *The Condition of Postmodernity*, published just four years before *The One, the Three, and the Many*, targeted a similar audience and, as a Marxist, offered a nuanced perspective on economic anthropology that could

---

19. Graphically described by Heron (*Century of Protestant Theology*, 70) as the "corrosive acids of modernity."

have enriched Gunton's work considerably. There's an irony here: one of Gunton's strengths was his ability to connect overlooked ideas—especially across theology, philosophy, and, to a lesser extent, science. Yet, his use of this skill in other fields was limited—a weakness that needs to be addressed if Gunton's resources are to make a meaningful impact in the field of Faith and Work.

Key Contributors to Gunton's Formation

For a theologian committed to the concept of perichoretic participation, it's fitting that Gunton placed a high value on the contributions of others. His work reveals a clear appreciation for collaborative input, seen in his role as a founding editor of the *International Journal of Systematic Theology* and his involvement in organizing activities through the Research Institute in Systematic Theology. These initiatives reflect Gunton's commitment to engaging a diversity of perspectives. Of particular interest, however, are those theologians who significantly influenced Gunton's thought—figures who stood out from the rest in shaping his theology.

His Mentors and Teachers

In the dedication of *The Promise of Trinitarian Theology*, Gunton personally acknowledges a select group of theologians who were particularly influential from his perspective: Robert W. Jenson, Daniel W. Hardy, Thomas F. Torrance, and John D. Zizioulas.[20] Jenson, as noted earlier, was Gunton's first PhD supervisor, and references to Hardy, Torrance, and Zizioulas will follow in this chapter. Additionally, Gunton's theology is deeply shaped by figures he encountered primarily through their writings—the Cappadocians, Irenaeus, Karl Barth, and Samuel Taylor Coleridge among them. While many others could be mentioned, these are the thinkers whose shoulders Gunton has stood on to build his theological framework. Their names will become familiar to the reader as the chapter unfolds.

---

20. Gunton (*Promise*, xiv) writes, "The dedication of the book is a small attempt to signal my debt to a number of my seniors who have helped shape my development in this rewarding craft, and in particular have impressed on me in different—some of them may think different—ways of the importance of thinking in a trinitarian way."

Gunton's "Opponents"

To complete the list of key influencers, we must also consider those theologians with whom Gunton frequently disagreed and felt compelled to engage throughout his career. Chief among these is Augustine, whose ideas Gunton critically examined on multiple occasions. Augustine's influence and Gunton's critiques will be explored in this chapter and again in chapter 3. Aquinas also warrants mention here. Although Gunton occasionally reads Aquinas sympathetically, he ultimately views Aquinas's theological contributions as largely negative.

Omissions: Those Whose Absence Is Surprising!

Gunton's work must also be evaluated for its notable omissions—those influential figures whose absence is conspicuous. Pannenberg, for instance, is a contemporary whom Gunton rarely engages. As a Trinitarian theologian, one might expect Gunton to interact more fully with others in this tradition, even from different theological backgrounds. Yet theologians such as Rahner, LaCugna, and Moltmann play surprisingly minimal roles in his work. Among these, the writer argues that Rahner's limited presence is perhaps the most significant missed opportunity, a point that will be explored in greater detail later in the chapter.

Gunton has already faced criticism for a certain philosophical myopia, with Harvey cited as an example of an overlooked peer. Other disciplines, such as economics, are similarly underrepresented in his work. Sociology receives slightly more attention, largely through Gunton's engagement with Charles Taylor, which brings some contemporary sociological issues into his theology. However, for a theologian addressing the culture of modernity, Gunton's scope of reading remains too narrow. Unlike past theologians, today's thinkers require a breadth of interdisciplinary exposure, one in which Gunton ultimately falls short.

Gunton's Peers and Critics

While Reformed theologians have often tended toward a defensive stance, Gunton stands as a refreshing exception, embracing criticism both given and received. His approach aligns with his role in establishing the *Journal of Systematic Theology*, a platform that invites theologians to rigorously test their ideas. Gunton writes, "The gospel will therefore not be served by the mere denunciation of modern rejection, but by probing how it came to happen. Christianity is indeed offensive to the natural human mind; and yet it is often made offensive by its representatives for the wrong reasons."[21] Gunton's critiques of both Augustine and Barth are cases in point—bold confrontations by any measure, even viewed as somewhat reckless by some. Many of his sharpest critics have come from within his own circle: peers invested deeply enough in his project to engage it rigorously. Then there are those outside his immediate sphere, drawn to respond precisely because Gunton ventured into their domains. Green and McNall are notable examples and will be examined in depth in the following chapter.

Gunton's openness to critique may, in part, reflect the influence of the deconstructionists of his time. When figures like Derrida were reducing truth to fragmented local narratives, a bold reevaluation of theological history felt far less daunting than it might have to Gunton's predecessors.

Though Gunton was no stranger to criticism, Nausner's remarks may have given him pause—not so much for the critique of his writings, but for his challenge to a Trinitarian perspective itself. While Nausner's view may not represent mainstream theological sentiment, it underscores that Trinitarian theology remains far from universally accepted. This is crucial to remember as we explore Gunton's development and core doctrines. While this theology may seem diminished in influence, it is revisited here to discern whether there are valuable aspects that may have previously been overlooked.

Gunton's Style

Structure Was Not a Strength

In a world that thrives on clarity, Gunton's writing has faced criticism for being dense, haphazard, and sometimes lacking in necessary detail. Webster affirmed this, observing that Gunton's prose was "sometimes clumsy

---

21. Gunton, *One*, 1. Here Gunton leads out his argument with an acknowledgement of Christianity's precarious existence in the world. It's a move we have seen before. The first sentence of his first publication in 1978 reads as follows: "The decline of the belief in God in the Western World has been documented and analysed in many way" (Gunton, *Becoming and Being*, 1). It is a theme that continues to drive the apologetic flavor of his writing.

and gave the impression that it was too hurried."[22] This "clumsiness" is particularly noticeable when he attempts to summarize his key positions, with arguments that often struggle to follow a clear structure. The reader may feel that Gunton focused heavily on addressing Christianity's critics but gave less attention to making his language accessible for readers within the church.

Gunton's Trinitarian "bus" has not picked up as many passengers as he might have hoped. While some have simply chosen not to align with his theological conclusions, the response could be markedly different if his writings were more accessible. In *Act and Being*,[23] for instance, there is a glimpse of what might have been possible: shorter sentences, a clearer structure, and adequate time devoted to each point before moving forward.

More Conductor Than Composer

Gunton is considered here as a representative of Trinitarian theology. While this approach has gained popularity in recent years, it offers little that is entirely new—a point that holds true for Gunton himself. To draw an analogy, Gunton is less a composer and more a conductor, orchestrating a fresh arrangement of earlier compositions. While Barth's "music" resonates within Gunton's work, it is far from a mere recital. Gunton incorporates other theological influences, crafting a symphony with a distinct sound of its own. This observation carries important implications for how his work is navigated and understood.

Concluding Comments on Gunton's Formation

The section aimed to contextualize and characterize Gunton's writings. Attention now shifts to identifying the theological concepts that anchored his conviction in Trinitarian principles, especially the implications of *perichoresis*.

---

22. Webster, "Gunton and Barth," 29.
23. Gunton, *Act and Being*.

GUNTON'S EPISTEMOLOGY AND ONTOLOGY[24]

In his office at King's College in London hung two portraits: one of Samuel Taylor Coleridge and the other of Karl Barth.[25] These two figures symbolize the dual theological foundations at the heart of Gunton's work: epistemology and ontology.[26] This emphasis was neither surprising nor unique, as both subjects were very much the focus of the era. Although trends have shifted—particularly in the realm of epistemology—keeping these two disciplines at the forefront helps us better understand their interaction within Gunton's context.

Gunton's preference for "epistemology" over "methodology" is significant. In a post-Kantian context, foundationalism has lost its relevance. Gunton, influenced by Barth's commitment to Reformed theology, moves away from foundationalist roots. This shift goes beyond questions of method; it probes the nature of knowledge itself and how we come to experience it. While Gunton was ultimately critical of Barth, particularly in relation to the doctrine of the Trinity, we see a consistent influence of, and appreciation for, Barthian methodology.

Samuel Taylor Coleridge played a crucial role in moving Gunton beyond Barth, arguably serving as a key figure behind the theological shift evident in Gunton's later work. Coleridge's influence helped solidify

---

24. This heading represents a choice to prioritize epistemology and ontology over other key themes found in Gunton. This could raise an objection from some of Gunton's commentators, Green in particular, who argue that creation is more important than ontology. However, any objection in favor of creation over ontology would be misguided. Yes, the doctrine of creation is significant to Gunton, and we will explore how Gunton extends his *analogia relationis* to all of creation. Nevertheless, those who elevate creation fail to recognize the centrality of perichoresis. This term is relational and primarily addresses the relational nature of God, enabling us to understand our own ontology. In terms of logical sequence, for Gunton, the ordering must be incarnation → ontology → creation. Furthermore, the term "creation" has too many other claimants that detract from the ontological emphasis required in this context. Ontology is the better choice, as Gunton's primary message pertains to our being in communion.

25. "Rev Professor Colin Gunton."

26. At this point, there may be an objection that Barth contributed both epistemology and ontology to the Reformed tradition and to Gunton. This note is a request for patience. Gunton (*Triune Creator*, 163) writes, "Barth's God, because he is eternally the God of Jesus Christ, has freely committed himself to the human race for eternity. We are on the verge of the Origenist-Augustinian doctrine of an eternal creation here; and although it is only the verge, there is a way in which Barth's Christ is dangerously close to becoming a near equivalent to the platonic forms, as Robert Jenson has argued." It is Coleridge (among others) who guides Gunton to Trinitarian theology with a greater pneumatology and relationality than that inherited from Barth. The impact of both Barth and Coleridge will be covered in later sections of this chapter.

the Trinitarian views Gunton inherited from Barth, while also adding a stronger emphasis on pneumatology and relationality—elements Gunton found lacking in Barth's writings. Coleridge's concept of "ideas" was particularly instrumental for Gunton, as it offered a way to bridge the analogical gap that emerged with his departure from classical theology. Though others, such as Zizioulas, also contributed to this development, it was Coleridge who catalyzed the shift. His influence on Gunton contrasts sharply with Barth's: while Barth's theology could be likened to a tidal wave in both volume and force, Coleridge's impact resembles a pebble dropping into a still pond, with small but far-reaching ripples across the theological landscape.

Yet, including Coleridge in Gunton's intellectual circle is not without challenges. Gunton's admiration for Coleridge seems to surpass Coleridge's direct influence on him, and, at times, Coleridge appears an unusual and even perplexing mentor. This complexity will be critically examined later in the chapter.

A doctoral study on Barthian methodology (as was the case for Gunton) naturally brings epistemology into sharp focus—yet, it seems this emphasis sparked a dissatisfaction that propelled him toward Coleridge, the Cappadocians, and ultimately an ontology grounded in *perichoresis*. In the critical context this chapter seeks to establish, the journey to *perichoresis* becomes nearly as significant as the concept itself.

Key Departures from Classical Theology

In exploring Gunton's "journey" to *perichoresis*, three significant "departures" merit further examination: *Rejection of a priori definitions of God*. Gunton pushes back against Greek-inspired definitions that cast a long shadow over Western theology. This departure primarily engages with epistemology, as it challenges foundational assumptions about knowing God; *the Gnostic subordination of matter* which relates to ontology; *a mediated view of relationships versus unmediated*. Gunton advocates for unmediated relationships and critiques the separation of act and being. This departure touches both epistemology and ontology.

The relationship among these points is circular, not linear, with the rejection of *a priori* functioning as the overarching category. This dismissal of classical *a priori* assumptions enables both the movement from analogy to direct mediation and a reconception of creation that no longer views matter through a Gnostic lens.

Rejection of A Priori Definitions of God, and Towards a Theology of Revelation

Classical theology traditionally relied on certain transcendentals as markers of divine identity, using them as a kind of plumb line to discern God's nature and actions.[27] However, with the advent of rationalism, this foundation came under intense scrutiny. Kant's *Critique of Pure Reason* dismantled the link to metaphysics, effectively severing the epistemological bridge to these long-held transcendentals.[28]

Gunton explains: "By tending to replace revelation by reason, or rather to displace it altogether, locating the source of revelation largely if not wholly in reason, it threw into question the historical basis of Christianity, and so opened up the modern debate about the epistemological basis for faith."[29] Kant's project aimed at restoring philosophy as a science,[30] but the impact on theology was profound, sparking a crisis of existence. In response, much of subsequent theology reflects efforts to redefine itself without reliance on these classical transcendentals.

In his doctoral thesis, Gunton examines two contrasting theologians—Barth and Hartshorne—who both grapple with the challenges facing classical theology. Although they agreed that something was "radically wrong" with the tradition, their theological starting points were diametrically opposed,[31] resulting in two vastly different responses to the theological crisis. Ultimately, Gunton finds both approaches inadequate, yet his assessments of each differ significantly.

---

27. In Gunton's view, Aquinas's *Summa Theologica* is a substantial foundation for the classical view. The core components of this view are as follows:

Supernaturalism: This involves a language of negativity or reverse engineering where we cannot know what God is, but only what he is not (Gunton, *Becoming and Being*, 2). This is addressed again in *The Triune Creator*. "Far from being the source of transcendental insight, God appears to be derived from a process of negating the essential characteristics of the world of time and becoming" (Gunton, *One*, 139).

Timeless: "Because the natural is necessarily temporal, and because God is the negation of the natural, his relation to time will be that of the timelessly eternal" (Gunton, *Becoming and Being*, 2).

Hierarchical: "The classical concept of God depends on a hierarchical ordering of reality" (Gunton, *Becoming and Being*, 3).

28. Rosemann, *Trinitarian Ontologies*.

29. Gunton, *Brief Theology of Revelation*, 2.

30. Rosemann, *Trinitarian Ontologies*.

31. "They agree that there is something radically wrong with the classical tradition. But in their starting points for reconstruction they could not be much further apart" (Gunton, *Becoming and Being*, 198).

Gunton's view of Hartshorne's theology is notably critical. He writes: "Hartshorne has fallen into exactly the same trap as his classical predecessors, of deciding in advance what is and is not possible for God, and has thus himself achieved a divorce between act and being."[32] In his view, Hartshorne's response not only fails to address the core issues but also does little to advance the theological project.

Gunton's response to Barth is of a different nature entirely. While he ultimately views Barth as flawed, he sees Barth as offering a viable alternative to classical theism's reliance on transcendentals through the inseparability of God's action in the economy.[33] Barth preferred to describe these as *a priori* assumptions, a term that cleverly opens the door to revelation while aligning with Kant's principles of scientific methodology. In Barth's use of *a priori*, we see a synthesis: an acknowledgment of the rationalist critique of classical theology, coupled with openness to an alternative framework for understanding God.

The Greek Influence: Separation of Act and Being

For Gunton, a specific kind of *a priori* conception has been a persistent obstacle in theology. Time and again, he seeks to disentangle theological thought from what he views as the negative influence of Greek philosophy—a theme that grows stronger in his later works. In the opening of *Act and Being*, Gunton writes, "It is one of the tragedies—one could almost say crimes—of Christian theological history that the Old Testament was effectively displaced by Greek philosophy as the theological basis of the doctrine of God, certainly so far as the doctrine of the divine attributes is concerned."[34] His writings are filled with frequent critical examinations of early theologians who, in his view, overlooked the signs and began interpreting theology through Greek paradigms. For Gunton, Augustine stands as the prime example of this misstep.

Here, we see epistemology and ontology tightly intertwined. Greek epistemology assumed that knowledge mirrored reality—more precisely, a mirror of *static* reality. To acquire knowledge, therefore, was to receive a representation rather than a dynamic encounter. Ontology mirrored this detachment, reinforcing a sense of separation. This led to what Gunton

---

32. Gunton, *Becoming and Being*, 149.
33. Webster, "Gunton and Barth."
34. Gunton, *Act and Being*, 3.

describes as theology's central "derailment": the division between God's being and God's acts.

For Barth, the core of divine identity lies in God's self-revelation in the person of Christ. God's identity isn't to be understood through predetermined attributes; rather, it's defined by God's actions toward humanity. Gunton's timing in approaching theological history critically couldn't have been better—few periods were as ripe for such an endeavor as the 1980s and 1990s, with postmodern reflexivity at its peak. In this context, Gunton's critique of Augustine, as detailed below, takes on a "Jonah principle." Kant's critique had dismissed Plato, and by association, Augustine. To preserve theology's course, it seemed necessary to "throw Augustine overboard" to save the ship.

Towards a Relational Identity of God: Reconnecting Act and Being

For Gunton, Barth's approach to revelation opened the way to a "radically different conception" of God's reality—one that underpinned the Trinitarian character of all his theology. This view sees "God as essentially relational being; in which the being of God for us is not something foreign to God's essence but is grounded in his very being."[35]

In other words, we need not approach the incarnation through a filter of predetermined markers of divine identity. The incarnation isn't something to which we apply knowledge; instead, it stands as the very epicenter of our knowledge of God. The direction is reversed: we don't come to the incarnation to "prove" God's existence; we come to receive God's self-revelation and, in turn, to be received by him. This revelation is not separate from God's identity—it is identical with it. There is no hidden deity behind the incarnation, no fallback on "foundations" or "transcendental markers."

We turn to a quote taken from the publication of Gunton's doctoral dissertation:

> There is no conceptual or ontological gulf between the being and the revelation of God, any more than there is an interest in the inner reality of God in abstraction from what he does in history. Why then must there be any distinction at all between the outward activity and essence, or between the "economic" and "immanent" trinity? ... An answer to this question brings us to

---

35. Gunton, *Becoming and Being*, 143.

the heart of Barth's doctrine of God. In this dipolar doctrine of God, there is what may be called an asymmetry of understanding, by which God's freedom is preserved. What God does is a sure guide to understanding of what God really is.[36]

It is worth restating the full extent of this shift. God is not an object we can study with detachment; God is relational and can only be known through God's relational acts among us.

This approach inevitably presents a degree of circularity, echoing Anselm's dictum and aligning with Barth's view that it is the only option God offers us. For Gunton, Barth's influence has been formative (to call it "foundational" might be a bit ironic!). Barth was the one to ignite Gunton's theological fire. Yet, even early in his career, it is clear that Gunton's appreciation for Barth is tempered by a critical stance. He was consciously stepping out of Barth's shadow.

OUT OF BARTH'S SHADOW

Both Gunton and Barth were fervent critics of Western theology, with Barth's iconic rejection of Brunner's natural theology standing as a prime example. For Gunton, however, the critique of Western theology took an even greater focus. His writings reveal that theological apologetics took precedence over the completion of a systematic theology—resulting in an incomplete overview of his systematic theology at the time of his death. Of those Gunton critiqued, Barth and Augustine receive the most attention, with Barth being the focus of this section and much of chapter 3 devoted to Augustine.

Barth's stature within Reformed theology, particularly concerning the doctrine of the Trinity, is hard to overstate. As Torrance noted, it is to Barth that we owe "the reintegration of revelation and the divine identity."[37] Barth's theological contribution to Reformed theology is so significant that it is easy to get lost in his shadows. Despite their differing emphases, Gunton and Barth played distinct, complementary roles. Barth's theology centers on the freedom of God, liberating theology from both its classical roots and its rationalist constraints (or outright

---

36. Gunton, *Becoming and Being*, 147.

37. Torrance, *Persons in Communion*, 58. Torrance's *Persons in Communion* is the publication of his second doctorate in which he focused on Barthian language in the doctrine of divine identity.

dismissal, depending on perspective). His most significant contribution was re-establishing the centrality of the doctrine of the Trinity.

Gunton's theology speaks to a different era, bringing with it a distinctive emphasis. His aim is to paint with a broader brush, integrating theology into God's larger creative purpose. While Barth focused on establishing the centrality of divine identity, Gunton sought to explore the implications of this divine identity on human identity and, indeed, on all of creation. In this respect, Gunton was more of a rehabilitator than a liberator.[38] If Barth's legacy marks the shift from *analogia entis* to *analogia fidei*, then Gunton's work marks the move from *analogia fidei* to *analogia relationis*.

Gunton's Criticisms of Barth

Gunton's movement beyond Barth becomes evident when examining his core criticisms. Some points may feel somewhat like putting the cart before the horse, as concepts important later in the chapter are engaged here before being fully introduced. This is because Barth serves as a foundational figure in the first half of Gunton's development. Gunton's more critical perspectives emerged as he gained exposure to thinkers like the Cappadocians, who will be introduced further on.

The Personal Nature of God Is Weakened

In *Becoming and Being*, Gunton describes Barth as a neoclassical theologian, suggesting that, despite the reforms Barth introduced, he couldn't fully escape his classical roots. Gunton acknowledges the value in Barth's effort to ground the knowledge of God's existence in revelation, noting it "has the merit of being rational without being rationalistic."[39] Yet, it is the outcome of this approach that concerns Gunton. *Analogia fidei*, in his view, feels too static, bearing a trace of Platonism. The unintended result,

---

38. Webster ("Gunton and Barth") supports this view in his comment on Gunton and Barth. "One of Gunton's worries was that Barth restricted the range of what Christian doctrine might achieve in interpreting the world, in part because his doctrine of God, oriented as it is to election and reconciliation does not press him outwards into engagement with the being of the creaturely world. There is a real difference here; where Barth was intensely (so some compulsively) focused, Gunton, especially in his later work, was an associative thinker more concerned to trace the ramifications of the gospel for the material and cultural world" (Webster, "Gunton and Barth," 19).

39. Gunton, *Becoming and Being*, 219.

Gunton argues, is that the personal dimension of faith is diminished to the point of near disappearance.[40] This early critique of Barth by Gunton is one that continues to develop throughout his later career.

Few examples illustrate Gunton's divergence from Barth more clearly than Barth's preference for *Seinsweise* ("mode of being") over "person" in describing the Trinity. Gunton, aligning with A. Torrance and others, considered Barth's language for the Trinity inadequate.[41] This initial dissatisfaction spurred Gunton's quest for a theology centered on divine identity. As his theology matured, this unease grew, with "person" becoming a non-negotiable term for Gunton.[42] While Gunton viewed this linguistic difference as a key departure from Barth, others argue the distinction is less pronounced. For Barth and Gunton, "person" carried distinct historical nuances, and within the same context, their positions may have aligned more closely.

---

40. Gunton, *Becoming and Being*, 221.

41. "Barth's concept of the trinitarian *Seinsweisen* obscures the concept of the communion of God. . . . If Barth is to adopt the term *Seinsweise* because of its apparent neutrality he risks the charge of naiveté here through his failing to appreciate the extent to which *Seinsweise* is less than neutral—to the extent that it undermines the notion of mutuality and of relatedness within the divine identity as they are conveyed by the term *person* when it is given in its proper theological currency" (Torrance, *Worship, Community*, 116).

42. Rahner (*Trinity*, 44) diverges from Barth's terminology, opting for "distinct manner of subsisting" as an alternative. Yet, he takes a pragmatic view on the term "person," noting, "the word 'Person' happens to be there, it has been consecrated by the use of more than 1500 years, and there is no really better word, which can be understood by all and would give rise to fewer misunderstandings." Rahner prefaces this by reminding us that we must often strip away the usual attributes we associate with "person" (Rahner, *Trinity*, 43). His insight is essential and resonates with Gunton's argument in *Actuality of Atonement*. The language we use to speak of God's acts and being stretches beyond its ordinary descriptive reach. Such language must be held lightly and enriched by a diversity of biblical terms, avoiding the exclusion of any one expression.

LaCugna introduces Rahner's English translation of *The Trinity* and is also reluctant to be too narrow in her definitions. "Theological definitions of person will continue to evolve, as they should. Personhood will remain notoriously difficult to define precisely, but that may be good reminder that no one concept is up to the task of defining the ineffable mystery of God" (Rahner, *Trinity*, xx). The claim that "no one concept is up to the task" could quite easily be the words of Gunton taken from *Actuality of Atonement*. A mature Gunton would stick with "person," but certainly acknowledge that it comes with terms and conditions.

Cunningham (*These Three Are One*, 71) too supports a more cautious approach. "Indeed, the biblical language for God is something of an architectural patchwork; it is greatly varied and widely unsystematic."

A Muted Role of the Spirit and Mediation

For Gunton, Barth's treatment of the Spirit was too static and retrospective. Gunton, instead, emphasized a more active, mediated role for the Spirit, focusing on relation and transformation. As Webster notes, "In short, for Gunton, both Barth's doctrine of creation and aspects of his Christology and soteriology remain caught in the briars of Neoplatonism and its divorce of the eternal from the temporal. The only means of release is a more consistently trinitarian, and especially pneumatological, doctrine of God's relation to the history of creatures."[43] However, in fairness to Barth, this difference may arise more from context than from underlying theological disagreement. Barth's focus leaned toward election and reconciliation, giving less attention to the mediation of grace post-reconciliation. Thus, while the Spirit's role may seem muted in Barth's work, it may reflect more of a contextual blind spot than a Neoplatonic influence.

A Response to Gunton's Barthian Critique

Gunton's engagement with Barth primarily focused on *Romans*, select writings from the 1920s, the *Anselm* book, and *Church Dogmatics*. His perspective was shaped by key figures in Barth interpretation from the 1950s and 1960s: T. F. Torrance and Robert Jenson in the Anglo-American sphere, along with continental voices such as Jüngel, Balthasar, and Barth's Lutheran and Roman Catholic critics.[44]

According to Webster, this selective reading led Gunton to seriously underestimate Barth's focus on time and history.[45] Webster suggests that Gunton may have had more common ground with Barth than he realized—a reminder that Gunton, at times, may have been too quick to draw his conclusions.

In concluding this section on Gunton's formation, it's clear that Gunton owed a substantial debt to Barth, especially in establishing the economic Trinity as central and holding that the doctrine of God is the foundation of systematic theology. Despite their apparent differences, Gunton's theology was fundamentally built on Barth's initial framework.

---

43. Webster, "Gunton and Barth," 26.
44. Webster, "Gunton and Barth," 18.
45. Webster, "Gunton and Barth," 29.

TOWARDS THE *ANALOGIA RELATIONIS*

When reviewing a theologian, examining the evolution of their views over time reveals their capacity to deepen their research and respond to critique. Some academics solidify their positions during doctoral studies, with the rest of their careers merely reinforcing these initial views. This is not the case with Gunton. Broadly speaking, the latter half of his career shows an increasing emphasis on identity and particularity. Using language that has gained traction in the doctrine of God, Gunton's shift might be described as a movement from *analogia fidei* to *analogia relationis*. This transition can be understood through two distinct movements, though, in practice, these shifts were interwoven and not easily separated into independent movements.

- The first shift is a turn toward the Cappadocians and the use of *perichoresis* in articulating the doctrine of God: Here, Gunton emphasizes the particularity and identity of each person within the Trinity. This represents a clear progression from his Barthian foundations and is accompanied by a growing dissatisfaction with Augustine. Augustine's perceived monism serves as a foil to the Cappadocians, whose emphasis on *hypostasis* underscores particularity within divine identity. This shift is arguably the most significant in Gunton's theology, requiring thorough engagement throughout this chapter and into the next.

- The second shift is a gradual moderation and broader application of the perichoretic concept. In this phase, Gunton takes a slightly more critical view of the Cappadocians yet extends *perichoresis* to encompass all of creation. Coleridge seems to be the initial catalyst for this broader application, though he recedes from focus as Gunton's project gains momentum. Gunton maintains a strong emphasis on relationality and particularity in persons, alongside a deepening appreciation for mediation—a theme largely influenced by Irenaeus, whose impact on Gunton nearly eclipses that of the Cappadocians (and even some of Coleridge's) in his later works.

Gunton expresses mounting discontent with certain theological choices in Western thought, using Augustine as both a focal point and a stand-in for key Western philosophical decisions. It is as though Gunton traces an intellectual thread from the Greeks through Augustine, Aquinas, Descartes, and even elements of Barth's work. His response, however, is uneven; at times, he engages directly with figures like Pseudo-Dionysius,[46] but largely concentrates his critique on Augustine's theology, where most of his critical focus lies.

There is a foil for this Greek "capture" in the Cappadocians. Yes, it is a position that did moderate in the latter half of Gunton's career. By his own admission, his early appreciation of the Cappadocians lacked enough critical reflection.[47] But even with this moderation of his Cappadocian appreciation, Augustine remained bad news for theology.

Holmes cites Gunton's 1985 inaugural lecture as Chair of Christian Doctrine as an early sign of this shift. "Alongside the concern for relationship and community that had always been there in the criticisms on alienation and suchlike, two new words come to prominence: 'person' and 'particularity.' These terms are almost wholly absent from the first decade of Gunton's published theology."[48] With Augustine emerging as the foil to the Cappadocians, he provides a fitting starting point for this exploration.

A Growing Discontent with Augustine (and What He Represents)

At the time of writing this chapter, South African politicians are retrospectively trying to understand the impact of State Capture—the control of the state by extra-governmental individuals through corruption. Analogously, this is the same as what Gunton sees in Augustine. Gunton's view is that Augustine has had his theology "captured" away from its Old Testament roots by Greek influence leading to a monistic concept of God and the effective displacement of the Trinity.

According to Gunton, this monistic concept of God has ultimately given rise to modern individualism.[49] He emphasizes this point in the

---

46. Gunton, *Act and Being*.

47. In the second edition to the *Promise of Trinitarian Theology* we see a more reflective Gunton. He writes, "I am less tempted than I was to run the risk of romanticizing the Eastern Tradition. That tradition, too, has a history of abstraction, and particularly of developing a breach between the being of God and his action in the economy of creation and redemption. But to the Cappadocians are owed crucial steps in the process of conceptual development which, despite some parallels in the West, has for the most part been neglected" (Gunton, *Promise*, xii).

48. Holmes, "Towards the Analogia Personae," 39.

49. Holmes observes how this theme was reiterated at Gunton's inaugural lecture as the chair of systematic theology. He paraphrases Gunton as follows: "Western theology has presented a monistic concept of God, which has resulted in an individualistic concept of what it is to be human" (Holmes, "Towards the Analogia Personae," 39).

opening chapter of this study: "In Augustine we are near the beginning of the era in which the church is conceived essentially as an institution mediating grace to the individual, rather than of the community formed on the analogy of the Trinity's interpersonal relationships."[50] Gunton finds the consequences of this shift so profound that he describes it with terms like "tragedy" and "crime."[51]

Gunton writes in a context marked by a post-Kantian rejection of metanarratives. In critiquing Augustine, he seizes this cultural moment to engage critically with one of Western Christianity's most influential figures. Though the era was more accommodating to iconoclasts and "dissenters" (as Gunton preferred to be known), his critique of Augustine remains among the boldest elements of his theology, leaving him in a notably exposed position. This underscores the importance of Gunton's assessment of Augustine, which forms a central focus of this study. However, some introductory remarks are essential to clarify the stakes of this debate.

Gunton's perspective on Augustine is foundational to his relational theology. It is as if he positions Augustine and his own views at opposite ends of a continuum. His stance is best captured in the following quote:

> We have seen that the achievement of the Cappadocians, an achievement which Augustine has failed adequately to understand, was to create a new conception of the being of God, in which God's being was seen to consist in personal communion. . . . Augustine has given us little reason to believe that God is to be known as he is from his manifestation in the economy. All the drive of his thought is aware from that to a knowledge derived from and based in the structures of human mentality: to essentially a singular deity for him community is epiphenomenal or secondary.[52]

The theological basis for this conclusion will be outlined below. As previously noted, Gunton's arguments are not always easily compartmentalized, and his critique of Augustine is a prime example. Following Gunton's intricate engagement with Augustine is a lengthy and challenging endeavor. For the purpose of this study, his conclusions about Augustine

---

50. Gunton, *Promise*, 51.

51. In the opening pages of *Act and Being*, Gunton writes, "It is one of the tragedies—one could almost say crimes—of Christian theological history that the Old Testament was effectively displaced by Greek philosophy as the theological basis of the doctrine of God, certainly so far as the doctrine of the divine attributes is concerned" (*Act and Being*, 3).

52. Gunton, *Promise*, 53.

rest on three foundational pillars—core elements without which the argument would collapse. Although these points are interrelated, expressing them separately clarifies the unique contributions each makes to the discussion. They are summarized below and will be expanded upon in the following sections:

- The Platonic influence, which elevates the intellectual over the material.
- The separation between the immanent and economic Trinity, effected through the use of *substantia*, which introduces an underlying reality within God's being, and the mediation of angels, which distances God from the revelation in Jesus.
- The prioritization of God's unity over the particularity of the three persons.

While Augustine frequently appears throughout Gunton's works, *The Promise of Trinitarian Theology* and *The One, the Three, and the Many* provide the most in-depth examinations. A more concise summary of these points appears in chapter 8 of *Act and Being*. Despite the considerable gap between the publications of *The Promise of Trinitarian Theology* and *Act and Being*, Gunton's convictions remain consistent; he readily refers readers to the former in the latter.[53] His chapter in *The Promise of Trinitarian Theology* was initially presented at a weekly research seminar at King's College before finding its way into the *Scottish Journal of Theology (SJT)*. The convictions expressed here persist into *Act and Being*, published in 2002.

Rahner: An Unlikely Resemblance

Before unpacking these points in more detail, it is essential to examine the similarities between Gunton and Rahner, especially given the objections some raise against Gunton's critique of Augustine[54]—more so, arguably, than against his criticisms of Barth. Although Rahner writes from a Catholic perspective, he shares Gunton's Reformed agenda. While Gunton doesn't cite Rahner directly, their work reflects striking thematic parallels:

53. See his comments in *Act and Being*, 135 n3.
54. Bradley Green being the most notable. His defense of Augustine is engaged in chapter 3.

- Rahner critiques the Neo-Scholastic influence of Thomas Aquinas, a later expression of the Platonic influence that Gunton identifies in Augustine.

- Rahner's preferred term, "distinct manner of subsisting," rests on his argument that the economic Trinity is the immanent Trinity. Section IC of his work is titled "The Axiomatic Unity of the 'Economic' and 'Immanent' Trinity." Rahner's summary reads: "The 'economic' Trinity is the 'immanent' Trinity and the 'immanent' Trinity is the 'economic' Trinity,"[55] a view closely aligned with Gunton's.

- Finally, on the third point regarding the elevation of the unity above the particularity, Rahner is also very clear. "It looks as if everything which matters for us in God has already been said in the treatise *On the One God*."[56]

Exploring why Gunton did not capitalize on this alignment lies beyond the scope of this study (though the similarity between these two "dissenters" presents a promising avenue for further research).[57] Here, this connection is highlighted to underscore the foundation of Gunton's critique of Augustine.

Augustine's Platonic Influence

Gunton observes that Augustine, influenced by Platonism, found it challenging to see the material world as genuinely real or as a vehicle for knowledge.[58] This philosophical stance, Gunton argues, had significant Christological implications: Augustine struggled to fully embrace the materiality of the incarnation.[59] For Gunton, this issue strikes at the

---

55. Rahner, *Trinity*, 22.

56. Rahner, *Trinity*, 17.

57. Gunton cites Rahner in chapter 3 of *The Promise of Trinitarian Theology*. The reference is to Rahner's comment, "It looks as if everything that matters for us in God has already been said in the treatise *On the One God*" (Rahner, *Trinity*, 17). This is it! None of the other concepts are introduced. The only other reference is found in *Enlightenment and Alienation* where Gunton aligns Rahner and Schleiermacher on the subject of transcendence and freedom (Gunton, *Triune Creator*, 96). Perhaps Gunton was nervous of too close an association with Rahner. Gunton was also not one to look for theological heavyweights to endorse his ideas. He was content to be backed up by his own convictions.

58. Gunton, *Promise*, 33.

59. Gunton, *Promise*, 34.

heart of theology, where a robust affirmation of Christ's humanity is foundational to a doctrine of the Trinity that remains grounded rather than veering into abstraction.[60] In this, Gunton's debt to Barth's insights is unmistakable.

A Separation of the Immanent and Economic Trinity

Gunton groups several of his critiques under the broader theme of the relationship between the immanent and economic Trinity, where he sees Platonism diluting Augustine's portrayal of God's active participation in the world. In discussing mediation, Gunton identifies two concerns centered on divine self-revelation. The "lesser" of these, he suggests, is Augustine's treatment of angels, where they risk overshadowing the Word's role as the mediator of God's relationship with the world. Gunton warns of a potential pitfall: creating the perception of an "unknown God working through the angels."[61] Essentially, Gunton questions why Augustine's God would need to send a messenger when he could be fully present himself.

The second, and far more significant, concern is Augustine's use of the Latin term *substantia* to translate the Greek *ousia*. This choice touches on a pivotal element in theological discourse: the language employed to articulate divine identity, a core issue at the heart of debates across theological schools. Here, Augustine diverges sharply from the Cappadocians, a decision with profound implications for the development of later doctrines.

Gunton observes of Augustine: "It is difficult for him to understand the meaning of the Greek *hypostasis*. One reason for this is that he can make nothing of the distinction so central to the Cappadocian ontology between *ousia* and *hypostasis*. . . . He prefers to say, with his Latin tradition, *unam essentiam* or *substantiam*."[62] While there are various ways to approach this debate, Gunton's core issue centers on *substantiam* and its implications for God's knowability. By grounding divine unity in this underlying *substantiam*, Augustine, according to Gunton, risks making God less accessible to human understanding—particularly because this *substantiam* resides within the immanent Trinity. Gunton clarifies this point further in *The One, the Three, and the Many*:

---

60. Gunton, *Promise*, 34.
61. Gunton, *Promise*, 34–35.
62. Gunton, *Promise*, 40.

> It could be argued that when the Western tradition took the decision to translate the Greek *ousia* by *substania*, which is in point of fact a literal translation of *hypostasis*, it effectively deprived the concept of the person of due weight because it introduced a stress on the *underlying* reality of God. On such a translation, the thought is encouraged that the real *substance* of God, what he substantially is, is the being that underlies the particular persons.[63]

The tension between the economic and immanent Trinity becomes especially evident here, and it is this divide that draws Gunton's strongest criticism. In contrasting Augustine with the Cappadocians, Gunton questions, "But if the Father is not the substratum of the Godhead, what is? What is it that the Spirit makes known through the Son? We are thrown back onto some unknown and unknowable substance underlying the economy."[64] Revelation is lost, and we are left with the predicament we were placed in by Kant.

Augustine's treatment of the Spirit, especially regarding its eschatological role, underscores another key critique from Gunton. Gunton argues, "In the economy it is the action of the Spirit not simply to relate the individual to God, but to realise in time the conditions of the age to come. Augustine's discussion of eschatology tends to lack this dimension, because it is essentially dualistic, tending to require a choice between this world and the next, rather than seeking a realisation of the next in the materiality of the present."[65]

The One over the Many

Augustine's starting point yields a doctrine of God rooted in Greek thought, prioritizing the unity of God over God's diversity—the one over the many. "What we see in the Origenist-Augustinian tradition is an elevating of the one over the many in respect of transcendental status. Unity but not plurality is transcendental."[66] Though a straightforward observation, it's crucial: this emphasis on unity is seen by Gunton as an artificial structure imposed on God's identity, diverging from the dynamic engagement we encounter in the *economic Trinity*.

63. Gunton, *One*, 191 (emphasis original).
64. Gunton, *Promise*, 54.
65. Gunton, *Promise*, 50.
66. Gunton, *One*, 138.

Gunton draws on Karl Rahner's critique of Augustine's separation in his treatises *On the One God* and *On the Triune God*. "It looks as if everything which matters of us in God has already been said in the treatise *On the One God*."[67] Here, Gunton underscores his point on the separation of the economic and immanent Trinity: "Because the one God is the real God, and known in a different way from the God who is three, God as he is in himself would appear to be, or at least conceivably is, other than the God made known in salvation history."[68]

Augustine's "Internal" Trinitarian Analogies

Augustine is renowned for his numerous Trinitarian analogies.[69] Gunton contends that these analogies "impose upon the doctrine of the Trinity a conception of the divine threeness which owes more to neoplatonic philosophy than to the triune economy, and that the outcome is, again, a view of an unknown substance supporting the three persons rather than being constituted by their relatedness."[70] Rahner, too, becomes a valuable ally here (or perhaps credit should go to his translator for the pointed emphasis). On this subject, Rahner argues that these "Augustinian-psychological speculations on the Trinity" lead to an "utterly vacuous" conclusion, grounded more in philosophical abstractions than in the economic Trinity.[71]

Interim Summary on Augustine

This brief overview of Gunton's critique of Augustine sets the stage for the next chapter, which explores the church's role in fostering individualism. Engaging with Gunton's assessment of Augustine here highlights a crucial point: Augustine, in Gunton's view, restricts access to the divine identity. Gunton summarizes, "Augustine has given us little reason to

---

67. Rahner, *Trinity*, 17.
68. Gunton, *Promise*, 32.
69. Cunningham (*These Three Are One*, 93) provides us with a brief summary of these. "As is well known, Augustine goes on in later books of *De Trinitate* to offer a large number of threefold *vestigia*: the lover, the beloved, and love; the mind, its knowledge, and its love; memory, understanding, and will; man, woman, and child; and many others."
70. Gunton, *Promise*, 42–43.
71. Rahner, *Trinity*, 19.

believe that God is to be known as he is from his manifestation in the economy."[72] This suggests that Augustine's approach remains grounded in classical methods, offering limited insights into the relationship between divine and human identity.[73]

Augustine has long been a central figure for Kantian criticism, and Gunton argues that this criticism is justified. Even in our post-Kantian landscape, there remains an Augustinian bias, which research on the Cappadocians must address. Engaging with Gunton, then—perhaps even challenging his conclusions—becomes essential for this line of inquiry. In many respects, Augustine remains an official gatekeeper of theology.

Perichoresis and the Cappadocians

Gunton's appreciation for the Cappadocians was profoundly shaped by his relationship with John Zizioulas, particularly during their collaboration on a paper for the British Council of Churches. Robert Jenson also played a role in deepening Gunton's engagement with Cappadocian thought. To the reader, it appears that Gunton discovered more than he

---

72. Gunton, *Promise*, 53.

73. Gunton is not alone in his critique of Augustine. We see strong support coming from Jenson in defending Gunton's views:

> What is *not* done by those who bash us Augustine-bashers is to face up to the truly disastrous propositions Augustine did in fact emphatically and insistently lay down, propositions that became maxims of subsequent Western theology. He *did* in fact say that the Cappadocian distinction of *ousia/hypostasis*—the very distinction that enabled the creedal doctrine of the Trinity—could be no more than a purely linguistic device, that it could tell us nothing about the reality of God. He did treat the works of God in the economy, in the history of God's saving work, as indivisible, in the sense that any of them *could* have been done by any of the three, thereby destroying the whole basis on which an immanent triunity could be affirmed in the first place (Jenson, *Decision Tree*, 12, emphasis original).

To Jenson we must add Schwöbel who also holds strong views on Augustine's influence of theology in the West:

> It would not be a gross exaggeration to see the mainstream history of Western trinitarian reflection as a series of footnotes on Augustine's conception of the Trinity in *De Trinitate*. Augustine's emphasis on the unity of the divine essence of God's triune being, his stress on the undivided mode of God's relating to what is not God and his attempt to trace the intelligibility of the doctrine of the Trinity through the *vestigial trinitas* in the human consciousness, mediating unity and differentiation, defined the parameters for the mainstream of Western trinitarian reflection" (Schwöbel, "Renaissance of Trinitarian Theology," 4–5, emphasis original).

initially sought in the Cappadocians' writings. Approaching their work as a theologian seeking an alternative doctrine of God, he found a model that better accounts for the particularity manifest in the economy. Not only did this search succeed, but it also led Gunton to a richer appreciation for personhood and the mediating role of soteriology.

The Cappadocians, contemporaries of Augustine, were born roughly twenty years before him—a narrow gap in the span of church history, yet enough for Augustine to be influenced by their writings. Their theological contributions emerged in response to the heresies of Sabellianism and Eunomianism,[74] and within their context, the Cappadocians' doctrinal innovations were transformative. Unlike the Greeks, the Cappadocians embraced an ontology grounded in personhood rather than substance. As Zizioulas states, "The philosophical scandal of the Trinity can be resolved or accepted only if substance gives way to personhood as the causing principle or *arche* in ontology."[75]

The Cappadocians used *perichoresis* to articulate their groundbreaking ontology. Gunton expands:

> In its origins, the concept was a way of showing ontological interdependence and reciprocity of the three persons of the Trinity: how they were only what they were by virtue of their interrelation and interanimation, so that for God to be did not involve an absolute simplicity but a unity deriving from a dynamic plurality of persons. . . . According to the teaching of perichoresis, the three divine persons are all bound up with each other, so that one is not one without the other two.[76]

---

74. Sabellianism is characterized by its singular use of the term "person," portraying the Trinity in a Modalist framework, where the one God assumes different roles or modes in the economy. Zizioulas outlines the theological implications as twofold: "[1] It would also make it impossible for the Christian to establish a fully personal dialogue and relationship with each of the three persons of the Trinity. [2] Furthermore, it would appear that God was somehow acting in the Economy, pretending, as it were, to be what He appeared to be, and note revealing or giving to us His true self, His very being" (Zizioulas, "Cappadocian Contribution," 46).

Eunomianism, on the other hand, has its roots in the Arian controversy and plays out through its particular handling of the substance of God and the persons of God. The divinity resides in the substance of God, and with the Son being begotten, He falls outside of the being or substance of God. Of the substance, little can be said (Zizioulas, "Cappadocian Contribution," 49).

75. Zizioulas, "Cappadocian Contribution," 52.

76. Gunton, *One*, 152–53.

Here, the possibility emerges for unity and particularity to function as co-determinants in defining divine identity—where neither the one nor the many serves as foundational. As Zizioulas asserts, "True being in its genuine metaphysical state, which concerns philosophy par excellence, is to be found in God, whose uncreated existence does not involve the priority of the *One* of the nature over the *Many* or the persons."[77]

Substance Replaced by Relationship

At the heart of this revolutionary doctrine lies a paradigm shift: the Cappadocians replace Augustine's focus on substance with a focus on relationship as the cause of being. Expressed in Gunton's words, "God is not God apart from the way in which Father, Son and Spirit in eternity give to and receive from each other what they essentially are."[78] Zizioulas[79] further connects this concept to the notion of personhood: "Entities no longer trace their being back to being itself—that is, being is not an absolute category in itself—but to the person, to precisely that which constitutes being. . . . In other words from an adjunct to being (a kind of mask) the person becomes the being itself and is simultaneously—a most significant point—the constitutive element (the 'principle' of 'cause') of all beings."[80]

For a fourth-century audience steeped in Greek philosophy, this was an enormous paradigm shift. Yet, to a generation on the cusp of the 4IR, it may seem less radical. Our organizations are already adopting this relational approach: the era of large corporate offices is giving way to brand-centric identities. A brand, inherently relational with attributes like trust and recognition, is now often the largest asset on a company's balance sheet. Many employers actively encourage remote work, forming businesses constituted purely by relationships among employees and with customers. These relational dynamics now serve as the constitutive elements of organizational identity.

What Gunton gains from the Cappadocians is an ontological paradigm shift, one that serves as a catalyst moving him from *analogia fides* to *analogia relationis*. Of course, catalysts, by definition, are never the

---

77. Zizioulas, "Cappadocian Contribution," 53 (emphasis added).
78. Gunton, *One*, 165.
79. Gunton, *One*, 165.
80. Gunton, *One*, 165.

entire ingredient. It is in this shift to *analogia relationis* that we see both the Cappadocians and Coleridge coming together. This is a crucial point. *Analogia* remains part of the equation but is transformed from *fides* to *relationis*. It is the Cappadocians who have provided the foundation for *relationis*, but it is to Coleridge that Gunton turns for *analogia*.

Coleridge and Revisionist Analogy

When it comes to analogy, Gunton seems almost to have painted himself into a corner. On one side, his theological work has been highly critical of the historical use of analogy,[81] especially regarding Platonist influences on transcendentals. Yet, Gunton recognizes that analogy can never be entirely excluded from theology. Clearly, the economic Trinity itself uses the analogous terms of Father and Son, and his own *Actuality of Atonement* centers on the Bible's analogous language surrounding the crucifixion.[82]

Gunton treads a delicate path. His challenge is to discuss analogy in a way that connects God's being with human personhood and soteriology, all while steering clear of Platonism and the classical or Thomistic use of analogy. His solution lies in the concept of the "open transcendental," where he draws extensively from the works of Samuel Taylor Coleridge.

Coleridge and Ideas

Coleridge is the enabler of Gunton's "open transcendental" through his notion of "ideas." Again, we encounter another commonly used word that needs to be "repositioned" into a new meaning. In Gunton's words, an "idea" is

> neither a timeless Platonic abstraction nor the particular mental datum of empirical experience beloved of so many of the philosophers in Coleridge's recent past. It is like the innate idea of the rationalist tradition, but not such as to succumb to Locke's critique, for it is concerned more with common ways in which

---

81. There are parallels here with Cranmer who saw the need for reform yet recognized the need to do so within the existing ecclesial structures. For example, if Cranmer discarded the concept of priesthood, he would have reduced too much—discounting the very platform from which he used to lead. Gunton is apprehensive of analogy, but without it we would lose the analogous relationship, particularly of Father and Son, that would help us understand *perichoresis*.

82. Gunton, *Actuality of Atonement*.

the human mind interacts with reality than with fixed or static concepts. For Coleridge ideas are not static, but dynamic.[83]

The emphasis on *dynamic* is crucial here. Coleridge resists any reduction to formula and is best understood in contrast to his contemporaries. Above all, Coleridge positions himself against Locke. As Gunton observes, Coleridge harbors a "suspicion of the doctrine of the passivity of perception, especially when that is linked up with a view of the world as a mechanism operating upon passive human senses."[84] Through Coleridge's notion of "ideas," Gunton finds an analogous link between the perichoretic relationship within the Trinity and our identity as persons-in-relation, formed through God's atoning work. This connection becomes a *dynamic universal note of being*: a concept to reference analogically, free from the static limitations of its Platonic predecessor.

Holmes observes that, while Coleridge was a prolific and varied writer, his impact on Gunton centers on a single, pivotal insight. "What Coleridge gave to Gunton was a hint—and in the dense and serpentine threads of logic that make up Coleridge's prose one never finds more than a hint—that ontologies, or, even better, protologies or archologies, define all that follows."[85] For much of Gunton's work, this observation by Holmes holds true. However, the depth of Gunton's appreciation for Coleridge becomes especially clear in *Enlightenment and Alienation*. This early work offers a more comprehensive look into Gunton's intellectual affinity with Coleridge, a scholar devoted to reversing the alienation of the Enlightenment, which Gunton describes as "the cutting of ourselves off from things as they really are."[86] On a more personal level, Coleridge's own journey from Unitarianism to Trinitarianism offered a solidarity that resonated deeply with Gunton.

---

83. Gunton, *One*, 143.

84. Gunton, *Enlightenment and Alienation*, 30.

85. Holmes, "Towards the Analogia Personae," 38. In an astonishingly dense lecture, unpromisingly entitled "On the Prometheus of Aeschylus: An Essay, Preparatory to a Series of Disquisitions Respecting the Egyptian in Connection with the Sacerdotal Theology, and in Contrast with the Mysteries of Ancient Greece," Coleridge offered a tabular contrast between worldviews (Holmes, "Towards the Analogia Personae," 38).

For further reading of Holmes on Gunton and Coleridge, see Holmes, "Gunton and Coleridge."

86. Gunton, *Triune Creator*, 7.

Using Coleridge to Create a Relational Analogy

Coleridge, like the Cappadocians, aids Gunton in achieving clarity, especially in his revisionist approach to analogy. In the extended quote below, Gunton situates his project by drawing on key historical figures, providing one of the rare instances where he defines his work through negation—stating what his project is not. Given his resistance to using negation in theological discourse, particularly regarding the doctrine of God, this choice stands out. Consequently, this reference becomes crucial for grasping the essence of Gunton's position.

> Only a concept of relationality based from the outset in God's economic involvement in the world of the many will be adequate. But Aquinas' aim is right. We do need to be able to conceive the way in which created structures of relationality are marked by the hand that made and upholds them. In that respect, Barth's programme, too, falls short. He is right to develop his theology of analogy on the basis—foundation—of the implications of God's triune relatedness to that which is not God. But his quest is too limited, being mainly, if not solely, restricted to a theology of how language may be predicated to God. In distinction from both of these paradigmatic theologians, my concern is to develop a trinitarian analogy of being (and becoming): a conception of the structure of the created world in the light of the dynamic of the being of the triune creator and redeemer.[87]

The quote is rich with significant references, many of which have been addressed in prior sections. These include Gunton's mention of "economic involvement," his recognition of Barth's success in conveying God's freedom (though limited by language), and terms like "concept of relationality," "dynamic," and "created world"—concepts that would gain even more prominence in Gunton's later theology. Here, Gunton affirms the value of analogy but rejects any notion of a static bridge bridging the gap.

To underscore the dynamic nature of this mediation, Gunton uses the concept of "mediation" to express his "non-foundationalist foundations." His language here is cautious and deliberate, rarely seen in his work—like a soldier navigating a minefield, carefully considering each step. Gunton is intent on stressing that these analogies are not static or fixed; rather, they unfold dynamically through God's actions in human history.

---

87. Gunton, *One*, 140–41.

In *The One, the Three, and the Many*, Gunton introduces perichoresis with a blend of conviction and caution, as if carefully guiding the reader. He notes, "It is important that when these transcendental concepts are used as a springboard for further thought, note should be taken of their extreme generality. They are, as in Coleridge's characterization of the most important ideas, both unfathomable and infinitely suggestive. They introduce a relational dynamic, but also bring with them all the problems associated with analogy."[88]

Gunton's language feels somewhat strained as he attempts to connect the doctrine of God with human identity. One might wonder if his task would have been easier through an analogy to music. Music has a unique mediatory quality—it conveys meaning without being substantive, resonating with ideas in a way that remains both mediatory and inexhaustible. Although neither Gunton nor Coleridge explicitly reference music, it could serve as a fitting illustration for Coleridge's concept of ideas that both mediate and remain boundless.

For Coleridge, the Trinity is the "idea of ideas," opening a transcendental space that connects humanity back to the identity of God. In Gunton's work, it is *perichoresis* that assumes this role, establishing an ontological link between God's being and human identity.[89] "Human being in the image of God is to be understood relationally rather than in terms of possession of fixed characteristics such as reason or will, as has been the almost universal tendency of the tradition."[90]

Coleridge as an Unlikely Partner

There's an irony in Coleridge's centrality within Gunton's work, given Coleridge's reputation as a staunch supporter of the Anglican establishment.[91] Had he encountered a dissenter like Gunton in person, their respect might not have been mutual! Despite some raised eyebrows among Gunton's critics over his reliance on Coleridge, few have offered direct

---

88. Gunton, *One*, 153.

89. "If, as I am suggesting, the concept of perichoresis is of transcendental status it must enable us to make a third step and begin to explore whether reality is on all its levels 'perichoretic,' a dynamism of relatedness" (Gunton, *One*, 153).

90. Gunton, *One*, 3.

91. Holmes describes Coleridge as an Anglican Zealot "who poured out scornful works in support of Anglican establishment" (Holmes, "Towards the Analogia Personae," 38).

critiques—a notable omission. While Gunton does offer occasional criticisms of Coleridge, his appreciation at times appears one-sided.

There's also room to explore the parallels between Coleridge and Schleiermacher. Though Coleridge moves beyond Schleiermacher by emphasizing the personal nature of God's being, he mirrors Schleiermacher in locating faith's essence within inner experience.[92] Even Augustine might have found valuable resources in Coleridge—a notion that Gunton would likely find unsatisfactory.

In a project that seeks to reposition analogy, Coleridge is a risky ally. His prose is dense and often challenging to navigate, with "idea" appearing prominently in only a single essay rather than as a consistent theme throughout his work.

Here, it's essential to introduce a key idea that will resonate into the next chapter: the debate around Coleridge—and, by extension, Barth, Irenaeus, and Augustine—is something of a distraction. In Gunton's writing, these influential figures seem to serve a symbolic function, with Gunton's engagement with each shaped by their alignment with his primary objective. This objective is to free theology from the constraints of foundationalism.

Barth is the first figure we encounter in Gunton's critique, yet he is faulted for not advancing far enough. Gunton's selective use of Barth overlooks potential common ground available in Barth's later writings. In contrast, Augustine, explored in the following chapter, is portrayed as the "father of foundationalism," and Gunton's assessment borders on contempt. On the other hand, figures like Coleridge, the Cappadocians, and Irenaeus receive Gunton's largely uncritical admiration, with Irenaeus holding a particularly favored position.

How does this idea impact our current assessment of Gunton and Coleridge? Coleridge presents a reversal of Cartesian alienation; where rationalism fostered isolation and an inward retreat, Coleridge counters with an emphasis on imagination and the relationality of the Trinity. In this way, Coleridge transcends the sum of his parts, serving as a catalyst that enables Gunton to move beyond mere "analogy" by offering a dynamic alternative. This raises the question: if Coleridge is an unexpected partner, is he nonetheless essential?

---

92. Heron, *Century of Protestant Theology*, 61.

A Conclusion: Was Coleridge Necessary?

Did Gunton truly need Coleridge? Ultimately, the answer is no. While Coleridge may have served as a catalyst for Gunton's own progression beyond certain paradigms, he is no longer essential for the transition to a mediated ontology today. Gunton, deeply invested in countering Platonism, sought an antidote that matched the offense. For him, Coleridge provided this antidote, enabling him to move beyond what he saw as Barth's limitations. However, Coleridge served primarily as a tool for Gunton, not for us. It's worth noting that Gunton's book emerged in a context of extreme relativism, where the idea of "universal marks of being" was a challenging concept, and Coleridge offered a way to bypass what Gunton perceived as an impassable barrier.

For today's reader, however, Coleridge acts more as a supplement to Barth than a necessity. Gunton viewed Barth's project as relationally limited, finding an alternative in the Cappadocian project but requiring Coleridge to apply *perichoresis* to soteriology. Yet, as Webster's critique suggests, Barth's later works addressed many relational gaps within *Church Dogmatics*. Here, Gunton arguably overextends by incorporating Coleridge, risking the credibility of the debate. Perhaps Gunton came to recognize this himself; though he never openly acknowledged it, Coleridge receives only a brief mention in *Act and Being*, and not in connection with the concept of ideas.

From Coleridge to Irenaeus and the Two Hands of God: A Transformed Pneumatology and Soteriology

Irenaeus is the final key contributor to be explored in detail. While it appears that a later Gunton may have lessened his reliance on Coleridge, the same cannot be said for Irenaeus. Just as Coleridge served as Gunton's counter to Descartes, Irenaeus acts as a foil to Augustine. Furthermore, Irenaeus supports Gunton in addressing what he perceived as a subdued role of the Spirit in Barth.

Ironically, while Gunton cautions against idealizing Irenaeus, he does not fully heed his own warning.[93] His use of Irenaeus lacks a

---

93. There are good examples of high praise for Irenaeus to be found in *The One, the Three, and the Many*. First is the reference to Irenaeus's "beautiful maintenance." "Because in his theology, the mediation by Christ as the Spirit, as well as the teleological directness of the creation, play too limited a role, a first effect is the link, so *beautifully*

critical dimension, at times bordering on romanticism. We previously noted Gunton's tendency toward polarization, and Irenaeus exemplifies this as well. For Gunton, Augustine could seemingly do no right, while Irenaeus could do no wrong. Chapter 3 will delve further into this topic, presenting a detailed comparison from *The One, the Three, and the Many* to demonstrate that 58 percent of Gunton's references to Augustine are counterbalanced by references to Irenaeus.

Gunton draws on Irenaeus and his "two hands" analogy to illustrate the soteriological dimensions of *perichoresis*—specifically, our participatory role within the life of God and the integral relationship between creation and redemption. Gunton critiques Western theology's approach to redemption, which he views as both narrow and transactional, primarily focused on dispensing grace to the individual. In his words, "Redemption means the completion of the whole project of creation, not the saving of a few souls from hell."[94] Irenaeus is pivotal in his response to this:

> It is arguable that few later theologies have achieved so adequate an integration of time and eternity, the one and the many, as Irenaeus. His work should not be idealised, for he is also bequeathed with problems to the tradition, but in general we shall not go far astray if we use him as a measure against which to assess prospective accounts of the economy. In contrast to him, some theologies are in danger of emphasising creation at the expense of redemption, and the reverse.[95]

The value of Irenaeus lies in the clarity of his "two hands" analogy, through which we understand that, by the Spirit, we are drawn into the very being of God. Ironically, however, Irenaeus's pneumatological emphasis introduces a Christological challenge for Gunton. This issue is notably raised by his former doctoral supervisor, Robert Jenson, who critiques Gunton's reception of Irenaeus. Jenson states, "Gunton's reception of Irenaeus brings him and us to yet another fork in the road. A key part of Irenaeus' fidelity to the economy is that he never speaks of the

---

maintained in Irenaeus between creation and redemption, becomes weakened to the point of disappearing, to that it is rarely adequately treated in Western theology after this time" (Gunton, *One*, 120, emphasis added). Later we read of Irenaeus's "remarkable coherence." "Irenaeus is able to give a *remarkably coherent* and satisfying account of the divine constitution of and involvement in the created world's time and space" (Gunton, *One*, 120, emphasis added). You don't need to be a form critic to pick up Gunton's appreciation.

94. Gunton, *Triune Creator*, 71.
95. Gunton, *One*, 159.

eternal Son as other than that Son who is the man Jesus."[96] In response to this, he remarks: "One way to cut the knot of Irenaeus' strange logic is of course to say with the apologists from Justin to Origen, that for all eternity the Son/Logos was unincarnate, a *Logos asarkos*, and that when Mary got pregnant this Logos became Jesus. Gunton chose instead to stick precisely with the oddity of Irenaeus' way of speaking."[97]

With access to Gunton's unpublished book on doctrine, Jenson offers insight into Gunton's reasoning for his stance on the "newness" of Jesus' birth. He writes, "If the Logos is not somehow other after the birth than he was before, what was the point of the birth?"[98] This question highlights a complex debate, one in which Gunton had multiple interpretive paths.[99] However, engaging in the debate itself is not the primary aim of this chapter. Instead, it illustrates that Gunton might have approached Irenaeus with a more critical lens. Furthermore, it raises the question of whether the outcome of this debate risks conflicting with God's perichoretic nature and the mediated nature of our relationship with God. Jenson's critique does not suggest such a conflict, indicating that this concern does not disqualify Irenaeus from being one of Gunton's core theological influences.

Irenaeus provides a fitting point at which to close this section. *Analogia relationis* emerges as a key departure from Barth, encapsulating Gunton's approach to *perichoresis*. The themes of relationality, mediation, and particularity are foregrounded as foundational to his theology. With the aim of offering a broad view of Gunton's theological framework, it is essential to briefly revisit some of the critiques raised before proceeding to a summative conclusion.

CRITICAL RESPONSES

Criticism held a prominent place in Gunton's theological approach. He writes, "The Christian faith is best defended, I believe, on the joint bases of a confidence in its truth and an openness to the reception of criticism and truth from whatever quarter. That has not always been the manner of

---

96. Jenson, *Decision Tree*, 14.
97. Jenson, *Decision Tree*, 14.
98. Jenson, *Decision Tree*, 14.
99. Does this debate not relate to the impassibility of God if we take the death of Christ as an extension of his incarnation? Using Gunton's language again we would need to say that if the Logos was not somehow other after his death on the cross then what was the point of the death. Perhaps the point is too simplistic.

things and it makes the task of contemporary defence more difficult than it might be."[100] In essence, he suggests that a lack of critical engagement weakens theology as a discipline. As the lens of critique now focuses on him, it is reassuring to think that Gunton himself might have found its absence disappointing.

Philosophical (Epistemic) Bias

Gunton's greatest strength also serves as his greatest limitation. His philosophical background provided him with critical insight into the development of doctrinal thought, enabling him to offer a distinctive perspective. However, this concentrated focus often resulted in peripheral blind spots. This is evident in his critique of Augustine, where he predominantly follows the epistemological thread, nearly to the exclusion of other factors. Here, Gunton arguably falls prey to the very "epistemic drive" he criticizes in Barth.[101] His analysis might have been more comprehensive with a deeper understanding of political and economic forces. Modernity, after all, involves not only the obscuring of the many but also the rise of the one. The dynamics of concentrated power in business and politics, notably absent from Gunton's work, are integral to this narrative. Economically, the rise of corporations, surplus income, and the stock exchange all played a crucial role in shaping modernity. These omissions ultimately narrow his audience and diminish his credibility in engaging with the full scope of modernity's impact.

Applying this to Gunton's engagement with Augustine highlights his careful construction of a significant challenge to Western Christianity—albeit one that overlooks other critical points. Gunton's overall approach to Augustine can thus be described as somewhat myopic. This rationale partly underlies chapter 3's focus on the Gunton/Augustine relationship, where the goal is to assess whether Gunton may have risked one of his most distinctive contributions by overextending his critique of one of Christianity's most celebrated figures.

Cunningham offers a related critique, particularly regarding *The One, the Three, and the Many*. Cunningham argues that Gunton creates an artificial dichotomy between "the One" and "the Many," forcing philosophy and theology into opposing camps.[102]

100. Gunton, *One*, 7.
101. Gunton, *Promise*.
102. Cunningham, *These Three Are One*, 39.

Polarization of Scholars

In addition to a philosophical bias, this chapter has also examined Gunton's tendency to polarize other scholars. Augustine provides a clear example, alongside Barth, as both receive significant critique. Yet, this tendency has a counterpart in Gunton's apparent idealization of certain figures, such as Coleridge and Irenaeus.

Critiques of Gunton's polarizing approach fall into two categories. First, there are critiques that agree with Gunton's identification of flawed theology, with Jenson's analysis of Gunton's take on the *Logos* and Irenaeus serving as an example. Second, there are critiques asserting that Gunton misreads sound theology—a category in which his critique of Augustine often falls, according to critics. Scholars like Green, McNall, and Webster suggest that the primary issue lies with Gunton's interpretation of Augustine rather than with his theology overall. Green, similar to Webster, does not dispute Gunton's conclusions but questions his portrayal of Augustine, whom he contends could serve as more of an ally to Gunton than an adversary. Gunton himself, however, would likely disagree with this assessment.

Cunningham is one of the more vocal critics of this tendency in Gunton's work. In his summary of Trinitarian theology, he labels this approach as historical "scapegoating," which he defines as "the apparent necessity felt by many theologians to explain the decline of trinitarian theology by casting aspersions on a particular theologian or theological movement."[103] Gunton and Jenson are among those he identifies as culprits, particularly in their critiques of Augustine. However, Cunningham's perspective could be seen as somewhat naïve. As an Episcopalian teaching at a Reformed institution (Hope College, Michigan), he indirectly benefits from the same scapegoating tactics practiced by Reformers such as Latimer and Ridley.

That said, it must be acknowledged that Gunton's redaction is frequently abrasive, and there are numerous points where a lighter touch would have served him well.

---

103. Cunningham, *These Three Are One*, 31.

Truncation!

Related to the above criticism is the observation that Gunton's critiques are not always grounded in a representative selection of works. In an earlier section, Webster criticized Gunton for basing his assessment of Barth on Barth's earlier writings. This is a valid point, though not a disqualifier. If Webster's argument reflects a tendency to equate Barth primarily with *Church Dogmatics*, then this is the appropriate place to raise such criticism. In Gunton's writings, however, we rarely see him engage with Barth's context in a way that might provide a more sympathetic view, though this does not imply it was absent. The criticism here is not of Gunton's direction or his perspective on early Barth but rather that he did not balance his critique with Barth's later, more mature works. Valid or not, this critique does not undermine the findings of this chapter.

Radical Ontology

Attention now turns to a central critique of Gunton's theology: his revisionist ontology. This section serves as an introduction, as the arguments involved are intricate and require the in-depth analysis provided in chapter 3 to reach a more conclusive assessment.

Among scholars supportive of Trinitarian theology, there exists a range of ontological perspectives. Many on the periphery appreciate the concept of relationality but struggle to connect it with ontology, marking the beginning of what we might call the relationality spectrum. Thompson contends that Gunton has positioned himself at the opposite end of this spectrum, advocating an ontology that is irreducibly relational. While generally appreciative, Thompson suggests that Gunton's radical ontology may go a step too far.[104] However, in this conclusion, Thompson appears to misinterpret Gunton. Although Gunton does imply irreducible relationality in several instances, his stance is ultimately more nuanced. On this specific point, Gunton clarifies, "It is at this stage of the argument, however, that we must be aware also of the way in which *perichoresis* is—only—an analogy. When used of the persons of the Godhead, it implies a total and eternal interanimation of being and energies. When

---

104. Thompson, *Has Colin Gunton's*.

used of those limited in time and space, changes in the intension of the concept necessarily follow."[105]

The best way to grasp this debate, at least from Gunton's perspective, is to delve deeper into his dispute with Augustine. At the core of this dispute lies the theological treatment of *ousia* and *hypostasis*. Narrowing it down further, the primary disagreements revolve around *ousia*. This debate is well illustrated in Nausner's critique of Gunton and Thompson's response. Although neither scholar agrees with Gunton's handling of *ousia*, Thompson maintains an appreciation for Gunton's broader contributions despite their divergence. His critique is particularly pointed, accusing Gunton of "violating" the distinction between *ousia* and *hypostasis*.[106] Thompson, in contrast, asserts that Gunton "collapses" *ousia* into *koinonia*.[107]

While Thompson may have misread Gunton or interpreted him without the benefit of his tempering remarks, he indirectly raises an intriguing question: Is there a middle ground in Gunton's ontology? Can *analogia relationis* be realized in a moderated form? Chapter 3 will explore this possibility, and chapter 6 will take up the task of arguing for its viability.

PRELIMINARY CONCLUSION ON GUNTON'S CONTRIBUTION: *PERICHORESIS*, RELATIONALITY, PARTICULARITY, AND MEDIATION

This is only a preliminary conclusion, as our examination of Gunton continues in chapter 3. While this chapter has offered a holistic overview of his works to clarify his theological positioning, chapter 3 will narrow its focus to his engagement with Augustine. Not only does this debate reach to the core of Gunton's theology, but it also contextualizes it within his broader project. Any assessment of Gunton is incomplete without expanding on this context.

In summarizing Gunton's theology, we borrow an analogy from Barth, who likened the writing of his *Epistle to the Romans* to stumbling in the dark of a church bell tower, accidentally grabbing the bell rope for support and inadvertently waking the whole village. Gunton, similarly roused by the bell, finds himself surprised that others are still sleeping.

---

105. Gunton, *One*, 170.
106. Nausner, *Failure of a Laudable Project*, 213.
107. Thompson, *Has Colin Gunton's*.

His career, then, has been a continuous effort to keep ringing the bell until all are fully awake—to bring about a renewed appreciation for Trinitarian theology. As Cunningham puts it: "The doctrine of the Trinity is a challenge to the modern cult of the individual."[108] In delivering this challenge, Gunton is more of a bell ringer than a builder. Though he aimed to provide both critique and constructive insight, it is his critique that stands out as the larger contribution, driven by a deep discontent with both secular and theological conceptions of the self. Both domains, in his view, are marred by distortions that demand redress.

Bell ringing serves an essential purpose. This book contends that contemporary society still struggles to balance *the one* and the many—a challenge intensified by today's radical individualism, which both fuels and results from this imbalance. Rather than bringing true freedom, individualism has isolated people and promoted a notion of identity far removed from the participatory vision of God's engagement with humanity. Modern individualism has little in common with the perichoretic doctrine of personhood, which emphasizes relational identity. Therefore, radical individualism must stand at the center of any theological critique of the market economy.

God does not hold a monopoly on mediation. Thinkers like James K. Smith, particularly within movements like Radical Orthodoxy, are pioneering fresh expressions of ontology and identity. Although Smith's focus is on the formative—or "liturgical," as he provocatively terms it—nature of retail spaces, his insights readily extend to the broader impact of the market economy. Smith exposes how our Cartesian heritage continues to erode our sense of self. Individualism, in this view, demands a remedy, yet the church remains too invested in classical theology to offer a viable alternative. Just as the American housing crisis stemmed from the misevaluation of bonds, much of today's theology of personhood and identity is grounded in concepts that have been similarly overvalued. The theology or personhood and identity needs a major overhaul if it is to play any role in God's mission.

Particularity and Relationality Are Not in Conflict

Gunton's aspirations extended beyond the role of a bell ringer; he sought to be a builder, guiding the church back to its Trinitarian roots

---

108. Cunningham, *These Three Are One*, 8.

in addressing today's crises. Yet, endorsing Gunton's theology cannot be done without reservations. His project is built around *analogia relationis*, the analogy of relationship. While one may support the shift from *analogia fidei* (the analogy of faith) to *analogia relationis*, this does not necessitate arriving at the same constructs as Gunton.

At the core of *analogia relationis* lies the concept of *perichoresis*, which emphasizes that particularity and relationality are not opposing forces but, rather, essential complements in understanding our identity. Gunton connects particularity directly to divine identity, stating, "The chief affirmation to be made here is that if persons are, like the persons of the Trinity and by virtue of their creation in the image of the triune God, hypostases, concrete and particular, then their particularity too is central to their being."[109] Yet, particularity remains an underappreciated concept. We see this in industries like fashion, where individuality is often shaped by fleeting trends rather than an authentic expression of self.

Gunton's critics often value relationality but stop short of agreeing that relationships alone constitute being, a position Gunton, following Zizioulas, takes perhaps too far. Gunton's approach leaves little room for a continuum, instead drawing a firm line in the sand. Yet, this overextension does not disqualify his contributions; one can disagree with his endpoint while appreciating his key emphases: mediation, particularity, and relationality. Gunton's primary contribution lies in his call for Western theology to "write back" these attributes into its framework. The challenge, however, is one of visibility—without recognizing the weaknesses in our theological heritage and thoughtfully applying Gunton's insights, we risk working at cross purposes, like pressing the brake and accelerator simultaneously. Even a partial embrace of Gunton's ideas demands a rigorous examination of our theological foundations. Nowhere is this more relevant than in addressing contemporary individualism, a pervasive paradigm that obstructs Gunton's three core contributions: *particularity*, *relationality*, and *mediation*.

Conclusion: Reconceiving the *Ordo Salutis*

A key task of this book is to critically examine Gunton's assertion that the contemporary Western church distributes grace merely to individuals. This idea begins to take shape in *Becoming and Being*, where Gunton

---

109. Gunton, *One*, 196.

writes, "Grace is not a semi-substantial entity as it sometimes appears to be conceived in theology, but a further specification of the act that God is. God is grace, and there can therefore be said to be in the essence of God a turning to man in condescension. . . . Grace is not a 'thing' or substance apart from himself that he gives, but an aspect of the becoming in which God is himself."[110]

This view contrasts sharply with much of Reformed theology, highlighting why Gunton embraced *perichoresis* as a model of grace that is relational rather than transactional. Alan Torrance notes that adopting a perichoretic model "would not only have addressed the dichotomies of so much traditional Western thought (not least by undermining the contractualism of the Western *ordo salutis* and the impersonalist notions of revelation), but would encourage a fuller appreciation of revelation as a creative, perichoretic and participative event, one whose *telos* is the integrated reordering of our humanity for the fullness of participation in the triune life of God."[111]

As we bring together our reflections on Gunton, we anticipate that his contributions of mediation, particularity, and relationality will be delivered through *perichoresis* as the primary framework. This contribution represents a shift away from a reliance on open transcendentals. Building on the previous discussion, Gunton's most significant impact may lie in his critique of the foundational assumptions of contemporary theology.

While the church does not set the agenda of the marketplace, it has the responsibility to act as a counterbalance. *Perichoresis* offers a vision of personhood that is non-contractual and leaves no room for the marketplace's *ordo salutis* of meritocracy. Instead, *perichoresis* fosters an ecclesiology centered on belonging rather than behaving.

Ultimately, *perichoresis* draws the church back to a deeper dependency on God. Gunton emphasizes that grace is mediated, not simply distributed. The role of *perichoresis* also connects directly with the critique of individualism discussed in chapter 3. For Gunton, Augustine represents the early roots of an obstruction to *perichoresis*, making it essential to examine this aspect of Gunton's theology more closely before addressing the limitations of Faith and Work theology.

---

110. Gunton, *Becoming and Being*, 199.
111. Torrance, *Persons in Communion*, 119.

3

Gunton's Biography of Individualism

Tracing the Path from Augustine to Adidas

INTRODUCTION: EXPLORING PURPOSE AND RISK

Gunton's hypothesis boldly suggests that the roots of modern individualism are found in the Christian tradition, particularly in Augustine. Gunton's disturbing hypothesis is explored further in *The Promise of Trinitarian Theology*, where he writes: "In Augustine we are near the beginning of the era in which the church is conceived essentially as an institution mediating grace to the individual rather than of the community formed on the analogy of the Trinity's interpersonal relationships."[1] This is, in essence, Gunton's reversal. Rather than defending theological principles against those of philosophy, he reinterprets these core ideas of modernity, turning them on their head. The aim of this chapter is to examine the validity of Gunton's claim, acknowledging that, even if only

---

1. Gunton, *Promise*, 51. Readers will note that this book refers to *Western theology*, while Gunton often speaks of *the church*. As a student of *Church Dogmatics*, Gunton likely reflects Barth's view that theology belongs within the church. However, *Western theology* is used here to emphasize Gunton's focus on the European and North American context.

partially accurate, it presents a profound challenge to the integration of faith and work.

This chapter offers a path to explore the foundations of Gunton's ontological convictions—specifically, the roots of *perichoresis*. Spanning the vast period from Augustine to Adidas, Gunton's work is at its most compelling here. His broad, confident approach enables him to tackle debates that would intimidate most. Put another way, Gunton suggests that a powerful secular doctrine of the self stands in direct contrast to his Trinitarian focus.[2] This doctrine, he argues, was not conjured *ex nihilo* by the Enlightenment, as often claimed, but has instead grown from a distorted theological root. In Gunton's view, certain core aspects of Western theology and the individualism driving the market economy share common origins. He challenges the notion that faith and the market operate from opposing paradigms; rather, he argues that their frameworks may be strikingly similar, even syncretistic.

The most contentious aspect of Gunton's argument is that, to make his case, he effectively sacrifices Augustine on the altar of theological criticism. Known for his bold claims, this is perhaps Gunton's boldest yet. Augustine stands as one of the most revered figures in church history, making any strong critique of him both a solitary and audacious endeavor—some might even call it reckless. Using this critique as a foundational element in a larger theological project carries significant risk. Any theologian aiming to challenge Augustine's legacy must present an exceptionally robust argument. To borrow a phrase from commerce, the theologian pursuing such a path must weigh carefully whether the potential "return" of a successful argument justifies the risk of the entire project's collapse.

We enter this debate with an understanding of Gunton's characteristic style, marked by a broad-brush approach. Critics have previously argued that this tendency has led to imprecise interpretations of figures like Barth and Augustine. Similarly, this approach often leaves Gunton less critical of his allies, notably Irenaeus, who features prominently in his critique of Augustine. Although a comprehensive analysis of Gunton's stance on Augustine is yet to be undertaken, there remains a suspicion that Gunton's research may not be sufficient to significantly challenge

---

2. This book does not aim to provide a comprehensive review of identity. Instead, it centers on the tension between constructive and subtractive views of individualism. The goal is to present an argument favoring a constructive perspective and to demonstrate that this perspective has deep theological roots.

Augustine's stature or influence. This initial hesitation represents one of the many challenges addressed in these opening pages, aiming to underscore the importance of the problem at hand.

Compounding these challenges is the vast historical distance between the two horizons under examination—Augustine and contemporary individualism. At the outset, we face two formidable obstacles: the near impossibility of tracing a direct causal link across such an extended period and the iconic status of Augustine himself. In short, this section summarizes the considerable risk involved. Yet the potential reward tips the balance. If Gunton's argument proves even partially valid, it opens the door to a possible revision—even reversal—of foundational aspects of the theology of Faith and Work.

The next section on structure and scope will explore how previous methodologies may have inclined others to overlook key aspects of Gunton's argument. This, however, defers the chapter's main content, and given the "high-risk" nature of the undertaking, a more thorough preamble is essential.

GUNTON'S NARRATIVE: A BIOGRAPHY OF INDIVIDUALISM

Augustine is the proverbial elephant in the room. This section aims to reposition the discussion and outline the methodology that will guide it. As noted, Gunton's approach is broad-brushed; using an analogy, one might liken it to a high-flying jet. The altitude allows a plane to travel farther, but at the cost of more fuel, less agility, and a requirement for a longer runway. Similarly, Gunton's work is best understood with an awareness of this "altitude."[3] In this context, altitude highlights that the debate does not center on Augustine. The true focal point is individualism and its

---

3. We find a similar sentiment in Holmes's introduction to *Revelation and Reason: Prolegomena to Systematic Theology*: "Colin's telling of intellectual history is often enough impressionistic, offering heightened contracts, bold colours and stark lines; like a great painting, however, if it distorted the appearance of reality somewhat it was only to reveal more clearly the essence of what was being looked at" (Gunton, *Revelation and Reason*, 5). And again, this time specifically with Augustine in mind: "Colin's approach to the history deserves comment. He was master of the grand historical narrative, and would tell big stories spanning centuries to illustrate what he regarded as the key historical developments" (Gunton, *Revelation and Reason*, 7).

development. Methodologically, centering the discussion on Augustine would divert it from its intended trajectory.[4]

The connection between this analogy and the method of this chapter needs to be clarified. Logically, the popular approach to addressing this sub-problem has been to break it down further, structuring the chapter around the specific nature of Gunton's criticisms of Augustine. Many of Gunton's critics have taken this route, isolating each component of Gunton's engagement with Augustine. Addressing these points individually and in sequence often leads to dismissing their overall validity. In essence, they are unraveling the strands of the cord and testing each one's independent strength, rather than assessing the strength of the chord as a whole.

Taking this approach is a mistake, revealing a failure to align method with content. By treating each component as an isolated problem to be solved, we risk pulling the Augustinian debate out of its broader context.[5] This approach accomplishes little more than stacking critique upon critique, merely to satisfy the examiner's expectation of critical thinking. To remain true to our goal—contributing meaningfully to the debate—a different path is essential.

Significant weight in this argument rests on the above point. Therefore, it is imperative that we take the time to bring absolute clarity to both this point, and the grand narrative that we interpret Gunton presenting—that of the biography of individualism.

Causality: Origins of Individualism

Gunton uses Augustine to assist in rewriting the biography of individualism, illustrating his conceptual reversal. While the modern understanding of individualism sees itself as emerging through a process of subtraction—stripping away external influences—Gunton interprets it as birthed through construction. The reference to Adidas in the chapter heading serves as a proxy for individualism, embodying its contradictions

---

4. See also Rae ("Introduction," 4), who underscores the risk of centering the debate on Augustine, stating, "one should not allow a defence of Augustine to deflect attention from what, for Gunton, was really at stake."

5. There is an irony here. Gunton's critics accuse him of isolating parts of Augustine's writings from the larger narrative—an accusation we'll explore further, particularly with Green. The irony, of course, is that in defending Augustine against Gunton, they employ the very method they criticize in him: addressing an argument in isolation from its broader context.

between proclamation and practice. With Adidas, we observe the drive for individuals to craft unique identities, yet they do so through a mass-produced brand, reliant on external recognition. The brand's global appeal, transcending economic and cultural boundaries, suggests that the "unique" modern individual may be less distinct than the original modernity project envisioned.[6]

For Gunton, individualism is the focal point, with significant credit owed to Taylor for his inspiration. Taylor's seminal work, *Sources of the Self*, emerged in the late 1980s, when paradigms were the topic of the day.[7] His opening chapter, "Inescapable Frameworks," lays a strong foundation for causality over subtraction, and Taylor remains a guiding presence in Gunton's argument, helping him trace the formation of individualism.

Gunton challenges the modern belief that the autonomous individual emerged by stripping away misguided influences—a concept known as the subtractionist theory of the self. In contrast, Gunton argues that individualism is not a natural state uncovered through reduction; rather, it is a constructed identity shaped by specific theological interpretations. Here, Augustine plays a key role, but not as a standalone figure—he is part of Gunton's broader critique of subtractionist theology in shaping modern individualism. To debate Gunton's perspective on Augustine without addressing his critique of subtraction misses a central part of Gunton's argument. As the title suggests, Augustine is not engaged merely as a historical figure; he is portrayed as the initiator of the path that ultimately leads us to Adidas.

---

6. Taylor (*Sources of Self*, 40) echoes this point in the following: "It is a critique that has often been made of modern consumer society that it tends to breed a herd of conformist individuals." There is not enough scope in this study to explore this point in detail; however, it is introduced here to set the stage for chapter 4, which examines how writings within the Work and Faith movement engage with this significant topic.

7. Taylor, *Sources of the Self*.

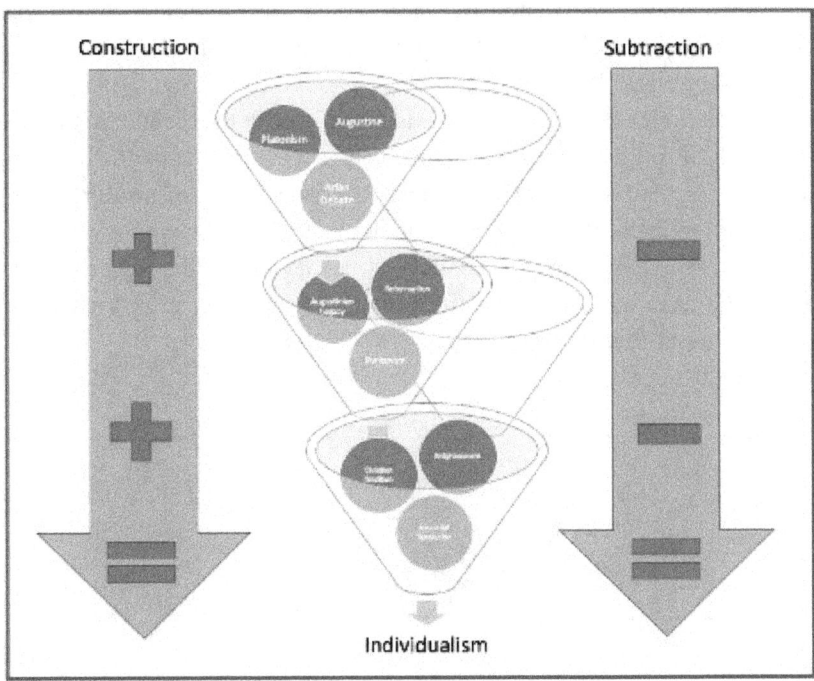

Figure 01: Gunton's Construction View of Individualism
Versus Predominant Subtraction Theories.

Contextualizing Criticisms Against Gunton

To recap, Augustine does not occupy the central role often attributed to him. Instead, this belongs to individualism—or, as Gunton prefers, foundationalism. This distinction is crucial for understanding Gunton's critics, particularly those focused on his treatment of Augustine. While he has faced considerable critique, two critics especially relevant to the Augustine debate will be examined here. Their approach is notably linear: they deconstruct Gunton's view of Augustine down to individual concepts or statements, each then scrutinized for validity.

The natural response to this method might seem to be an appellate approach, where each point is re-examined to identify potential gaps and arrive at a revised judgment. However, this would not engage Gunton on his own terms. His broad-brushed style loses its effectiveness when reduced to a series of isolated arguments. Instead, Gunton's work requires assessment from a higher vantage point, one that encompasses the larger narrative of individualism's evolution.

With individualism, or foundationalism, at the center, Gunton's approach to Augustine shifts. Rather than examining Augustine in isolation, Gunton works backward from the "crime scene" of modern individualism to locate its source, ultimately identifying Augustine—or more precisely, as McNall reminds us, Augustine's *legacy*—as the culprit.[8] This legacy, Gunton suggests, is distinct from Augustine himself, creating a nuanced view that demands analysis within the broader framework of individualism's biography.

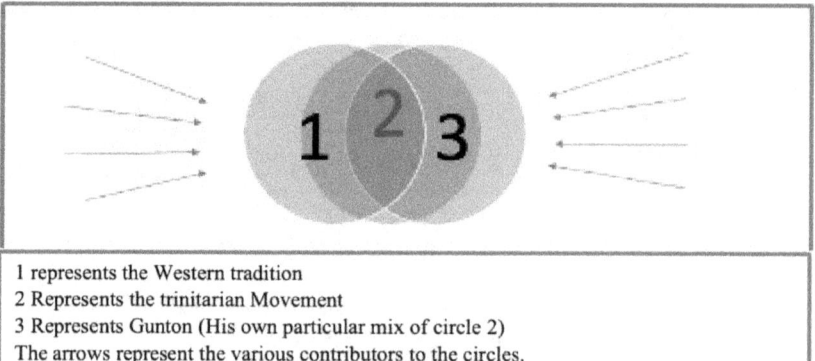

1 represents the Western tradition
2 Represents the trinitarian Movement
3 Represents Gunton (His own particular mix of circle 2)
The arrows represent the various contributors to the circles.
In this diagram, Augustine only gets to be an arrow. The Reformation must be there too.
In terms of circle 3, Irenaeus must be a contributor, so too must Coleridge and Barth.

Figure 02: Illustration of Gunton's Position Relative to the Broader Trinitarian Renaissance.

What this approach clarifies is that even if Augustine is ultimately acquitted of Gunton's criticisms, the broader argument regarding the flaws within Western theology can still stand. Gunton's perspective begins with Barth and is interwoven with influences from the Cappadocians, Irenaeus, Coleridge, and Zizioulas, among others. What truly challenges Gunton's model is not necessarily a rejection of his critique of Augustine, but rather his inference of a causal link between individualism and the Christian tradition. The findings of this study must address this critical point.

---

8. McNall, *Free Corrector*, 246.

Clarifying the Purpose of the Chapter

In summary, let's revisit the key question driving this exploration: "To what extent can Christian tradition(s) be held responsible for the radical individualism we encounter in today's global market economy?" While Gunton raises specific criticisms about Augustine's influence, these should not overshadow the broader discussion.

Gunton's critique of Augustine is indeed one of his boldest claims, yet it must be appreciated within the broader context of his critique of Western Christianity. For Gunton, these critiques sometimes verge on synonymous. Thus, this chapter aims to examine both his treatment of Augustine and the suggested causal link between individualism and the Christian tradition—two arguments that can stand independently.

This does not dismiss the scholarly views of those who defend Augustine. Their insights, as we will see, hold essential implications for theology's legacy. However, methodologically, these views shift the focus. With a nod to Barth's influence, we encounter questions like: "What of Barth's reversal?" "What causality was he writing against?" "What of Gunton's *Becoming and Being*?" This chapter's hypothesis suggests that there are causal drivers within Christianity that may need revision, and the critical question becomes whether these drivers share common ground with modern expressions of individualism.

INDIVIDUALISM AND CAUSALITY: THE BROADER DEBATE ON CONSTRUCTION AND SUBTRACTION

This section now shifts from describing the problem to actively engaging with it. While having introduced the two opposing views on the origins of individualism: the "construction" view, where individualism is a built-up ideal, and the "subtraction" view, where individualism emerges from the stripping away of traditional structures, they now need to be expanded on. Gunton sees the history of individualism as a central narrative, it's crucial to unpack the concept of "subtraction" before exploring his alternative view.

Individualism as Subtraction: "A Curious Blindness"

At its core, individualism revolves around the autonomy of self-determination, often celebrated as pure identity—what remains after all transcendent or Platonic notions of order are deconstructed (or destroyed!).[9]

According to Taylor, the effect of subtraction is that individualism becomes an unquestioned norm, perceived as "just common sense."[10] This perspective makes the issue of causality appear somewhat contrived. While various terms could describe this stance, "subtraction" best encapsulates the rejection of causality. As Taylor writes,

> The mistake of moderns is to take this understanding of the individual so much for granted that it is taken to be our first-off self-understanding "naturally." . . . This makes it easy to understand the emergence of modern individualism by a kind of subtraction story: the old horizons were eroded and burned away, and what emerges is the underlying sense of ourselves as individuals.[11]

While a detailed analysis of subtractionist theory is beyond this discussion, referencing it here underscores the "mistake of moderns"—the curious blindness, perhaps subconscious, that has shaped a dominant paradigm in our understanding of self and identity.

"Curious Blindness" has been coined by Taylor, and reveals his own bias on the position. He writes,

> The rejection of the higher can be presented as a liberation, as a recovery of the true value of human life. Of course, the moral

---

9. Taylor's perspective reinforces this view, encapsulating two essential ideas in subtraction theory. The first is the idea of individualism as a form of *recovery*. This concept aligns with the notion of deconstruction, suggesting that individualism isn't merely about independence and autonomy but is also a reclaiming of identity from previous limitations or oppressions. The second idea Taylor presents is a counterpoint to this recovery: the notion of *curious blindness*. This term, though subtler than Gunton's critique, points to the same underlying issue:
> Modern culture has developed conceptions of individualism which picture the human person as, at least potentially, finding his or her own bearings within, declaring independence from the web of interlocution which have originally formed him/her, or at least neutralising them. It's as though the dimension of interlocution were of significance only for the genesis of individuality, like the training wheels of nursery school, to be left behind and to play no part in the finished person (Taylor, *Sources of Self*, 36).

10. Taylor, *Sources of Self*, 64.

11. Taylor, *Modern Social Imaginaries*, 64.

value attaching to this liberating move itself presupposes another context of strong good. But with that curious blindness to the assumption behind their own moral attitudes, utilitarians and modern naturalists in general can just focus on the negation of the older distinctions and see themselves as freeing themselves altogether from distinctions as such.[12]

This paradigm is not confined to our constitutions or textbooks—it permeates every "terms and conditions" checkbox we mindlessly accept when visiting a new website, every receipt we receive at checkout. Subtraction becomes the foundation for building a consumerism based on an alleged meritocracy. Here we see strong Lockean and Nietzschean undercurrents.

Later, I will explore James K. Smith's work, which extends beyond Taylor and Gunton's critiques.[13] In *Desiring the Kingdom: Worship, Worldview, and Cultural Formation*, Smith argues that the subtractionist paradigm has become a subconscious liturgy shaping our very desires and worldview. According to Smith, the emphasis on freedom and emancipation is embedded within the fibers of our society, subtly constructing the modern self even as it claims to dismantle structures.

Individualism presents itself as a rebellion against Augustinian or other medieval influences, yet Gunton argues it is actually *neo-Augustinian*. In other words, individualism is less a reaction against flawed theology than it is its own evolution of it. Gunton's *The One, the Three, and the Many* reiterates his doctoral thesis, asserting that modern individualism mirrors the approach of neoclassical theologians. Only now, instead of defining God with a priori assumptions, it is humanity that is defined by them.

The implications are profound: individualism, far from being a path to emancipation, merely reenacts the same methodological reflexivity it claims to reject from classical theology. Subtraction is, in reality, a construction—a construction steeped in self-deception. As Gunton warns, it offers an illusion of freedom, masking what he calls a "cloak for tyranny, its creed a pretext for the suppression of the authentic human quest for truth."[14]

---

12. Taylor, *Sources of Self*, 81.
13. Smith, *Desiring the Kingdom*.
14. Gunton, *One*, 23.

Individualism and Construction (Necessary Frameworks)

Gunton's critique is not aimed at individualism itself. His thorough analysis reveals both an awareness of historical abuses of influence and a genuine sympathy for individualism's foundational ideals. His challenge, instead, is directed at *how* Christianity has interpreted individualism—and, equally, at how individualism interprets itself.

- In general, the church in the West gives the paradigm of individualism too much validity.
- Individualism gives itself too much validity.

Gunton and Taylor share a central conviction: individualism is the by-product of a constructed history. Both argue that individualism emerges as a result of preceding developments, reflecting the cultural paradigm shifts of their times. Writing during the late 1980s and early 1990s, when "subtraction" was at its peak, they viewed prevailing paradigms as potentially oppressive forces.[15] These paradigms were often perceived as inherently dangerous vehicles of control.

Today, we have largely moved beyond this debate, seeing the irony in rejecting metanarratives altogether. Derrida and Lyotard are read more for historical context than for radical insight. Yet, in doing so, we risk misunderstanding the ongoing relevance of this discourse. Taylor's work on *Social Imaginaries* in the early 2000s revitalized the conversation, and scholars like Smith contend that these debates are deeply embedded in our cultural actions rather than just our words.[16] They are woven into the fabric of our market-driven society, subtly shaping contemporary individualism. This legacy now forms part of our collective DNA, profoundly manifest in today's individualistic values.

Gunton is less concerned than Taylor with defending frameworks, perhaps assuming his audience already acknowledges them. This assumption poses no issue for his readership, but the same cannot be taken for granted when addressing a market-driven context. In this environment,

---

15. Taylor prefers the term "framework." Kuhn's seminal work on *The Structure of Scientific Revolutions* put "paradigms" on the map as a popular term (Kuhn, *Structure*). By the '90s the trend had shifted to "narratives" and "metanarratives." It is not necessary to back one of them, but the stronger influence of Taylor sees "frameworks" dominating this study.

16. Taylor, *Modern Social Imaginaries*.

theology may encounter a "curious blindness" as found in subtraction theory and the individualistic paradigm that prevails. Here, theology risks being subsumed or overlooked within the market's dominant ideology.

The "curious" nature of this blindness lies in its sense of déjà vu, a familiar echo when examining the history of frameworks. After the Enlightenment, humanity experienced a reconfiguration—and in some cases, a dismantling—of frameworks once believed to share the same ontological foundation as the very structure of the universe.[17] This upheaval offered a clue that identity was not embedded in the structure (or "form," invoking its Platonic heritage) of being but was often the result of human interpretation.

Subtraction theory leaves us like a hiker lost in the woods, circling back to the same spot, realizing that the notion of the autonomous individual as the foundational unit of society is strikingly familiar. Rather than being dismantled, the same underlying assumptions persist, merely reinterpreted and reasserted in a different guise.

Into this context, Taylor presents his core argument: "Doing without frameworks is utterly impossible for us; otherwise put, that the horizons within which we live our lives and which make sense of them have to include these strong qualitative discriminations."[18] Taylor himself, of course, operates within certain frameworks—some of which he acknowledges, while others remain implicit. His theory aligns closely with the Cartesian legacy, where much of human experience appears to unfold within the realm of the mind.

While this brings certain limitations, Taylor's research on the "qualitative discriminations" above offers valuable resources for this project. Two aspects of these discriminations are particularly relevant here. The first is Taylor's account of the history of modern identity. The second connects this history to prevalent themes in contemporary identity. Notably, the "liberated" individual today often resembles their neighbor—a somewhat ironic similarity. Although these two aspects are interdependent and resist clear separation, an attempt will be made to outline them separately.

17. Taylor, *Sources of the Self*, 26.

18. Taylor, *Sources of the Self*, 26–27. Elsewhere we see Taylor expressing the same point, again emphasizing the complexity of identifying frameworks that others simply do not see. "We could conclude from the fact that some people operate without a philosophically defined framework that they are quite without a framework at all. And that might be totally untrue (indeed, I want to claim, always is untrue)" (Taylor, *Sources of the Self*, 21).

The reader may question yet another detour before arriving at Gunton's engagement with Augustine. However, these introductory remarks serve a purpose that should start becoming clear. While debates on causality are crucial, they are also fraught with challenges. Ironically, the more one investigates, the less definitive the outcomes become; deeper research tends to add complexity rather than yielding decisive conclusions. Bearing this in mind, one final discussion on methodology will follow—this time focusing on the inherent difficulties in establishing causality—before delving into the specifics of Gunton's debate with Augustine.

Complexity as a Challenge to Establishing Causality

Taylor is particularly candid when outlining the limitations of causality. He warns us that "the order of causation is difficult to trace in this domain."[19] Again, in *Modern Social Imaginaries*, he writes, "The only general rule in history is that there is no general rule identifying one order of motivation as always the driving force."[20] Taylor's approach is particularly insightful, as he openly addresses the limitations in his focus on tracing the roots of modern identity primarily through philosophical rather than economic paradigms. Instead of shying away from these challenges, Taylor reimagines causality in a more flexible, nuanced way. He uses terms like "wake," "orbit," and "nudge" to describe a type of causality that influences without directly driving—suggesting forces that shape identity in subtle, often indirect ways yet still leave a lasting impact.[21]

---

19. Taylor, *Sources of the Self*, 393.

20. Taylor, *Modern Social Imaginaries*, 33.

21. To demonstrate the use of his terminology in context, Taylor (*Sources of the Self*, 393) is quoted at length below:

> These two big and many-sided cultural transformations, the Enlightenment and Romanticism with its accompanying expressive conception of man, have made us what we are. I don't mean this as a causal hypothesis, of course. As I have often said, the order of causation is difficult to trace in this domain. If we were looking for causes, we would have to mention a great many other things like the industrial revolution and the rise of modern nationalism. What I mean is rather that our cultural life, our self-conceptions, our moral outlooks still operate in the *wake* of these great events. We still wait another large-scale cultural upheaval which might carry us out of their orbit, as we sense ourselves to have already departed from the *orbit* of Deism, Lockean or Hutchesonian, let along such seventeenth-century notions as the divine right of kings. (emphasis added)

These terms are valuable tools in navigating the debate between Gunton and Augustine. McNall wisely reminds us that Gunton's critique is not directed at Augustine himself but rather at the "Augustinian Legacy"—a distinction worth noting. The "wake" Augustine left behind does not always offer a fair or balanced representation of his theological body of work. This issue will be explored in a later section.

When considering complexity in relation to Gunton, it becomes evident that his arguments face certain challenges. One critique carried over from chapter 2 concerns notable omissions. Among these are the influences of economics and technology—undeniably significant forces in shaping the modern individual. Another example is the Reformation. Although it holds a crucial place within Gunton's scholarly framework, its role in his causality arguments is surprisingly understated. This chapter will contend that the limited emphasis on the Reformation should be added to the list of key omissions in Gunton's work.

Any omission weakens an argument, yet it is the task of this chapter to determine whether Gunton's strengths help outweigh these omissions, providing us with valuable resources with which to critically examine identity in the market economy. The reader can expect two areas of argument:

- From a theological and philosophical perspective, it will be necessary to trace the lines of causality or influence from Augustine, through Descartes, the Reformation, and modernity, up to the present day.

- From an epistemological perspective, there must be a critical examination of underlying assumptions. Here, Taylor provides valuable insight, highlighting the dichotomy between the proclaimed truths of modern individualism and the truths enacted in practice.

In summary, modern individualism represents a convergence of flawed theology and epistemology. This discussion will trace a causal line from Augustine, through Descartes, the Reformation, and Modernity, right up to the present. The argument is that modern individualism remains within Augustine's "orbit," with enough gravitational pull to influence its daily expressions. Additionally, a closer epistemological examination of individualism's self-assumptions is essential, as Gunton contends that Augustine's influence has shaped reality itself, not merely our perception of it.

Stickiness as a Challenge to Establishing Causality

There is yet another layer of complexity to add to the discussion on causality. It's often assumed that ideas gain traction based on their inherent merit, but, in reality, substance and popularity don't always go hand in hand. This underscores the need to recognize that causality isn't always linear or rational; thus, a logical argument may not always be the best tool for understanding it.

Gladwell's appearance in theological arguments is, undoubtedly, very rare. He is a journalist for *The New Yorker* magazine and has established a reputation as a "left field" social commentator. For the purposes of this discussion, he could be classified as an anthropologist. His popularity is well deserved as he consistently delivers blockbuster volumes to challenge social perceptions.

In the year 2000, he published a collection of articles under the title *The Tipping Point: How Little Things Can Make a Big Difference*.[22] The articles examine topics from epidemics to trends. Of particular interest here is the sixth chapter titled, "Rumours, Sneakers, and the Power of Translation," where he looks at why a particular type of sneaker established iconic status in the United States of America. Essentially, Gladwell's task is the same as that of this chapter. He is interested in the causality of an idea.

Central to his argument is key role players. He calls them the "connectors" or "mavens." They are the ones who are able to create that critical momentum allowing one idea or concept to become more "sticky" than another. "They are the ones who make it possible for innovations to overcome this problem of chasm. They are the translators: they take the ideas and information from a highly specialised world and translate them into a language the rest of us can understand."[23]

Our role here is not to unpack Gladwell's argument, but to consider his theory as a reality for theological ideas. Why should the same phenomenon that influences the popularity of a particular Adidas shoe not impact the "stickiness" of Augustine.[24] The legacy of Augustine may

---

22. Gladwell, *Tipping Point*.
23. Gladwell, *Tipping Point*, 199–200.
24. The writer has personal experience of tipping points. As a retailer, Adidas is a listed vendor. There are a number of styles in the Adidas pool sandals range, but it is the oldest item, the "Adilette," that has the strongest demand. Logically, the newer shoes have better fabrication and are more comfortable. Nevertheless, the customer will pay a premium for the Adilette. It has a weighting beyond its functionality. What's more, this

attribute some of its popularity to simply getting across the threshold of an invisible tipping point. If that is case, the direction and interpretation belong to the translator and not the author.

Dissonance, Delusion, and Dead Ends as a Challenge to Establishing Causality

We have previously discussed Taylor's notion of "curious blindness." Here, we must revisit it, considering it not only as an obstacle to establishing causality but also as a defining feature of modern individualism. This perspective will be applied to Gunton's work and will carry forward into the next chapter, which examines the intersection of theology and the market economy. A key question throughout will be to what extent any theological engagement with the market economy may inadvertently reinforce these very characteristics.

Taylor considers this issue central to understanding the self. While we have already noted his commitment to articulating frameworks, he repeatedly highlights the circular nature of this debate. In many ways, we are addressing a concern that most people do not consciously recognize. In his introduction to *Sources of the Self*, Taylor describes this as a "lack of fit between what people as it were officially and consciously believe, even pride themselves on believing, on the one hand, and what they need to make sense of some of the moral reactions, on the other."[25] This disconnect results in what Taylor calls an "ideologically induced illusion." However, illusion might be too gentle a term; when a belief persists despite contradictions from reality, it verges on delusion.

Taylor observes, "As long as the naturalist picture, by which having a moral outlook is an optional extra, continues as plausible, the place of these frameworks in our lives will be obscured."[26] In his later writings, however, his tone intensifies. By 2004, he conveys a similar idea with

---

weighting is inconsistent across provinces. In KwaZulu-Natal (KZN), the Adilette has a much higher demand than in other provinces, a difference that cannot be explained by climatic differences. The shoe has somehow developed the stickiness outlined by Gladwell.

25. Taylor, *Sources of the Self*, 9.
26. Taylor, *Sources of the Self*, 42. "My identity is defined by the commitments and identifications which provide the frame or horizon within which I can try to determine from case to case what is good, or valuable, or what ought to be done, or what I endorse of oppose. In other words, it is the horizon within which I am capable of taking a stand" (Taylor, *Sources of the Self*, 27).

heightened urgency: "Not only the troubling aspects, like some forms of nationalism or purifying violence, but other, virtually unchallenged benchmarks of legitimacy in our contemporary world—liberty, equality, human rights, democracy—can demonstrate how strong a hold this modern order exercises on our social imaginary. It constitutes a horizon we are virtually incapable of thinking beyond."[27] This last sentence is, at least for this book, the most important insight that Taylor has to contribute. While he remains engaged in the debate on frameworks, there is a palpable resignation: this debate seems to reach a dead end, constrained by a paradigm that resists shift and cannot be overturned by argument alone.

These discussions on modern individualism have brought deeper insight to Gunton's arguments. In a way, Gunton seeks to prompt an epiphany—a revelation of a harmful paradigm to which even the church has fallen prey. While we trace causality back to Augustine, we begin with the reality of the paradigm itself. This paradigm, a product of causation, has a remarkable tendency to shield itself from scrutiny—a pattern we'll also see reflected in the critiques of Gunton's work.

Recap and Preparing to Engage with Augustine

This section has outlined the challenge of establishing causality, as well as the subtle, almost subconscious acceptance of individualism as simply "the way things are." We introduced the notion that Augustine's legacy may not fully reflect Augustine himself—there are forces at play here that are difficult to articulate. These complexities apply to both sides of the argument; while Gunton may need to temper his confidence, his critics must do the same. With the grand narrative of individualism now positioned and its inherent complexities reviewed, we are prepared to engage with Augustine.

GUNTON'S PROCLAMATION OF AUGUSTINE AS THE FATHER OF INDIVIDUALISM

This section revisits and expands upon the introductory comments from the earlier section titled "A Growing Discontent with Augustine." This serves as an essential starting point, as the strong opposition to Augustine

---

27. Taylor, *Modern Social Imaginaries*, 185.

seen in Gunton's later works was not always so pronounced. To be fair, there was little in the form of appreciation, but certainly not the scale of opposition we encounter in later writings.

Gunton's redactive approach, first evident in his initial publications, rejected classical theology yet simultaneously voiced concern that newer authorities (notably Barth) had not gone far enough. As Augustine moves increasingly from the periphery to the forefront in Gunton's works, additional layers of revision shift the trajectory of his earlier assumptions. In this sense, Gunton resembles an archaeologist, articulating his findings before fully unearthing them.

For Gunton, discontent is a powerful motivator. In reviewing his earlier works, it becomes evident that the seeds of his critique are present, and as these seeds grow, they reshape his perspective. This dynamic, emphasized in the introductory sections, is crucial: while Augustine becomes a focal point in Gunton's thought, he remains secondary to the issue of individualism, which is paramount. This prioritization has significant implications for any critique of Gunton's work.

Recap: We are Dealing with a Subset of Gunton's Complaints Against Augustine

This section diverges from the section titled "A Growing Discontent with Augustine" by specifically tracing the lineage of individualism within Gunton's writings and linking this trajectory back to Augustine. Gunton's most definitive articulation of individualism appears in *The One, the Three, and the Many*,[28] with additional significant claims found in *The Promise of Trinitarian Theology*.[29] Here, the goal is to "join the dots," establishing the foundational framework upon which Gunton bases his strong assertions.

This focus on the "dotted line" will selectively address critiques, prioritizing those relevant to Gunton's hypothesis about Augustine's influence on individualism. While other critiques of Gunton's broader assessment of Augustine are valid, they will receive less emphasis here. The dotted line itself represents two primary movements: one leading into the Enlightenment and the other emerging from it:

---

28. Gunton, *One*.
29. Gunton, *Promise*.

- Into the Enlightenment: The need for a link between Augustine and both the Enlightenment and Reformation.
- Out of the Enlightenment: An affirmation of the impact of the Enlightenment and Reformation on modernity.

Descartes and Locke serve as pivotal figures within these two movements: the trajectory toward the Enlightenment and the transition from the Enlightenment into modernity. In the earlier phase, Ockham represents a crucial milestone, setting the stage for shifts that would later be developed by Descartes and Locke.

Bringing Augustinian Complaints and Individualism Together: A Tabular View of the Hypothesis

As we move toward a more detailed analysis, it is helpful to revisit the articulation of Gunton's complaints presented in the section titled 'A Growing Discontent with Augustine.' This framework does not originate from Gunton himself but emerges from this book. Here, we will review these complaints and then illustrate how they connect to the lineage of individualism. The complaints are as follows:

- **Complaint 1:** The Platonic influence of the intellectual being superior to the material.
- **Complaint 2:** The separation of the immanent and economic Trinity, both through the use of *substantia,* which effectively introduces a focus on an underlying reality within the being of God, and through the mediation of angels which distances God from revelation in Jesus.
- **Complaint 3:** The elevation of the unity of God above the particularity of the three persons.

Presenting these complaints in a linear manner has its limitations. They do not represent isolated aspects of Augustinian theology but are interdependent, each highlighting a distinct dimension of Augustine's legacy. As we delve into Gunton's writings, it is useful to engage in a mapping process that aligns these complaints with his critiques of individualism. This approach underscores that Gunton is not offering a general critique of Augustine; rather, he is focused on those elements of Augustine's legacy that influence contemporary identity. Only these specific Augustinian descendants, as they appear in modern individualism, are of primary concern to him.

By "correspondence" in the above paragraph, we once again invoke Taylor's concept of "orbit" or "nudge." When tracing the source of a river, one is often met with numerous tributaries, each contributing as meaningfully as the source itself, though they don't extend as far back. Similarly, in identifying the foundational characteristics of individualism, we encounter many contributing influences. As we outline these characteristics, we simultaneously set the stage to assess whether Gunton is justified in tracing their origins to the Augustinian legacy.

- **Shift of focus to the individual:** This chapter argues that the emphasis on the individual finds its roots in Complaint 1—namely, the suspicion of the material world, which relegates key decision-making to the intellect of the individual.
- **The individual as society's foundational unit:** Here, we see the "naturalist" or subtractionist perspective that individualism represents humanity in its raw, original state. This corresponds to Complaints 2 and 3: prioritizing the one over the many dismisses the need for others, while a diminished role for mediated pneumatology undermines the necessity of a relational, mediated ontology.
- **Erosion of particularity:** As the focus shifts to the autonomous individual, particularity fades—especially any form of particularity that involves transcendental intent or supports a relational ontology.

Were Gunton to read this section, he would be asking why so much fuss was being made about issues of structure. The response would be, "Why so much fuss about Augustine!" Simply put, the detail of the argument is important. This is a very broad section of the debate, and without clarity, it is hard for the reader to ensure that I am doing what was promised: joining the dots!

Table 1. Gunton's Three Main Complaints Against Augustine

Complaint (against Augustine and Western Theology)	Foundation of Individualism	Gunton's Theological Contribution (The Antidote!)	The Complemented (Irenaeus and others)
Complaint 1: The platonic influence of the intellectual being superior to the material.	There is a shift in the center of gravity toward the individual. The beginning of Cartesian inwardness.	Mediation is a key response here.	• Irenaeus's "two hands" • Coleridge's "idea" • Doctrine of creation • Pneumatology
Complaint 2: The separation between the immanent and economic Trinity, both through the use of *substantia*, which effectively introduces a stress on an underlying reality within the being of God, and through the mediation of angels that distances God from revelation in Jesus.	The view that the individual is the building block of society. A "theology of satisfaction" results in too much weight being apportioned to Jesus' action toward the Father. Focus on the legal and the moral. Salvation becomes transactional and individual. Pneumatology becomes transactional. A focus on transformation vs. mediation.	*Perichoresis*, Relationality, Particularity, Mediation. A reconception of the *ordo salutis*. Our participation in the fellowship of the Trinity. A reconception of ontology as interdependence.	• Barth • Rahner • Owen • Irving • Zizioulas
Complaint 3: The elevation of the unity of God above the particularity of the three persons.	The monistic view of the individual	*Perichoresis*, Particularity, Mediation.	• Coleridge

Unpacking Gunton's work enabled the construction of this table and established a crucial foundation for engaging with his critics. This chapter can then integrate these insights by incorporating perspectives on individualism beyond a strictly theological lens, setting the stage for a well-rounded conclusion.

Early Gunton and Augustine: The Seeds of Discontent (pre-1988)

Earlier, it was noted that epistemology played a foundational role in Gunton's intellectual journey. His early writings contain minimal engagement with Augustine, which aligns with their predominantly epistemological focus. These writings touch on the strong Platonic influence, which, in my view, represents the first of Gunton's three complaints against Augustine. Although brief, these references are worth citing in full, as they not only bolster the argument but also support the response to his critics. In particular, against Green, the argument holds that without an understanding of this epistemological shift, one cannot fully grasp Gunton's reading of Augustine.

Becoming and Being (1978)

In *Becoming and Being*, Augustine receives only a brief mention, primarily in relation to the Platonic influence noted in Barth's thought. Gunton references Prenter's critique of Barthian Platonism, stating: "He [Prenter] concludes that there is a noticeably platonic tendency in Barth's thought, and ascribes this in part to Barth's interest in medieval Augustinianism, particularly Anselm, although he does not wish to stress this side of Barth at the expense of historical actualism."[30] This remains the sole mention of Augustine, and it is not a central issue for Barth. Gunton refrains from adding his own views to Prenter's comment, instead pivoting to discuss Barth's restrained role for the Spirit. At this stage, Augustine is not yet on Gunton's radar.

Yesterday and Today (1983)

Gunton draws on Cochrane's *Christianity and Classical Culture*, endorsing Cochrane's view that figures like Athanasius and Augustine gained influence partly due to Classicism's need for structured paradigms. Gunton

---

30. Gunton, *Becoming and Being*, 183.

notes, "Historically, that is to say, Christianity conquered, particularly in the West, because in certain respects it proved itself intellectually superior to a bankrupt alternative."[31] This sentiment resurfaces in *The Promise of Trinitarian Theology*, where he remarks, "The tragedy is that Augustine's work is so brilliant that it blinded generations of theologians to its damaging weaknesses."[32]

Two key points emerge here. First, Augustine's influence appears partly circumstantial—a meeting of genius with a landscape lacking strong alternatives. Erasmus's proverb about the "one-eyed man" ruling in the land of the blind comes to mind! Second, this offers a subtle theological precursor to the Christological focus seen in *Actuality of Atonement*.[33] At this stage, Augustine remains in the background, and Gunton's Trinitarian theology is still developing. Though we lack Gunton's own reflections on this period, one might speculate that as his theological vision took shape, Augustine increasingly became a focal point for critique.

Enlightenment and Alienation (1985)

Although not typically regarded as one of Gunton's more influential works, it serves as a reminder of his deep engagement with Enlightenment scholarship. This is significant, as the Enlightenment occupies a central role in Gunton's trajectory from Augustine to the rise of individualism. In the opening sections, he quotes Augustine in an epistemological reference.

> Augustine had taught that "unless you believe you will not understand," a view that was both developed and criticized by different thinkers in the centuries after him. In the Enlightenment, it was reversed. "If you believe you will not understand" has some claim to represent one of its chief mottoes. The Enlightenment was right to attack the credulity and superstition. But in the process it produced a view of the human mind that falsified its relation to the world, especially in suggesting that there could be attained an absolute objectivity and impartiality: A God's eye view.[34]

---

31. Gunton, *Yesterday and Today*, 1.
32. Gunton, *Promise*, 39.
33. Gunton, *Actuality of the Atonement*.
34. Gunton, *Enlightenment and Alienation*, 3–4.

If anything, this suggests a discontinuity rather than a direct causality between Augustine and the Enlightenment, a point Gunton reinforces later in the book when he critiques Augustine's weak exegesis as a factor fueling the Enlightenment's disdain for the church.[35] Gunton is comfortable acknowledging both continuities and discontinuities between Augustine and the Enlightenment.

This perspective also exposes a foundational element central to the Enlightenment and the rise of modernity: the shifting focus toward individual perception. Just a few years after this publication, Gunton will lay much of the responsibility for this shift squarely on Augustine. The key to this critique is the Cartesian link; it is Augustine's focus on internalization that, according to Gunton, lays the groundwork for rationalism. Here, we see Gunton establishing a single thread linking Augustine, Locke, Coleridge, and Descartes.

> Augustine's observation of the way in which we make sight the model for all perception enables us to see why the problem arose. For when we take sight as a model for all perception, develop a picture or metaphor with its assistance, and then turn that into a theory or doctrine, the outcome is the alienation about which Coleridge complained.... Take the example we have already met, Locke's view of the mind as a white paper or an empty cabinet.... Although the "doors" in the box admit items from the world, we are within and the world is without, so that there is no way of knowing whether what enters is a true representation of what remains inside.... We are shut up inside our heads as Descartes spent his famous day enclosed within his stove. We thus alienate ourselves from our world, and cannot restore ourselves to it: it is a "despotism of the eye" precisely because a concentration on sight encourages dependence on a picture that represents only part of the truth.[36]

---

35. "Partly as a result of the Enlightenment's assaults, the history of the church we tend to remember is rather in conflict with the theology.... It is unfortunate that Augustine's bad exegesis of the words of the parable 'compel them to come in' has accompanied, caused even, a development of Christianity from persecuted minority into persecuting majority. We have the Enlightenment to thank for trying to ensure that it will not happen again. But the credibility of Christianity depends more upon its capacity to create uncoerced community, and to enable society to do the same" (Gunton, *Enlightenment and Alienation*, 104).

36. Gunton, *Enlightenment and Alienation*, 36–37.

In summary, Augustine's view of perception serves as a precursor to Cartesian rationalism. Missing from this trajectory, however, is the role of Ockham, who is only introduced later in *The One, the Three, and the Many*.

Actuality of Atonement (1988)

Here, we encounter a work published the same year as Gunton's seminar on Augustine, which later appeared in *The Promise of Trinitarian Theology*.[37] Notably, there is a gap between the perspectives in these two works, suggesting that *The Actuality of Atonement* required a longer developmental trajectory.[38] In *Actuality of Atonement*, Gunton also identifies a discontinuous link between Augustine and the Enlightenment—a refreshing reminder that, despite his focused approach, Gunton acknowledges the complexity of this relationship.[39]

Gunton then maps out patterns of rationalism, reinforcing the causal connection he sees between Augustine and Descartes. In this instance, the link is epistemological, demonstrating how Gunton traces an intellectual lineage grounded in ways of knowing.

> It has long been held that some ways of expressing meaning and truth are superior to others, often that particular kinds of words are the only ones truly fitted to show things as they are. One favourite way of showing this is to argue that meaning and truth are successfully conveyed only by means of concepts of an intellectual kind which have been purified as completely as possible from all imaginative or pictorial content. On such an account, concepts are strictly distinguished from and opposed to pictures and images: while the former are fitted to convey the truth, the latter are, because of their unclarity, the source of

---

37. Gunton, *Promise*.

38. Gunton, *Actuality of Atonement*.

39. "The Augustinian and Reformation traditions alike teach a radical fallenness, and the corresponding need for a historical redemption. It is to this teaching that modern rationalism, which tends to be tied to an optimistic belief in human capabilities, has taken severest exception. . . . The Enlightenment in that way produced a radical version of the Pelagianism against which Augustine had struggled. Whether or not Pelagius was guilty of the heresy which bears his name, there is little down that his modern successors have come to believe that we may realise our humanity without divine grace, healing or redemption. . . . In all this, the central concept for our purposes is autonomy, the doctrine that each person is individually and completely responsible for moral action and should be free of all 'external' authorities like tradition and the church" (Gunton, *Actuality of the Atonement*, 4).

deceit and confusion. Both Plato and Augustine were strongly attracted to versions of this doctrine, largely because they believed that information conveyed by the senses was inherently untrustworthy. The father of the modern variation on the theme is Descartes, who held that anything he could conceive with utter clarity and distinctiveness was true, anything less than that essentially unreliable.[40]

Later in the book, we encounter a shift toward theological causality—an important addition to Gunton's argument that reflects his evolving Trinitarian views and growing critique of Augustine. This insight surfaces in Gunton's critique of Anselm's atonement theology, specifically his concern that "too much weight is thrown on the action of Jesus Christ towards the Father, too little on the notion of salvation being realised through involvement of the triune God in human history. . . . More important is the often noted weakness that Anselm appears to equate salvation with the remission of penalty."[41]

Gunton labels this perspective a "theology of satisfaction," establishing another link between Augustine and Western theological individualism. He argues that this theology centers on individual experience, particularly through its focus on the soul's health. "The theology of satisfaction tends to concentrate on the legal and moral rather than the cosmic aspects of the divine-human relationship. In that respect, it is a characteristically Western development, and is bounded on one side by Augustine's preoccupation with the health of the soul and on the other by Luther's preoccupation with justification."[42]

Summary of Augustine in pre-1988 Literature

In Gunton's early writings, Augustine faces no more criticism than other figures. Epistemology takes precedence, with Gunton even acknowledging points of discontinuity between Augustine and the Enlightenment, positioning Augustine more as a reactionary influence than a causal one in that context. These early concerns primarily relate to Augustine's Platonism, aligning with the first of Gunton's eventual complaints.

---

40. Gunton, *Actuality of Atonement*, 17.
41. Gunton, *Actuality of Atonement*, 93.
42. Gunton, *Actuality of Atonement*, 95.

A notable focus in this period is Augustine's inward journey, with minimal engagement with his Trinitarian constructs. However, in *Actuality of Atonement*, Gunton begins to extend the "dotted line" from Augustine to individualism, providing a foundation for his later, more comprehensive critiques. This sets the stage for the deeper engagement in *The Promise of Trinitarian Theology* and beyond, where additional complaints come to the forefront.

Augustine in *The Promise of Trinitarian Theology*

After 1988, we encounter the mature version of Gunton's critique of Augustine, with two central works to examine: *The Promise of Trinitarian Theology* and *The One, the Three, and the Many*. The latter will be reviewed in the following section.

Though *The Promise of Trinitarian Theology* was published in 1991, its third chapter, focused on Augustine, originated from a seminar presented at King's College in 1988. Notably, Gunton acknowledges the contributions of Zizioulas and Schwöbel, whose influences were discussed in chapter 2. Another key element is Gunton's deliberate comparison of Augustine with Irenaeus. While he makes a brief comparison in *Actuality of Atonement*,[43] *The Promise of Trinitarian Theology* presents a far more intentional contrast—one that would become a central theme in *The One, the Three, and the Many*.

The chapter title, "Augustine, the Trinity, and the Theological Crisis of the West," validates the previous work of contextualizing Gunton's engagement with Augustine. Stripped of Augustine's name, it could almost serve as an alternative title for the entire book—a collection of essays contributing to early Trinitarian scholarship. Gunton identifies the purpose of his chapter on Augustine as an exploration of the "problem of the knowledge of God," questioning to what extent issues surrounding this knowledge, and the relegation of the Trinity to a secondary role, can be attributed to Augustine.[44]

For Gunton, the issue lies in the contrasting approaches to the Trinity within Eastern and Western traditions. At some point, a divergence created a significant gap between the two, with Augustine emerging as the central obstacle in Gunton's view. While Gunton is known for his

---

43. Gunton, *Actuality of Atonement*, 146.
44. Gunton, *Promise*, 31.

assertiveness in staking claims and engaging in conflict, he displays an uncharacteristic caution in the opening paragraphs. He writes: "On the face of it, to accuse of undermining the doctrine of the Trinity one whose treatment of the topic is among the glories of Western theology may appear to be perverse."[45] Clearly, Gunton anticipated pushback on this contentious argument.

Alongside acknowledging Augustine's stature, Gunton identifies two additional challenges in critiquing him. First, Augustine is a "many-sided" figure, an apt observation given his vast body of work.[46] This raises the question of whether any critique accurately represents the larger corpus. Second, the nature of Platonic influence complicates interpretation, as statements cannot always be taken at face value. There may be a gap between what Augustine explicitly states and what he implies. Gunton describes this tension, asking: "The questions to Augustine concerns similarly [to Arianism] the impact of platonising doctrines upon his thought. Are they such as to take away with the left hand what had already been given with the right, to undermine the doctrine of God known as triune even while it is being stated?"[47]

Gunton's analogy of "giving and taking" can be likened to driving with both the accelerator and brake pressed simultaneously. He suggests that Augustine's writing is propelled by two opposing forces working against each other. Here, Gunton's emphasis on frameworks provides valuable context: he sees Augustine as a visionary attempting to reframe Christian thought, yet unable to fully break free from his Platonic presuppositions. This critique mirrors Gunton's assessment of classical theology in *Becoming and Being*—he is tracing this tension back to what he perceives as its origin in Augustine's approach.

The focus on assumed paradigms adds a layer of complexity to Gunton's engagement with Augustine. He is essentially addressing Augustine on two levels: the explicit statements and the underlying presuppositions, or *a priori* assumptions. He acknowledges this approach in his opening argument, signaling to the reader that the emphasis must be on the "underlying presuppositions which give the doctrine the shape it has."[48]

Gunton's argument, as summarized in his three main complaints against Augustine, is familiar to us. In this book, however, we see these

45. Gunton, *Promise*, 3.
46. Gunton, *Promise*, 32.
47. Gunton, *Promise*, 33.
48. Gunton, *Promise*, 32.

complaints being expanded and engaged with more deeply for the first time. Gunton's two opening sections introduce the contemporary issue of the knowability of God and outline Augustine's distrust of the material—a theme that sets the tone for the entire engagement. The subsequent sections are as follows:

- "*Substance and persons*": Gunton argues that Augustine is unable to escape the "stranglehold of dualistic ontology," leaving him unable to grasp the Cappadocian distinction between *ousia* and *hypostasis*.[49]
- "*The trinitarian analogies*": This section examines Augustine's inward journey through his analogies "between the inner structure of the human mind and the inner being of God."[50] Gunton contends that this approach undermines the Trinity and weakens the link with others.
- "*The third person of the Trinity*": Here, Gunton addresses what he sees as Augustine's "Achilles heel" or the "*most contested of his theologoumena.*" This is where Gunton finds a direct link between Augustine's theology and the individualism of Western theology today. Among Augustine's omissions, Gunton cites "a conception of the Spirit as realising the condition of the age to come particularly through the creation of community."[51] This is followed by a foundational statement for this study: "In Augustine we are near the beginning of an era in which the church is conceived essentially as an institution mediating grace to the individual rather than of the community formed on the analogy of the Trinity's interpersonal relationships."[52]

Causality

The chapter is relatively light on causation. In the opening lines, Gunton notes that the issue of God's knowability did not originate with Kant. Beyond this, however, there is no attempt to trace a path between the two historical horizons. Owen and Irving receive acknowledgment for ensuring "due prominence to Christ's full humanity,"[53] but this recognition is

49. Gunton, *Promise*, 40–41.
50. Gunton, *Promise*, 45.
51. Gunton, *Promise*, 51.
52. Gunton, *Promise*, 51.
53. Gunton, *Promise*, 34.

a response to broader theological issues beyond just Augustine and is not intended to bolster the causality argument.

At this point, the emphasis is on theological method as the central link. Here, Gunton identifies Augustine's "individualism and intellectualism,"[54] where individualism marks a shift from relying on the economic Trinity as the primary source of knowledge of God to relying on the individual human mind. Although Gunton's comparison of the Trinity to the human mind is less developed than Taylor's, the critical issue here is the shift of the individual from the periphery to the center. This shift, more than the theology's content, seems to represent the first glimmers of Enlightenment concepts of the self.

To underscore the emphasis on method over content, Gunton[55] clarifies that he does not "wish to deny that Augustine has a view of intellect very different from the typical post Enlightenment concept of the calculating machine. His notion of the mind is strongly religious in character." He concludes his chapter with the following:

> It is not being suggested that Augustine is propounding straightforward versions of the various heresies to which he is near. That is perhaps the problem, for the subtlety of his approach disguises its underlying problematic. Thus, for example, he is aware of the danger of Eunomianism, as he is of Arianism and modalism. The question which this chapter is designed to ask is whether he has the conceptual equipment to avoid a final collapse into something like them, and the answer must be that he has not. And if he has not, then how are we to avoid the conclusion that the road which he took did in fact lead, albeit by many twists and turns, to that deep-seated problematic about the knowledge of God with which we now so anxiously wrestle?[56]

Conclusion of The Promise of Trinitarian Theology

In our first in-depth engagement with Augustine, we encounter an argument closely aligned with that of *Becoming and Being*. With Barth as a catalyst, Gunton argues for sourcing the knowledge of God from the economic Trinity. It is as though he has traced the underlying presuppositions

---

54. Gunton, *Promise*, 43.
55. Gunton, *Promise*, 43.
56. Gunton, *Promise*, 55.

of classical theology back to Augustine, whose devout intentions, Gunton suggests, remain constrained by his paradigm of Platonic dualism.

Augustine in *The One, the Three, and the Many*

By the time Gunton published *The One, the Three, and the Many*, his critique of Augustine had reached full maturity. A key question, then, is what changed since *The Promise of Trinitarian Theology*. While Augustine's dualism remains a central theme, certain aspects have evolved.[57]

Between the two publications, an increased polarization between Augustine and Irenaeus emerges. Speculatively, Gunton's growing focus on creation may have aligned him more closely with Irenaeus as an ally. Gunton himself acknowledges this polarization, even defensively noting, "I do not wish to idealize Irenaeus, but to use his insights to reveal certain indispensable resources available in the doctrine of creation for the development of our theme of human life in the world."[58] However, empirical evidence challenges Gunton's claim; when their references are viewed in parallel (see the table below), nearly 60 percent of them feature Irenaeus and Augustine together, indicating a sustained engagement with both figures.

---

57. Continuation of the dualist theme is supported in the following references.
- "Creation is one and not dual. In a number of places in Augustine, the Genesis account is taken as indicating a double creation, first of the Platonic or 'intellectual' world, second of the material world" (*One*, 2).
- Page 23 contains a discussion on presocratic tradition's dualism of rational and moral functions in the Divine. Gunton argues that this is retained in Augustine (*One*, 23).
- Augustine is linked to Platonic teaching. "The true person is the soul, so that the material body comes to be understood as that which *divides* one human being from another rather than *relates* them to each other" (*One*, 48, emphasis original).

Page 51 contains a discussion on "The West's Double Mind" referencing Augustine's dual creation account.
- "The root of the modern disarray is accordingly to be located in the divorce of the willing of creation from the historical economy of salvation" (*One*, 55).
- "The long-term effects can hardly be exaggerated, for the tradition was saddled with the view that creation involved the production of timeless forms" (*One*, 56)

58. Gunton, *One*, 53.

Table 2. Parallel Page References for Augustine and Irenaeus in *The One, the Three, and the Many*.

Parallel References in *The One, the Three, and the Many* 58 percent of Augustinian sections engage with Irenaeus	
Augustine	Irenaeus
2	2
	23
	28
	48
53, 53	52–56
	58
66	72
80, 81, 84	81–84
97	86
119, 120	120
137	138, 140
151	
158–63	159
197	190

More significantly, the book deepens the connection between Platonic dualism and Augustine's inward journey, positioning Augustine as a precursor to Descartes, the father of modern individualism. Approaching the book from its conclusion clarifies the links Gunton is drawing. He writes, "We tend to see the thing as constituted by its externality or external relations, the person as internally constituted, largely, I suspect, because we believe that we know ourselves not by observing our relatedness with the other but by some kind of introspection, as a powerful tradition from Plato, through Augustine, Descartes, Kant to Freud."[59] This insight resonates with Charles Taylor's work, and Gunton acknowledges Taylor's influence in leading up to this conclusion.[60] In this intellectual lineage, Augustine is the first to turn the search inward, laying the groundwork for Descartes. Gunton explains, "The link between the particulars of our experience is made by a God essentially conceived after the image of the

---

59. Gunton, *One*, 202–3.

60. Taylor's contributions are acknowledged in eight of the sections in *The One, the Three, and the Many*.

individual rational will so prominent in theological anthropology after Augustine. It is so applied to God that it makes the world appear to be simply the arbitrary product of the divine will, abstractly conceived and essentially unknown."[61]

The link between Augustine's inward focus and Descartes becomes the cornerstone of Gunton's critique of Augustine. It is the one aspect that must hold firm for Gunton's argument on the theological lineage of individualism to remain intact.

Summary of Key Issues

Beyond *The One, the Three, and the Many*, Augustine begins to recede from Gunton's focus, though he remains part of the theological landscape. For instance, in *Act and Being*, Gunton references Augustine only three times—a relatively light treatment by his previous standards. Expanding on these references here adds little, as the overview above provides a sufficiently clear picture of Gunton's stance.

Among Gunton's numerous engagements with Augustine, two themes stand out. When Gunton critiques or references Augustine, it ultimately supports one of these two points. The first is the detachment of creation, linked to Platonic dualism—a theme that traces back to Gunton's earliest writings. The second is Augustine's inward focus, a theme that gained importance as Gunton's Trinitarian theology evolved. The remaining question is whether these themes retain their relevance after considering Gunton's critics.

GUNTON'S SUPPORTERS AND CRITICS

Gunton has amassed a number of critics, and for this study, I have chosen to focus on Green and McNall, both of whom began their work on Gunton as doctoral research. While these doctoral projects may lack the breadth of work by more established academics, they offer a distinct advantage: they can prioritize critical rigor over commercial appeal or readability, writing for a specialized audience.

For more appreciative perspectives, I will engage with Jenson, Taylor, and Rahner, with the latter positioned as a potential ally for Gunton—a role that will be further explored here. In the chapter's opening

---

61. Gunton, *One*, 58.

sections, it is noted that these critics cannot always be engaged on their terms, as they often miss Gunton's broader narrative—a point that will be reinforced in the following analysis.

Bradley Green

Green's critique of Gunton is rooted in his own theological journey, as he notes being "initially quite smitten with Gunton's theological reconstruction."[62] This early attraction led Green to a closer examination of Augustine, where he found "insights from Augustine that had not been appropriated or appreciated by Gunton."[63] For the reader, the real challenge lies in interpreting Green's conclusions, as his assessment delivers a somewhat mixed message about the extent of Gunton's missteps.

In chapter 6, for example, Green concludes, "At times Gunton appears to misread Augustine, and to fail to take into consideration the complexity and genuine insights of Augustine's thought."[64] This statement, while critical, isn't particularly surprising, especially considering Gunton's known tendency to selectively read Barth in earlier works—one could almost substitute "Barth" for "Augustine" and retain a true statement. However, if we contrast this measured critique with Green's broader implication that Gunton misinterprets Augustine on virtually every major doctrinal point, a gap emerges. Other than a few concessions, Green seems to suggest that Gunton consistently misreads Augustine. Perhaps, instead of saying, "At times Gunton appears to misread Augustine," Green might have intended to say, "At *all* times Gunton appears. . ."

This inconsistency in Green's handling of Gunton culminates in a somewhat surprising reversal when he suggests that "at points Gunton is actually rather Augustinian in his theology, and Gunton can find a friend not a foe in the bishop of Hippo."[65] Misidentifying a friend as a foe is a significant oversight, and despite Green's guarded language, he implies that Gunton fundamentally misunderstood Augustine. Given this, one might expect Green to recommend dismissing Gunton's broader theological project—perhaps not with the bluntness of Nausner, but a dismissal nonetheless. Yet, what is surprising is that, despite Green's view

---

62. Green, *Colin Gunton*, 202.
63. Green, *Colin Gunton*, 202.
64. Green, *Colin Gunton*, 201.
65. Green, *Colin Gunton*, 203.

that Gunton misinterpreted Augustine, he still finds value in Gunton's larger theological project.[66] While Green believes the West indeed faces a theological crisis, he suggests that Augustine, properly understood, could play a role in addressing it, positioning him as part of the solution rather than the problem.

Green, and to a lesser extent McNall, contribute indirectly to the extensive introductory sections. The central point, emphasized there and reiterated here, is that Gunton's argument must be properly framed before it can be critically engaged. Both authors categorize Gunton's response into specific complaints, addressing each sequentially. While the identification of distinct complaints is helpful—and mirrors the approach taken in this study—a methodological gap remains in treating these complaints as isolated issues rather than as interconnected elements within Gunton's broader theological study.

In evaluating Green's work, priority is given to understanding the macro context before examining specific complaints. For continuity, the response to Green will be structured around the three complaints outlined in this book. Before that, however, some general issues will be discussed.

Overstating Augustine and Understating Causation

Green notes being struck by Augustine's "towering presence" in Gunton's work,[67] but this assessment seems overstated. While it is clear that Augustine plays a significant role in Gunton's later writings, he was hardly even in the wings for the first act.[68] Surely the likes of Barth, the Cappadocians,

---

66. He concludes his critique of Gunton with the caveat that the criticisms "do not ultimately undermine the theology of Colin Gunton" (Green, *Colin Gunton*, 201).

67. Green, *Colin Gunton*, 202.

68. Does this point become a separate section on Green's reading of the Gunton corpus?
What makes this even more unusual is Green's quote that "one of the clearest expositions of Gunton's position on Augustine is found in The Promise of Trinitarian Theology" (Green, *Colin Gunton*, 30). What makes this unusual is that this was an early engagement with Augustine. It lacks the input from Taylor and the growing focus on mediation. It also has an underdeveloped work on the argument of causation which we see expanded in *The One, the Three, and the Many*.
There is further evidence that Green's reading of Gunton may have been too narrow. He writes that *The One, the Three, and the Many* is "the conceptual backdrop for Gunton's understanding of the history of Western thought" (Green, *Colin Gunton*, 33). This is not the case as both *Enlightenment and Alienation* as well as *God and Freedom* are also significant contributions here. Both of these appear in Green's bibliography but are not cited anywhere in the body of his work.

and Coleridge need to be ahead of Augustine for the "towering" accolade! On this point is it quite clear that there is little to no awareness in Green of the shift in Gunton's writing, and no engagement on the influential roles of Barth and Coleridge (although Zizioulas does receive some recognition). These omissions detract from the quality of his research.

On the topic of omissions, Green also offers limited engagement with causation and Augustine's legacy. Charles Taylor's work, which influenced some of Gunton's later thoughts on Augustine, receives only a footnote mention on p. 84.[69] Taylor's central hypothesis—and arguably Gunton's chief concern—is Augustine's focus on inwardness. For both scholars, Augustine repositions the self at the center, shifting the theological "center of gravity." Additionally, Gunton's *Triune Creator* dedicates much of its content to bridging gaps in the causality argument, yet Green does not address this part of Gunton's work.[70]

It appears that Green misunderstood the context within which Gunton referenced Augustine. Gunton's primary opponent was the contemporary theological paradigm, and through redaction, he argued that its source could be traced back to Augustine. Here, McNall demonstrates an awareness that Green lacks. For Gunton, the true issue lies in Augustine's theological legacy. Admittedly, Gunton's articulation could have been clearer, yet this conclusion is reasonably deducible within Gunton's broader project. This agenda is clearly outlined in *The One, the Three, and the Many* and is strongly reinforced in *Enlightenment and Alienation* as well as *God and Freedom*. Had Green recognized this context, he might have offered an alternative historical reading.[71] Instead, he acquits Augustine but leaves the unresolved challenge of modern individualism.

69. Green, *Colin Gunton*, 84.
70. Gunton, *Triune Creator*.
71. Green's best summation of causality can be found on p. 171. Here he commends Gunton for his redactive approach. "Gunton is concerned to ask, how do certain ideas show up repeatedly in history, and how do different ideas yield different social, cultural and political consequences. . . . A Christian view of history should certainly take 'the long view,' and ask how current trends are a reflection of, or a reworking of, very old ideas or tendencies in human history" (Green, *Colin Gunton*, 171). On reading this, the logical expectation of the reader is to expect Green's version of the "long view," especially since he is depriving us of Gunton's.

To Green's credit he does put something on the table here, albeit rather gingerly. He echoes Cunningham's critique that Gunton's critique of The One vs The Many has bought too deeply into the Hegelian paradigm. As an alternative he suggests *Belief* and *Unbelief*. Green argues, "Gunton's schema appears to give inadequate attention to the central importance of belief and unbelief, and that Scripture is centrally concerned to point out the connection that exists between the state of a culture and its spiritual state"

Overstating Creation

Green writes, "At the heart of Gunton's theology is a strong doctrine of creation. In the sense that creation is perhaps the central doctrine in Gunton's thought, he echoes H. H. Schmid's assertion that 'all theology is creation theology.'"[72] This raises the question of why Green views creation as central to Gunton's theology. If Green's assessment is correct, it challenges the understanding of Gunton's theological project in this study. It is true that Gunton wrote two books with creation in the title, *The Triune Creator* and *Christ and Creation*.

The Triune Creator specifically addresses the lack of mediation in contemporary theology. Within it, Gunton presents a familiar critique: the Enlightenment fostered a "belief that God made the world as a machine-maker makes a machine—with perhaps an eschatology of rewards and punishment after death—was made into the whole of rational religion. This effectively ruled out those aspects of the doctrine of creation which make it a basis for a continuing involvement of the creator with the world, as is supposed by the doctrines of Christ, the atonement, grace, the church and the sacraments."[73] This point aligns closely with the analysis of Gunton in chapter 2. For Gunton, his focus on creation is a response to dualism and a firm affirmation of the mediated nature of humanity's relationship with God.

There is more to be said about *The Triune Creator*. Here, we find Gunton's theory of causality in its most developed form, as he traces the evolving theology of creation and nature across the centuries to effectively link us to Augustine. This underscores a key conclusion from the previous section: creation is not the central theme of Gunton's theology. Green's interpretation may stem from over-reliance on selected works, leading him to miss the broader scope of Gunton's larger project.

(Green, *Colin Gunton*, 172–73). It's hard to give weight to this suggestion given the extensive covering of epistemology in Gunton. Green really needed to support this with a more detailed engagement with a *Brief Theology of Revelation* (only two references in this book) and *Becoming and Being*.

72. Green, *Colin Gunton*, 32. Green (Green, *Colin Gunton*, 33) goes on to add: "One could say that this doctrine [creation] is a cornerstone to the rest of Gunton's thought."

73. Gunton, *Triune Creator*, 6.

Complaint 1: The Platonic Influence of the Intellectual Being Superior to the Material

The ordering of Gunton's complaints in this book is intentional. By placing the Platonic complaint first, the focus is on the role of the presuppositions Gunton identifies in Augustine. This is followed by the source of our knowledge of God in the handling of the economic and immanent Trinity. Finally, a mishandling of the Trinity in Complaint 2 can lead to Complaint 3: the emphasis on the unity of God. In responding to Green, I will translate his work into this structure, as Green's arrangement—based on the thesis that creation is central to Gunton's work—is less suitable for this critique. Green categorizes Gunton's writings under 1) *Creation and Redemption*, and then 2) *Being and Ontology*, but given the disagreement over the centrality of creation, this structuring would be inappropriate.

Green rightly observes that, "At the heart of Augustine's troubles, as Gunton sees it, is Augustine's platonic (or neoplatonic) background, and what might be called an 'anti-materialism,' or aversion to the material world."[74] Green further expands on how Gunton views this aversion as undermining the Incarnation, effectively creating a gap between the immanent and economic Trinity. This theme appears in *The Promise of Trinitarian Theology* under the section titled "The Problem of the Unknowability of God." According to Gunton, when a gap emerges between the economic and immanent Trinity, the knowability of God is challenged.

While the writer agrees with Gunton's point regarding the challenges of knowability, his approach here was unwise. To open with "unknowability" as a critique of Augustine is more than unwise—it's potentially irresponsible. This language could be taken to imply that Augustine did not truly know God. By extending Gunton's argument to the Western theological crisis he outlines, one might infer that countless Christians also fall short of knowing God, an implication Gunton surely did not intend. Gunton's language lacks balance, focused solely on the notion that Augustine is insufficiently Trinitarian, without acknowledging, for instance, Augustine's response to the Arian heresy.

If we acknowledge Gunton's tendency to overreach and return to the question of Augustine's Platonism, does Gunton have a point? Green comments: "Perhaps one of the first things that should be said in response to Gunton is that in Augustine's theology the created order is good, even

---

74. Green, *Colin Gunton*, 80.

if it is a lesser good, even if it is a lessor good than ultimate spiritual realities. That is, in Augustine there appears to be limited dualism."[75] Here, Green seems to take away with the left hand what he has just given with the right. While he does not agree with Gunton's conclusion about the unknowability of God, he concedes that the Platonic dualism Gunton identifies is indeed present in Augustine's thought.

What Green acknowledges is a measure of dualism in Augustine—a concession to Gunton's conclusion but also a necessary moderation. Green's detailed study of Augustine offers a more nuanced view, one that appreciates Augustine's broader theological agenda. Gunton's portrayal of Augustine is relatively narrow, focused on a specific critique. Our conclusion, therefore, must recognize the presence of dualism in Augustine and its potential contribution to individualism. However, it also needs to note that Gunton's critique overreaches. Ironically, Gunton's analysis lacks the balance and appreciation that this book seeks to afford him. In short, the "sentence" Gunton has given Augustine does not fit the "crime."

Complaint 2: Immanent and Economic

Gunton's second complaint builds on the first: he argues that Augustine's dualism creates a gap between the economic and immanent Trinity. At the heart of this debate lies the question of an underlying substance supporting intra-Trinitarian relations, centering on Augustine's handling of *substantia* versus *ousia*. Green addresses this issue at length, providing an impressive overview of the origins of *ousia* and its contemporary interpretations. Green's key points include:

- Augustine's use of language can sometimes lead to misunderstanding. Following Durant, Green argues that "Augustine, like the Greek fathers, muddles and confuses Aristotle's notion of substance." Thus, Green suggests that a careful reading of Augustine is required, supported by corroborative insights from his broader writings. Additionally, Augustine begins book 5 with an admission of his own trepidation regarding the nature or being of God. Green combines this with his earlier point, noting, "Unless both (1) Augustine's

---

75. Green, *Colin Gunton*, 174. Green wants to reposition Augustine's Christian Platonism. He wants to separate Augustine from those who see the material world as bad. For Augustine, the material world is indeed good; it's simply that the nonmaterial is "better" (Green, *Colin Gunton*, 89).

trepidation and reticence, as well as (2) the eschatological nature of our vision of God are kept in mind, Augustine's analogies and quest for knowledge of God are likely to be misunderstood."[76]

- Augustine's focus was directed toward refuting Arianism. Therefore, his emphasis on the unity of God should be understood as a defense of Christ's divinity, rather than as a demotion of the Holy Spirit or a denial of the particularity within the Trinity.

In addition to these two contextual factors distorting our reading of Augustine, Green also affirms the presence of a relational ontology. He writes, "We should also note that while a type of *perichoresis* is often found in the Cappadocians (and more fully John of Damascus), at least a trace of the concept can be found in De Trinitate. Augustine here is concerned to affirm the simplicity of God as well as the individuality of the three persons and their intimate relationship with one another."[77]

Green deserves commendation for bringing greater "substance" to the debate. He demonstrates a depth and persistence with Augustine that we do not see in Gunton. Particularly significant is Green's emphasis on the impact of the Arian context and Augustine's trepidation regarding the nature of God. These points remind us that Augustine was not a self-proclaimed spokesman nor a systematic theologian; rather, he was a theologian responding to the pressing reality of the Arian threat.

These insights primarily critique Gunton's method of conveying his argument, as his tendency to overreach is evident here too. While Gunton's approach is redactive, one could argue that it has not been sufficiently so; he has not gone far enough to consider the broader forces shaping Augustine's reality. In this respect, Green's perspective provides valuable corrective insight.

On Augustine's relational ontology, however, we can be more skeptical. Although Green devotes two chapters to being and ontology, his reference to *perichoresis* on p. 161 is only one of three in the entire book.[78] Moreover, here he acknowledges only a "trace" of relational ontology. Green anticipates Gunton's critique of the relationship between Augustine's "trace" of relational ontology and his inward focus, particularly regarding Trinitarian images. Green responds, "What Augustine appears

---

76. Green, *Colin Gunton*, 147.
77. Green, *Colin Gunton*, 161.
78. Green, *Colin Gunton*, 161.

to be saying here is somehow the intimate relations of the three persons constitute the being of God."[79]

This assertion is difficult to accept. Gunton does not argue that Augustine disregards relationships, but to suggest that they are constitutive in a perichoretic sense seems to overstate the case. Green's generosity toward Augustine may be misguiding him here. If Gunton—and many others—have not found this relational ontology in Augustine's writings, perhaps it is because it simply is not there.

Green is again helpful in moderating Gunton's critique, but he does not fully exonerate Augustine. He concludes that we may be unfairly judging Augustine and argues that "on Augustine's own terms, and given his presuppositions, Augustine's position generally makes sense."[80] Here, McNall's often-repeated point is relevant: it is Augustine's *legacy* that is under scrutiny. If Augustine is so easily misinterpreted, it's plausible that his legacy diverged from his original intent. Indeed, we can observe the early signs of diminished relationality in Augustine's thought.

Complaint 3: Emphasis on the Unity

As previously noted, Augustine's emphasis on God's unity reflects his response to the Arian controversy, where the oneness of God received greater focus than particularity. Green is less critical here, but he acknowledges the issue in his chapter on Augustine's ontology, beginning his conclusion with, "Let us draw together Augustine's general position on essence/substance, nature, persons and relations. There is little doubt that Augustine does emphasize the oneness of God."[81] Here, Gunton's complaint finds more support in Green's analysis.

We now move beyond the complaints to areas that would have benefited from deeper exploration in Green's book. His treatment of satisfaction theory is too brief, missing the connection to Gunton's emphasis on ontology and mediation in soteriology. Another topic given limited attention is the person of the Holy Spirit. Although Green disagrees with Gunton's assessment of Augustine here, he overlooks the link to Gunton's focus on the Spirit's mediatory role.

---

79. Green, *Colin Gunton*, 153.
80. Green, *Colin Gunton*, 167.
81. Green, *Colin Gunton*, 165.

Conclusion

Green's contribution provides a useful corrective to Gunton's reading of Augustine, highlighting several areas where Gunton overreaches, seeing issues in Augustine's work that may not truly be there. Gunton's tendency for broad-stroke critiques often seems hasty and, at times, irresponsible. With more care, he might have tempered his points and balanced them with a greater acknowledgment of Augustine's contributions. There would have been much more for Gunton to lament if the Arian heresy had gained traction over Augustine's influence.

However, Green's arguments are weakened by a limited grasp of Gunton's broader theological project. His approach—lining up Gunton's points on Augustine only to dismantle them—misses the larger framework. While Green recovers some of Augustine's complexity, he loses Gunton's. As discussed in the opening chapter, Gunton's project was not simply about discrediting Augustine but about addressing the contemporary theological crisis. Green's limited engagement with the evolution of Gunton's journey and focus on the contemporary paradigm underscores this disconnect. Gunton made clear in *The Promise of Trinitarian Theology* that Augustine must be engaged on his presuppositions—a level at which Green's critique falls short.[82]

Green's argument is further weakened by inconsistency. While he aims to elevate Augustine from foe to friend and dismiss Gunton's assessment, he simultaneously asserts, "the criticisms do not ultimately undermine the theology of Colin Gunton."[83] This leaves the reader confused—how can Gunton's theology remain intact if, as Green suggests, his understanding of Augustine was fundamentally flawed?

Most critically, Green pays little attention to causation. He seems to believe that by challenging Gunton's view, he has resolved the matter. Yet for Gunton, modernity remains the real fire, with Augustine as a primary source. If Green removes Augustine from this role, he should offer stronger recommendations for other causal factors. Even if he had, his case would be weakened by his light handling of Augustine's inwardness.[84] Despite his supposed misreading at the hands of Gunton, is there

---

82. Gunton, *Promise*.

83. Green, *Colin Gunton*, 20.

84. There is an acknowledgement that books 8 and following turn inward to enable humanity to trace humanity's Trinitary in the image of God (Green, *Colin Gunton*, 163).

a possibility that Augustine's inwardness had unforeseen consequences? This question appears to have been left off Green's agenda.

Joshua McNall: "A Free Corrector"

McNall's book, originally submitted as a doctoral thesis in 2013,[85] presents itself as a "Free Corrector," a term Augustine invites, with McNall arguing that Gunton may have taken this freedom too far. The purpose here is to critically engage McNall, not to praise him. That said, his work is impressive and offers a meaningful contribution to the Gunton-Augustine debate. The quality of McNall's scholarship may be attributed to the fact that he was already a professor of theology when he wrote it. While he acknowledges reading Green, he demonstrates a much broader understanding of Gunton's project. McNall not only distills the key issues but also thoroughly examines them, persistently turning debates over to reach the most balanced conclusion possible.

Green, McNall, and Gunton converge in recognizing the profound influence Augustine has had on nearly the entirety of Western theology. However, the debate centers not on the *extent* of this influence but on its *nature*—the primary focus of this project. McNall consistently maintains a distinction between what Augustine originally articulated and how tradition has remembered him. McNall has an appreciation for Gunton's theological intent in approaching causation. He appreciates Gunton's intent in exploring causation, noting the value in how Gunton's work demonstrates that the gospel "provides a lens for viewing even a grand sweep of history."[86] While McNall may not fully grasp the overarching theme of Gunton's project, he offers a thorough engagement with Gunton's approach to causation.[87] By carefully separating Augustine from his legacy (or "Afterlife"), McNall addresses a key omission in Green's study.

In this, McNall's critique mirrors aspects of Green's: both find that Gunton's broad-stroke approach often overreaches, sometimes unfairly diminishing Augustine. These critiques are not unique to Green and McNall, as many scholars have similarly noted Gunton's tendency toward sweeping generalizations.

---

85. It is this thesis that is referenced here.
86. McNall, *Free Corrector*, 248.
87. McNall, *Free Corrector*, 245.

McNall remains polite yet critical. His suggestion that Gunton turns past thinkers into caricatures sends an important message: for all his insight, Gunton's critique of Augustine oversteps. If Gunton had applied this approach consistently across all his subjects, it might have been easier to accept, "dilute," or factor into a reading. However, when juxtaposed with his generous interpretation of the Cappadocians and near idolization of Irenaeus, as discussed in chapter 2, Gunton's evident bias weakens his overall argument.

McNall, unlike Green, offers a constructive alternative. By separating Augustine from his legacy, McNall allows us to appreciate Augustine on his own terms while acknowledging how, in the hands of later thinkers, aspects of his work contributed to the theology Gunton finds problematic.

Sources

This section highlights significant differences between Green and McNall, particularly regarding their access to scholarship. McNall benefits from having a wider array of resources at his disposal, including key works published after Green completed his studies. For example, while Green draws extensively on Ayres, the 2010 publication of Ayres—*Augustine and the Trinity*[88]—came too late to inform his PhD significantly. Likewise, Harvey's *Theology of Colin Gunton* was unavailable to Green during his research.

Two additional sources merit attention: Hanby and Pelikan. Hanby's work is only briefly mentioned in Green's analysis but features more prominently in McNall's. Even so, McNall carefully critiques Hanby's approach, noting its limitations: "*Thus while Gunton went too far in blaming Augustine for the failures of his progeny, Hanby seemingly errs in the opposite direction. In the end, we will come to see that the 'all-or-nothing' approach of both histories stands in need of some revision.*"[89]

Pelikan's absence from Green's work is striking, given his centrality in McNall's study. McNall positions Pelikan as a leading authority on Augustine, relying on him heavily to frame his analysis. However, this reliance introduces a potential vulnerability in McNall's argument. By allowing Pelikan's perspective to dominate, McNall risks undermining the independence of his critique. The reader may question the criteria

---

88. Ayres, *Augustine and the Trinity*.
89. McNall, *Free Corrector*, 139.

that elevate Pelikan to such prominence and whether his views should overshadow more critical interpretations, such as Taylor's. McNall might have strengthened his position by engaging more critically with Pelikan and balancing his insights with alternative perspectives.

Qualified Affirmation of Dualism

A central element of Gunton's critique of Augustine is his alleged dualism. Both Green and McNall argue that Gunton overstates his case, contending that Augustine's dualism is far more nuanced and limited than Gunton suggests. McNall illustrates this with Augustine's references to angels, writing,

> Augustine's treatment of the angels should be framed in the context of a pro-Nicene polemic. Yet in defence to Gunton, Augustine's way of defending the tradition can be seen to further a dualistic imbalance in which the immaterial and invisible trumps that which may be seen. Thus again, we find a kernel of truth in Gunton's somewhat uncontextualized critique.[90]

This approach is characteristic of McNall's perspective. By situating Augustine's arguments within their historical and theological context, McNall seeks to preserve the integrity of Augustine's contribution while simultaneously granting the legitimacy of Gunton's observation.

McNall consistently distinguishes between Augustine himself and the legacy that emerged from his thought, recognizing how Augustine's limited dualism could become amplified in the hands of his successors. He writes: "Thus, while Augustine's resulting dualism was of course 'limited,' it is not sufficient to conclude that this does away with Gunton's charge. On the contrary, for Gunton it was precisely the limited nature of Augustine's dualism which allowed it to be passed on to future generations."[91]

Gunton's Projectionism

McNall tempers his concession to Gunton with a critique of what he identifies as Gunton's projectionism, suggesting it as the driving force behind some of Gunton's overreaching theological claims. Projectionism, McNall argues, appears consistently in Gunton's work. To explore this tendency, McNall turns to Gunton's reading of the Cappadocians—a

90. McNall, *Free Corrector*, 117.
91. McNall, *Free Corrector*, 125.

strategic move to examine the other end of the theological spectrum. Drawing on Holmes, McNall critiques Gunton's interpretation of the Cappadocians, particularly his view of an analogical relationship between divine and human persons. While this critique holds some merit, it cannot fully engage Gunton's position without factoring in the influence of Coleridge, who was instrumental in Gunton's development of his *analogia relationis* framework.

McNall deserves credit for including Coleridge in the discussion—something Green entirely omits—but he does not connect Coleridge to Augustine's role in shaping the *analogia relationis*. McNall deserves credit for including Coleridge in the discussion—something Green entirely omits—but he does not connect Coleridge to Augustine's role in shaping the *analogia relationis*. This oversight weakens McNall's argument. Despite offering a more comprehensive study of Gunton than Green provides, McNall fails to capture Gunton's intellectual trajectory. For instance, although he references Ayres's acknowledgment of Gunton's growing appreciation for the complexity of Augustine's thought, McNall stops short of fully exploring how Gunton's views evolved over time.[92]

The Elevation of the Unity Above the Particularity

Gunton's third critique focuses on Augustine's alleged overemphasis on the unity of the Trinity at the expense of its particularity. While bypassing the detailed discussion of substance that leads to this issue, McNall's argument here provides sufficient clarity to justify this shortcut. The core of McNall's position lies in advocating for a balanced reading of Augustine, a method reminiscent of Childs's canonical criticism.

McNall acknowledges that in the passages highlighted by Gunton, the particularity of the Trinity may indeed appear obscured. However, he contends that these passages cannot be treated as representative of the entirety of Augustine's thought—what might be called his "canon." McNall writes,

> The problem with this charge is that there are other passages in Augustine (indeed there are always other passages in Augustine!), which would go on to affirm the distinct actions of particular persons within the godhead.[93]

92. McNall, *Free Corrector*, 41.
93. McNall, *Free Corrector*, 74.

If we follow McNall's reasoning, the natural conclusion is that if Gunton misread Augustine, others in Augustine's legacy might also have drawn similar, potentially flawed conclusions. McNall seems to anticipate this critique, acknowledging the possibility: "In such instance, Augustine's emphasis on the undivided nature of the divine action may have come to unwittingly marginalize the particularity of the triune persons."[94]

To develop a truly balanced response, further exploration of this theme is necessary. While there is a risk of over-referencing, additional examples will help clarify how a more measured reading of Augustine can address Gunton's concerns without succumbing to the same pitfalls.

- On the polemical nature or *De Trinitate*: "Polemics, after all, are meant to swing the pendulum of public opinion in the desired direction, yet if history is any indicator, such pendulums are sometimes difficult to stop. . . . It seems at least possible that *De Trinitate's* polemic emphasis may have had some unintended consequences."[95]
- On engaging Augustine's Platonism: "Gunton largely ignored this Augustine, and it is therefore yet another example of a highly biased reading."[96]
- On Augustine's inability to distinguish the temporal from the fallen: "For Augustine, the way to defend his flock from Manichean heresy was to conceive of God as timeless, and creation as an instantaneous act. This is not to say that Augustine's conclusion is an altogether happy one, yet it does explain the pastoral intent behind this position. Gunton never notes this point, and in so doing, he ends up accusing Augustine of the very thing he was trying to refute (a lingering Manichaeism)."[97]
- On Gunton's reading of the Cappadocians: "Gunton's use of the Cappadocians was almost as selective as his use of Augustine. In both cases, key phrases were seized upon and quoted frequently without extensive background."[98]

These points culminate in a conclusion that encapsulates their sentiment: "What is not fair, however, is that despite the good and bad of

---

94. McNall, *Free Corrector*, 76.
95. McNall, *Free Corrector*, 81.
96. McNall, *Free Corrector*, 100.
97. McNall, *Free Corrector*, 105.
98. McNall, *Free Corrector*, 228.

Augustine's many-sided doctrine, Gunton chose to focus almost solely on the negative."[99] Having examined Gunton's work in detail, it is clear that his broad-brushed approach often led to prematurely reached conclusions. A previous section illustrated the shortcomings of his treatment of Augustine, which was notably weak, and highlighted his overly idealized view of Irenaeus. The same critique applies to his engagement with Barth and Coleridge, though the latter fared much better under his scrutiny than the former.

However, these acknowledgments do not necessarily validate McNall's critique. Was *The One, the Three, and the Many* not itself a polemical work? Was Gunton not also attempting to redress an imbalance and shift the theological pendulum? Should he not be granted the same grace and interpretive charity that is so generously extended to Augustine?

In my view, we must have the same openness about both Augustine and Gunton. While Gunton's scholarship was occasionally shoddy, omitting important details, the same critique can be applied to Augustine. Perhaps Augustine's issue is not a broad brush but rather a prolific one. In producing such a vast corpus, it is possible that insufficient care was given to maintaining consistency across his positions.

To be fair, Augustine did not write with the expectation that his work would later be subjected to the intense scrutiny it has received. However, acknowledging this does not mean we should continue to place him on a pedestal. Both Augustine and Gunton must be subject to the same level of examination and critique, stepping down from the pedestal to take their place in the broader dialogue of theological inquiry.

While this paragraph has the tone of a conclusion, it is premature in this context. The purpose of this section has been to engage with McNall's argument for a balanced reading of Augustine. Though McNall's perspective is valuable, it inadvertently risks affirming Gunton's criticisms of the Augustinian legacy rather than undermining them. The next section will shift focus to a more significant issue: the connection to Cartesian thought.

Affirmation of a Cartesian Link

The primary focus of this chapter is the exploration of causation, specifically Gunton's thesis that Augustine's influence can be traced through

---

99. McNall, *Free Corrector,* 112.

history to modern phenomena, even as far as contemporary institutions like Adidas. McNall, to his credit, recognizes this dimension of Gunton's project. For Gunton, critique alone was insufficient—he sought to trace the trajectory of these issues from an Augustinian source to their modern manifestations. Central to this argument are the roles of Ockham and Descartes as key intermediaries.[100] Here, McNall offers a measured concession to Gunton's thesis:

> As Gunton has argued, certain modern maladies could be linked to both Augustine and his harvesters. As we have seen, this charge is only partly viable. While Augustine's doctrine of God was not overtly monistic, his decision to look inward (in order to find an echo of the Trinity), would contribute to consequences over time. Some fruit (while only a blemish on the tree) would grow rotten in the hands of the later harvesters.[101]

This aligns McNall with Charles Taylor, who similarly suggests that Augustine's inward turn laid the groundwork for later philosophical developments, including Descartes's centering of the individual. While McNall makes a similar point to Taylor, he acknowledges Augustine's provision of "important clues." The section is quoted in full:

> While the Reformers drew heavily upon Augustine's anti-Pelagian corpus, Descartes (with his Jesuit education at La Flèche) drew key insights from other works. Thus the relative optimism of *De Libero Arbitrio* was combined with the interiority of the *Confessions*, and the latter sections of *De Trinitate*. Thus while Augustine did not provide Descartes with a comprehensive system, he did furnish some important clues as to where one looks in order to perceive the indubitable truth.[102]

This important conclusion is not made lightly. McNall engages with both Lewis Ayres and Rowan Williams, who argue against Gunton by viewing Augustine's introspective method as distinct from modern forms of

---

100. To remain within the scope of this study, there is no space for a detailed discussion of both Ockham and Descartes. However, the treatment of each follows a similar pattern: Gunton is critiqued for being "too free" in his corrections while some merit is still acknowledged in his argument (McNall, *Free Corrector*, 158). Gunton in a *Brief Theology of Revelation* proposes that "the arbitrary will of the Ockhamist deity [was] metamorphosed into the arbitrary will of the human agent" (Gunton, *Brief Theology*, 48). It is the apparently arbitrary and monistic will of Augustine's God that is evident here in Ockham (McNall, *Free Corrector*, 156).

101. McNall, *Free Corrector*, 246.

102. McNall, *Free Corrector*, 243.

inwardness.[103] However, McNall's analysis notably omits engagement with Charles Taylor, whose insights might have allowed him to support Gunton's conclusion while maintaining Augustine's distinction from Descartes. Taylor, for instance, underscores that Augustine's inward journey was purely a quest to find God. The shift of the individual to the center was an unintended and, unfortunately, catastrophic consequence.

Concluding Comments

In summary, McNall defends Augustine while providing a measured critique of Gunton's approach, yet he acknowledges the validity of Gunton's broader concerns about Augustine's legacy. As McNall states, "The line from Hippo Regius to the later centuries is not as direct as Gunton often supposed."[104] He effectively advocates for a more balanced reading of Augustine, demonstrating that Gunton's critique may have overreached. Similar to Green, McNall perceives the gap between Augustine and Gunton as narrower than Gunton had envisioned.

What McNall overlooks is the opportunity to engage meaningfully with Gunton's broader project. Put simply, for Gunton, Augustine serves as a means to an end. Put simply, for Gunton, Augustine serves as a means to an end. While McNall successfully identifies and critiques Gunton's caricature of Augustine, he risks undermining aspects of Gunton's theology by failing to situate this critique within the larger framework of Gunton's thought.

This raises an important question: How should we understand individualism—as a development with ecclesial roots rather than solely the product of an iconoclast? If we apply Gunton's own broad critique to Gunton himself, we can agree with McNall's assessment of his overreach on Augustine while still acknowledging that Augustine's influence lingers, albeit indirectly, in the intellectual trajectory leading to Descartes.

Charles Taylor and the Nudge[105]

It is appropriate to follow McNall with Taylor. While McNall's contribution lies in tempering Gunton, Taylor's strength is in rethinking causation.

---

103. McNall, *Free Corrector*, 41.
104. McNall, *Free Corrector*, 162.
105. "The New Testament is full of calls to leave or relativise solidarities of family,

If McNall had engaged more meaningfully with Taylor's approach, he might have found a less adversarial way to interpret Gunton's views on causation. Instead, McNall's analysis tends to adopt a win-lose framework in reviewing Gunton. In contrast, Taylor takes a markedly different approach. He prioritizes nuance and detail over sweeping generalizations and focuses on the concept of causation itself rather than on any particular figure's role in it. While Taylor may exhibit a subtle appreciation for Cartesian thought, there is little indication that Augustine is implicated in any specific theological agenda within his work.

Taylor views causation as a subtle "nudge" in history rather than a forceful hammer.[106] He readily acknowledges the complexity of the topic, emphasizing the interplay of numerous significant forces in shaping modern identity. As noted earlier, Taylor is a strong proponent of the "construction" school of thought, viewing historical developments as multilayered and interconnected. For him, frameworks are inescapable. While Taylor has much to say about Augustine's impact on modern individualism, he also adopts a broader perspective than Gunton's study, highlighting the significant influence of other Christian scholars and movements on contemporary individualism. Gunton's fixation on Augustine risks diverting attention from his broader theological agenda, which, as emphasized, aims at addressing a much wider Christian impact. In contrast, Taylor's scholarship belongs to a select group of ambitious thinkers who invite us to step back and view the entire landscape of identity formation. His work serves as an invaluable resource for critically assessing Gunton's contributions.

An Overview of Taylor's Causation Hypothesis

Before turning the particulars on Augustine, its useful to understand Taylor's overarching project, which can be categorized into two key areas: 1) attributes, and 2) events. Regarding *attributes*, Taylor focuses on the presuppositions and choices that shape the *construction* of *"the good life"*

---

clan, and society and be part of the Kingdom. We see this seriously reflected in the way certain Protestant churches operated, where one was not simply a member by virtue of birth but had to join by answering a personal call. . . . But my thesis is that the effect of the Christian, or Christian-Stoic, attempt to remake society in bringing about the modern 'individual in the world' was much more pervasive and multitracked. It helped to nudge first the moral, then the social imaginary in the direction of modern individualism" (Taylor, *Modern Social Imaginaries*, 62).

106. Taylor, *Sources of the Self*, 393.

within the "*ordinary*," contrasting this with Plato's ideal of self-mastery. While significant, a detailed exploration of this aspect lies outside the scope of this study and will be addressed only briefly to consider the Reformation's role in elevating the significance of the ordinary.

More pertinent to this discussion are the events and their long-term impact. Taylor identifies both the Enlightenment and Romanticism as pivotal moments in shaping modern notions of the self. His primary focus, however, is on the post-Enlightenment influences on identity formation. Within this framework, Taylor sees in Descartes the distinct shadow of Augustine,[107] drawing Augustine into the debate. This perspective offers a markedly different view of Augustine compared to Gunton. Much like Gunton, Augustine appears here as the product of a certain level of redaction. However, Taylor's aim is the illumination of Descartes rather than a theological critique. His approach reflects a higher degree of detachment, as Augustine's role is not a personal concern for him.

This different perspective is evident in Taylor's language. Included here is an extended reference to show Taylor's style of conviction interlaced with caution. Words like "tilt" and "wake" are combined with phrases like "difficult to trace." Taylor spoke of the "curious blindness" of the modern self-conception. Reading his words below, maybe "curious causation" is another appropriate expression. It would certainly be a lot more palatable than Gunton's critical review. We can give Taylor the credit of taking the reduction out of redaction!

> These two big and many-sided cultural transformations, the Enlightenment and Romanticism which tilts accompanying expressive conception of man, have made us what we are. . . . As I have often said, the order of causation is difficult to trace in this domain. If we were looking for causes, we would have to mention a great many other things like the industrial revolution and the rise of modern nationalism. What I mean is rather that our cultural life, our self-conceptions, our moral outlooks still operate in the wake of these great events. We are still visibly working out their implications or exploring possibilities which they opened up for us.[108]

---

107. "On the way from Plato to Descartes stands Augustine. . . . Henceforth, for Augustine, the Christian opposition between spirit and flesh was to be understood with the aid of the Platonic distinction between the bodily and the non-bodily" (Taylor, *Sources of the Self*, 127).

108. Taylor, *Sources of the Self*, 393.

This is a simplistic summary of Taylor. In reality, his exploration of influence extends far beyond these two events. Taylor offers significant insights into the impact of Christianity, particularly through the Reformation and Puritanism—topics that will be addressed later. Here, the focus shifts to the relationship between Augustine and the Enlightenment, or more specifically, between Augustine and Descartes. For Taylor, inwardness is a defining feature of the modern "moral topography." This concept serves as his starting point, which he traces back through Descartes to Augustine. By examining Augustine through the lens of inwardness, Taylor adopts a focus that is narrower than Gunton's but also more penetrating.

As a preamble to his exploration of inwardness, Taylor examines Augustine's conception of the inner and outer worlds. While both Gunton and his critics have acknowledged this dualism, Taylor frames it as a "precondition" for the internalization that follows.[109]

The importance of beginning with Platonic dualism lies in its role as the foundation for Augustine's inward journey. Taylor traces this dichotomy to Plato's oppositions: "soul against body, of the immaterial as against the bodily, and of the eternal as against changing."[110] These oppositions, central to Plato's philosophy, clearly influenced Augustine's development. In Augustine's thought, "the goods of the soul are stressed over those of worldly action," articulating a dichotomy between the inner and outer realms.[111] Taylor takes care to highlight the selective nature of the transmission of this framework. While there is continuity, he also identifies a break that paves the way for Augustine's journey inward. Just as some argue for a discontinuity between Augustine and his legacy, one can imagine fifth-century philosophers lamenting Augustine's perceived corruption of Platonic ideals!

---

109. Taylor, *Sources of the Self*, 120.

110. Taylor, *Sources of the Self*, 121.

111. Taylor, *Sources of the Self*, 121. "Plato's distinction stands at the heads of a large family of views which see the good life as a mastery of self which consists in the dominance of reason over desire. . . . The framework of self-mastery through reason has also developed theistic variants, in Jewish and Christian thought. . . . But the marriage of Platonism, or with Greek philosophy in general, was always uneasy; and another, specifically Christian, these has also been very influential in our civilisation. This is the understanding of the higher life as coming from a transformation of the will. In the original theological conception, this change is the work of grace, but is has also gone through a number of secularising transpositions. And variants of both forms, theological and secular, structure people's lives today" (Taylor, *Sources of the Self*, 22).

To reiterate, it is the dichotomy between the inner and outer that propels Augustine inward. Taylor identifies this dynamic in *De Trinitate* 12.1, where Augustine draws a distinction between the inner and outer man.

> The outer is the bodily, what we have in common with the beasts, including even our senses, and the memory storage of our images of outer things. The inner is the soul. And this is not just one way of describing the difference for Augustine. It is in a sense the most important one of our spiritual purposes, because the road from lower to higher, the crucial shift in direction, passes through our attending to ourselves as inner."[112]

Inwardness and the First-Person Dimension

The thread of this discussion is important, as Taylor guides us through three key shifts: from Plato, through Augustine, to Descartes. Previously, the focus was on the continuity and discontinuity of Platonic dualism in Augustine's thought. This sets the stage for Augustine's inward journey, the second key shift, which heralds the advent of the first-person standpoint. From here, the third shift emerges in Descartes, where this first-person perspective undergoes a "gravitational shift" toward the center, positioning the individual as the epicenter of reality. The purpose of this section is to explore the second shift—the emergence of the first-person standpoint—in greater depth.

Taylor is keen to stress just how pivotal Augustine was in the formation of the first-person standpoint and its subsequent influence on Western culture. Unlike Gunton, who focuses on complaints, Taylor is more oriented towards observations, which suggests a much more muted style. However, when addressing Augustine's role in the transition to the first-person standpoint, Taylor abandons his usual guarded approach and becomes quite emphatic:

---

112. Taylor, *Sources of the Self*, 129. It is important to stress both the continuities and discontinuities between Augustine and Plato. This is something missed by Green and McNall, who are seemingly pursuant of a binary resolution. This will be revisited in the conclusion, as more coverage on the discontinuities may have left the writer with less to debate. Taylor provides an example of this discontinuity here: "God is not just what we long to see, but what powers the eye which sees. So the light of God is not just 'out there,' illuminating the order of being, as it is for Plato; it is also the inner light" (Taylor, *Sources of the Self*, 129).

> Augustine's turn to the self was a turn to radical reflexivity, and that is what made the language of inwardness irresistible. The inner light is the one which shines in our presence to ourselves; it is the one inseparable from which being creatures with a first-person standpoint. . . . It is hardly an exaggeration to say that it was Augustine who introduced the inwardness of radical reflexivity and bequeathed it to the Western tradition of thought. The step was a fateful one, because we have certainly made a big thing of the first-person standpoint. The modern epistemological tradition from Descartes, and all that has flowed from it in the modern culture, has made this standpoint fundamental—to the point of aberration, one might think.[113]

This is not an isolated reference; Taylor considers this particular transition to be pivotal in the formation of modern individualism.[114] Just as Platonic dualism enabled the inward journey, this transition also facilitates further development. We can observe both continuity and discontinuity as this process unfolds.

Descartes's "Radical Twist" of Inwardness

At the heart of the debate surrounding continuity and discontinuity lies the figure of Descartes. Taylor highlights examples where Descartes can be seen as "profoundly Augustinian," referencing Augustine's radical reflexivity, the centrality of the *cogito*, and the inward journey to find God.[115] Yet, embedded within this continuity is a significant discontinuity—a "radical twist" that results in Descartes's concept of disengaged reason. As Taylor explains: "But Descartes gives Augustinian inwardness a radical twist and takes it in a quite new direction, which has also been epoch-making. The change might be described by saying that Descartes

---

113. Taylor, *Sources of the Self*, 131.

114. Taylor provides additional references to underscore the significance he attributes to Augustine's impact on "the entire Western culture": "But somewhere between these two reactions lies a just appreciation of the change he wrought. This was to make a turn to the self in the first-person dimension crucial to our access to a higher condition—because in fact it is a step on our road back to God—and hence to inaugurate a new line of development in our understanding of moral sources, one which has been formative for our entire Western culture" (Taylor, *Sources of the Self*, 132).

"Augustine was the first to make the first-person standpoint fundamental to our search for the truth" (Taylor, *Sources of the Self*, 133).

115. Taylor, *Sources of the Self*, 143.

situates the moral sources within us."[116] This twist shifts the gravity of inwardness from Augustine's theological framework to the individual and their reason.[117]

From Descartes, Taylor traces the theme of disengagement further, linking it to Locke. Locke, moving beyond Descartes, "rejected any form of the doctrine of innate ideas."[118] This marks a firm establishment of the subtractionist view of identity within Locke's framework. Locke's conviction in the possibility of disengagement—or what might be termed an impartial standpoint—enabled the metaphorical "demolition and rebuilding" of identity."[119] Building metaphors resonate throughout Locke's work, reflecting his belief in an individual's power to reconstruct their world on their own terms. Taylor underscores both the foundational nature of Locke's subtractionist position and its enduring influence on modern conceptions of the self.[120]

The driving force behind Locke's radical disengagement is the pursuit of control. To extend his building metaphor, this process is akin to demolishing a house built by others and reconstructing it anew—a house where one feels fully in control. While the term "Enlightenment" may, in hindsight, seem presumptuous, it aptly conveys the intent of its proponents: an opening of the eyes and an empowerment of freedom through the mastery and control of one's circumstances.[121]

---

116. Taylor, *Sources of the Self*, 143.

117. The reference to gravitational shift appears later in Taylor's work as he discusses the Lockean development of Descartes. He states, "Of course, the chain of reasoning shows that I rely on a veracious God for my knowledge of the external world. But note how different this is from the traditional Augustinian order of dependence. The thesis is not that I gain knowledge when turned towards God in faith. Rather the certainty of clear and distinct perception is unconditional and self-generated. What has happened is rather that God's existence has become a stage in my progress towards science through the methodological ordering of evident insight. God's existence is a theorem in *my* system of perfect science. The centre of gravity has decisively shifted" (Taylor, *Sources of the Self*, 157, emphasis original).

118. Taylor, *Sources of the Self*, 164.

119. Taylor, *Sources of the Self*, 166.

120. Taylor emphasizes the extent of Locke's disengagement through the term "radical disengagement" (Taylor, *Sources of the Self*, 173). He argues that Locke "reifies the mind to an extraordinary degree" (Taylor, *Sources of the Self*, 166).

121. "Radical reflexivity is central to this stance because we have to focus on first-person experience in order so to transpose it. The point of the whole operation is to gain a kind of control. Instead of being swept along to error by the ordinary bent of our experience, we stand back from it, withdraw from it, reconstrue it objectively, and then learn to draw defensible conclusions from it" (Taylor, *Sources of the Self*, 163).

Before turning to look at other Christian influences on contemporary identity, it is valuable to summarize what Taylor is saying. The discontinuity is an important starting point, as it is abundantly clear that the possession of freedom or control was not Augustine's intent. However, Taylor makes a strong case in support of Gunton by demonstrating the link from Augustinian inwardness through Descartes to Locke.

Taylor on the Reformation Influence

Taylor's exploration of the self reveals more than a linear progression of influence through Augustine, Descartes, and Locke. At the outset of this section, I noted Taylor's candid acknowledgment of omissions, particularly regarding the roles of technology and economics. Equally important, however, are Taylor's deliberate inclusions—specifically, his broader consideration of Christianity's influence on the modern conception of the self. These inclusions are significant because they align with and bolster Gunton's hypothesis: that the modern self is more a consequence of bad theology than the progeny of its rejection.

Taylor focuses specifically on the Reformation's affirmation of the ordinary and Puritanism's emphasis on the will. This discussion begins with the influence of the Reformation, which can be explored through two key sub-themes:

a. *The removal of the mediation of salvation*: From a Reformed perspective, the rejection of mediation is often seen as one of its most positive contributions. It dismantled the power of the clergy and the institutional church as mediators of grace, while also challenging practices such as the veneration of relics and adherence to rituals. Taylor highlights these aspects in his analysis.[122] Going

---

"Holding the package together is an ideal of freedom or independence, backed by a conception of disengagement and procedural reason. This has given Locke's outlook its tremendous influence, not only in the eighteenth century, but right through to today" (Taylor, *Sources of the Self*, 174).

122. "The affirmation of ordinary life finds its origins in the Judaeo-Christian spirituality, and the particular impetus it receives in the modern era comes first of all from the Reformation.... The rejection of mediation was closely connected to their rejection of the medieval understanding of the sacred" (Taylor, *Sources of the Self*, 215).

"Therefore Protestants (particularly Calvinist) churches swept away pilgrimages, veneration of relics, visits to holy places, and a vast panorama of traditional Catholic rituals and pieties.... Each person stands alone in relation to God; his or her fate—salvation or damnation is separately decided" (Taylor, *Sources of the Self*, 216).

beyond Taylor, we see the danger in over-correction. By targeting mediation instead of addressing a poor theology of mediation, the Reformation did little more than create an ecclesial version of the Enlightenment. Its focus on *sola fides, sola gratia,* and *sola scriptura* inadvertently supported the Cartesian shift that moved the center of gravity inward.

b. *The affirmation of the ordinary*: It is hard to overstate the importance of this for Taylor. He describes its secularized form as "one of the most powerful ideas in modern civilization."[123] This was a change that was co-dependent on the removal of mediation, and subsequently evolved into a secular form. He writes: "With the Reformation, we find a modern, Christian-inspired sense that ordinary life was on the contrary the very center of the good life. . . . The previous 'higher' forms of life were dethroned, as it were."[124]

While some argue that this represents a break from Platonic influence and its call to higher forms of life, others view it as a simple democratization of Platonism. Does it truly offer a departure from these higher forms? Although not part of Smith's discussion in *Desiring the Kingdom*, his argument could be used to support Platonic continuity. The Platonic ideals are not gone; they are merely presented deceptively as attainable while never actually being within reach. This is where Taylor would have benefited from a reading of Gunton. Even with the supposed contemporary affirmation of the ordinary, satisfaction remains the enemy of the market economy. Self-help books serve as a perfect example: everyone qualifies to read a book on becoming a better leader or parent.

"Where a mediated salvation is no longer possible, the personal commitment of the believer becomes all important. Salvation by faith thus not only reflected a theological proposition about the inanity of human works but also reflected the new sense of the crucial importance of personal commitment" (Taylor, *Sources of the Self*, 217).

"But for Protestantism, there can be no passengers. This is because there is no ship in the Catholic sense, no common movement carrying humans to salvation. Each believer rows his or her own boat" (Taylor, *Sources of the Self*, 17).

123. Taylor, *Sources of the Self*, 14.
124. Taylor, *Sources of the Self*, 13.

Taylor on the Puritans

In Taylor's analysis, the Puritans are treated distinctly from the Reformers. He sees in them a clear reflection of Locke's *Demolish and Rebuild*. While this theme resonates with familiar Scriptural motifs, it is accompanied here by a significant "reification" of the will. Taylor observes, "The society of the Godly ought to be one of willed consent. Some went to great lengths, including crossing the ocean to the wilds of New England, to separate themselves from the ungodly and set up a Christian society. . . . The central significance of personal commitment meant that all these communities were now understood in a more consensual light."[125]

In this context, Augustine's influence appears considerably diluted, filtered through Locke, Descartes, and beyond. However, what emerges is a clearer connection to the modern self—not necessarily reinforcing the Augustinian link (though not detracting from it either), but rather underscoring the broader theological influence on contemporary identity.

Alongside the reification of the will, the Puritans also significantly contributed to the development of the modern work ethic. Taylor connects this to Weber's seminal research, noting: "Weber thought that the Puritan notion of the calling helped to foster a way of life focussed on disciplined and rationalized and regular work, coupled with frugal habits of consumption, and that this form of life greatly facilitated the implantation of industrial capitalism."[126] Here lies an opportunity for further study in understanding the overlap between Taylor and Bellah et al.[127] The latter's focus is specifically on North American individualism, which is influenced to a much greater extent by Puritanism than European individualism. This is linked to the American notion of "leaving home" as a marker of maturity and career progression in terms of professional development. Of course, these concepts are several iterations removed from Augustine. Using Taylor's terminology, it would be fair to say that we are out of his orbit. Nonetheless, they are useful in highlighting the importance of theological presuppositions, which receive only cursory treatment in the theology of faith and work.[128]

---

125. Taylor, Sources of the Self, 194.
126. Taylor, *Sources of the Self*, 225–26.
127. Bellah et al., *Habits of the Heart*.
128. "The notion of progress and the emphasis on rationally planned improvement came from the Enlightenment. But the inspiration and driving force still came largely from the Christian faith, and the sense of exceptionalism attached to Christian (or often to Protestant) civilisation. . . . We have already seen how the demands of the Christian

Conclusion of Taylor

Taylor is clear that his research on modern identity represents only a part of the picture. The reality is that there are myriad contributing sources.[129] Yet he also emphasizes that modern identity is akin to scrambled eggs; once scrambled, identifying the separate eggs is impossible. With modern identity, redactive analysis is a real possibility. Here, moderated redaction is an asset in assessing Gunton's thesis because it supports much of Gunton's argument without the same aggression. As we have seen, Gunton undermines the value of his own contribution by being imbalanced in his views—perhaps occasionally a bit bigoted! In this context, Taylor's position serves as a valuable belay to secure the journey to the summit.

Taylor is not without his faults. He seems to be firmly situated in a post-Cartesian school, and his response is a considerable distance from Gunton's ontological reconception.

Summary of the Section

This review has been comprehensive without being exhaustive. Some argue that the fourth century is one of the most significant periods for theology outside of the era of biblical authorship. Gunton is not alone in his interest in this time, as Ayres notes, "It became all too common for theologians to make an easy Eastward turn, rejecting the complex discussions of the Latin discussion and argument, and yet never really engaging the complexities and differences within Eastern Theology."[130]

---

faith were redefined to incorporate a heavy dose of social reform, often conceived in terms of utilitarian calculation. This built on an already existing tradition in English Protestantism which went back to the strong Calvinist link between godliness, regeneration, and an ordered social life" (Taylor, *Sources of the Self*, 399).

129. "The modern identity arose because changes in the self-understandings connected with a wide range of practices—religious, political, economic, familial, intellectual, artistic—converged and reinforced each other to produce it: the practices, for instance, of religious prayer and ritual, of spiritual discipline as a member of a Christian congregation, of self-scrutiny as one of the regenerate, of the politics of consent, of the family life of the companionate marriage, of the new child-rearing which develops from the eighteenth century, of artistic creation under the demands of originality, of the demarcation and defence of privacy, of markets and contracts, of voluntary associations, of the cultivation and display of sentiment, of the pursuit of self-knowledge" (Taylor, *Sources of the Self*, 206).

130. Ayres, "Foreword," xi.

My purpose was not to defend Gunton from his critics but, arguably, to rescue Gunton from himself. This study has shown that certain elements of Gunton's grand narrative retain relevance, the importance of which will be highlighted in the chapter conclusion below.

CONCLUSION: THE PROBLEM OF INDIVIDUALISM

The connection between Augustine and Adidas may seem absurd to some and offensive to others, yet this is a logical deduction from Gunton's argument. From the outset, the focus has been on preserving Gunton's grand narrative, even as his handling of Augustine falters. Central to this narrative is the assertion that the self, positioned at the center of reality, has a theological ancestry. Whether this lineage stems directly from Augustine, his legacy, or the Reformation's emphasis on independence, a clear resemblance exists. Contemporary paradigms claim to have liberated identity from its metaphysical entrapments, but in reality, they have merely replaced old presuppositions with new ones. Foundationalism's impact extends far beyond theology.

Reframed, the question should not be whether Augustine is to blame, but whether we face a problem with identity and our relationship to the world. The answer is undoubtedly yes—just not in the way Gunton portrays it. Gunton's fixation on Augustine ultimately undermines his argument. He could have structured his critique to reduce this dependence and missed an opportunity to deeply engage with the Reformation, an event that both transformed and contextualized theological legacy for its time.

Gunton, however, rightly identifies a significant issue: modern individualism often fosters alienation more than emancipation. In this respect, his work is pioneering. He took the problem of alienation seriously and sought to identify its roots. While I do not share Gunton's indictment of Augustine, much credit is due to his redactive approach and his emphasis on the theological lineage of individualism. Gunton's work challenges us to be far more critical of contemporary paradigms and to expand our engagement beyond theology, incorporating philosophy and sociology into the conversation.

More than simply identifying a culprit, Gunton aimed to bring the issue back to its theological core. Through concepts such as *perichoresis*, relationality, mediation, and particularity, he highlighted ideas that are fundamentally at odds with individualism—concepts that challenge its very framework.

Western theology, however, has often been complicit, granting excessive legitimacy to individualism and the structures of the market economy. It exhibits a "curious blindness" to individualism's ancestry.[131] Simply put, the same theology that has infused Western society with individualism cannot be used to dismantle it. Addressing individualism requires a different theology—or at the very least, a different approach to doing theology.

Thus, while this chapter has explored the link between Augustine and Adidas, its broader purpose has been to critically reflect on the dominant theologies underpinning the market economy. Having sided with Gunton in acknowledging the problem, the discussion now turns to chapter 4, which will evaluate these issues within contemporary faith and work theology.

---

131. Bellah et al. is discussed in chapter 5 as a source consulted by Keller. His study precedes Taylor and comes from the position of sociological research which lends itself to a more pragmatic style than Taylor's weave of sociology and psychology. He supports Taylor's "curious blindness" with the following: "Yet in our desperate effort to free ourselves from the constrictions of the past, we have jettisoned too much, forgotten a history that we cannot abandon" (Bellah et al., *Habits of the Heart*, 85).

4

Limitations and Blind Spots in Faith and Work Theology

INTRODUCTION: BRIDGING THEOLOGY AND PUBLIC LIFE

THIS CHAPTER MARKS A pivotal shift in the progression of my discussion. To guide you effectively, I want to highlight both the continuities and discontinuities, ensuring the flow remains coherent. Without these clear connections, the argument risks appearing fragmented.

In chapter 2, I began with an overview of Gunton's theology, followed by a focused and in-depth exploration of Augustine and the formation of individualism in chapter 3—an intra-theological debate. In this chapter, however, I move into the realm of public theology as I critically examine Reformed literature on faith and work. This shift is significant because public theology is the context where this broader discussion ultimately unfolds.

The groundwork I laid in chapters 2 and 3 was crucial, equipping me to engage meaningfully in this critique. The interplay between theological reflection and practical application is at the heart of this transition, bridging the academic and public dimensions of the discourse.

The concept that links chapter 4 with chapter 2 is the concern that faith and work theology is dominated by the genres of ethics and evangelism. Furthermore, the centrality of ethics and evangelism is as a logical consequence of a theology dominated by individualism and an epistemic bias: the autonomous self is making rational choices. The dominance of ethics must also be clarified as personal ethics as opposed to structural ethics.[1] This focus is less a deliberate choice and more what Taylor describes as a "curious blindness." In other words, the attention naturally gravitates toward the individual and the integration of their *personal* faith with the workplace. At the same time, criticism of social structures is conspicuously absent—not because these structures are deemed irrelevant, but because they are simply unseen.

Just as chapter 2 served as a stepping stone for chapter 3, chapter 4 lays the groundwork for chapter 5, where I will examine Tim Keller's particular contribution. Ultimately, this progression allows me to use chapter 6 to explore how Gunton's perspectives might engage Keller's, offering fresh insights into identity and the market economy.

The hypothesis—that faith and work theology is dominated by ethics and mission—provides both the link and the structure for this chapter. Any validation of this hypothesis compels us to critically examine our public theology. Gunton's warning resonates here: "But it may be that in our desire to impose form on the world and our lives we have lost the capacity to see the form that is there; and in that lies not liberation but alienation, the cutting of ourselves off from things as they really are."[2] Gunton, of course, was not addressing the Faith and Work movement specifically, but the alienation he describes is not confined to the secular mind. There is a very real danger that many of us operate with a diminished or distorted view of reality.

In this discussion, we must heed Volf's[3] warning about the complexity of these issues. However, complexity also brings opportunity. This chapter, in particular, benefits from the inclusion of contemporary thinkers from other disciplines. Social evolution has blurred traditional boundaries, especially regarding identity, where work has become deeply entwined with other forces, playing a significant role in our formation. Analogically speaking, the eggs are already scrambled—we can no longer separate them into distinct parts.

---

1. The purpose of this book is to represent the use of the term "ethics" as used by the theologians engaged. They determine the definition. Of importance to this book is the predominant place given to the individual. A mapping of the encountered ethical theories within the landscape of ethical genres is beyond the scope of this study.

2. Gunton, *Enlightenment and Alienation*, 7.

3. Volf, *Work in the Spirit*, 188.

In this context, models like Niebuhr's, which distinguish between Christ "for" culture and Christ "against" culture, have become far less applicable. The clear dichotomies they once provided no longer capture the complexities of our current reality. The solution is not to retreat into simpler frameworks but to proceed cautiously, acknowledging and addressing potential challenges as the argument unfolds.

Structure of the Chapter

At the heart of this chapter is the need for a broad overview of the genres within the Faith and Work movement—essentially, a classification guide, for lack of a better term. This framework provides the basis for evaluating the hypothesis that ethics and evangelism dominate the field. Since the Faith and Work movement is not static, a broad historical overview will serve as a critical foundation for this analysis.

Among those who have attempted to document this history, Miller stands out for his effort to approach the topic with neutrality. His research is extensive, and his account is rich with detail. From the resources available, Miller's *God at Work* emerges as the most suitable choice for this purpose.

To summarize the navigational points outlined above, the reader can expect the argument to flow as follows:

- **The emergence of the Faith and Work movement:** This section explores the origins and development of the movement, alongside the evolution of work itself, providing historical and contextual grounding.

- **Review of key genres:** A classification of the primary genres within the movement, examining their possible reasons for emergence and relative prominence. This section also introduces key authors, including Keller, and offers preliminary conclusions regarding the hypothesis of ethics and mission.

- **Engagement beyond faith:** An exploration of contemporary perspectives on work, drawing on insights from other disciplines to broaden the discussion.

- **Critical consideration of the hypothesis:** An evaluation of the proposed dominance of ethics and evangelism, connecting this dominance to Gunton's critique of modernity.

- **Concluding insights:** Reflections on how the findings from this chapter contribute to a deeper understanding of identity and the market economy, setting the stage for the chapters to follow.

A successful chapter will leave the reader confident that the Faith and Work movement has been represented fairly and summarized clearly. Furthermore, it should provide a solid understanding of the key themes and their respective priorities within Christian literature.

THE HISTORICAL FOUNDATIONS OF THE FAITH AND WORK MOVEMENT

The academic contributions addressing the history of the Faith and Work field are limited. In this context, Miller's work stands out as a thorough and detailed review of the subject. His work will serve as a scaffold for the historical section of this chapter, though this is not an endorsement of his views, which will be critically engaged throughout the discussion.

Miller's title, *God at Work: The History and Promise of the Faith at Work Movement*,[4] reflects his intent to provide a biographical overview of the movement. In the opening paragraphs of chapter 4, he shares his personal journey, describing his transition at age 38 from a partner in a private equity firm to a theological leader in this field. This detail is significant. Success in private equity requires a sharp ability to analyze causation and context, identifying patterns and potential that others might overlook. Private equity professionals succeed by discerning whether a business's historical performance contains sufficient indicators for future growth that will surpass market expectations.

Miller has effectively applied these analytical skills to documenting the evolution of the Faith and Work movement, offering insights and a level of detail that set his work apart in this field.

At the time of his writing, Miller served as the executive director of the Yale Center for Faith and Culture and as an assistant professor of business ethics. The mere fact that Yale established a position dedicated to business ethics underscores the chapter's hypothesis about the dominance of ethics within the Faith and Work movement—a point that will be revisited later in the discussion.

Miller's affiliation with Yale places him at one of the central hubs of the Faith and Work movement. He is a contemporary and peer of

4. Miller, *God at Work*, 63.

Miroslav Volf, often credited as one of the founding academics in this field. What makes Miller particularly noteworthy is his dual expertise: he is both a theological academic and someone with substantial business experience. It is rare to encounter an academic whose bookshelf includes both Moltmann and Mintzberg, reflecting a synthesis of theological depth and practical insight. This unique combination of perspectives further enriches his contribution to the discourse.

Miller has an additional tie to this project through Keller who also valued his contribution and relied on his book extensively in the writing of *Every Good Endeavor*. All these points serve to add credibility to Miller's contribution.[5]

Paradigms, Movements, and Models

This title encapsulates the three core components of Miller's approach. Using the concept of "paradigms," Miller classifies Faith and Work as a movement and segments it into three historical phases. He offers a valuable mapping of how social movements are influenced by their underlying paradigms. Miller then dedicates the remainder of his work to developing a model that maps the theological spectrum within the Faith and Work movement. While the latter is of particular interest, as Miller points out, the two processes are best understood together. The respective genres within the movement are more comprehensible when viewed in the context of their historical formation.

Beginning with Miller's paradigms and movements, the following sections guide us through his framework, culminating in his model, which he terms "The Integration Box." This model of the Faith and Work landscape provides a foundation for engaging with the broader body of literature. It allows us to question which genres are represented in other works but absent in Miller's or whether some genres might be expressed differently by others.

It is important to emphasize that using Miller's framework in this way does not constitute an endorsement of his views. Rather, it reflects an appreciation for his goal of offering a comprehensive overview of the field.

---

5. Through Miller, Volf, and later Markovits, this chapter shows an imbalance towards Yale. To a critical reader, this may seem like an overrepresentation of a North American perspective; however, this conclusion would be a mistake. Miller is British, and Volf is Croatian. Markovits is also British and holds a PhD from Oxford (Yale Law School, "Daniel Markovits").

Miller approaches his subject as an analyst, stepping back rather than forward to gain perspective. According to him, movements have three main components: "(1) a loosely networked collection of individuals or groups that are (2) reacting against something they find unsatisfactory and unlikely to be resolved by normal cultural institutions or resources, and are (3) grounded in some common identity, world view, or organising principle."[6] This is a refreshingly simple definition, with the emphasis on "reaction" being key.

To unpack the reaction central to his analysis, Miller draws on two influential scholars from distinct disciplines. Robert Wuthnow's *Poor Richard's Principle: Recovering the American Dream Through the Moral Dimensions of Work, Business, and Money* provides a sociological perspective. Wuthnow's research offers Miller access to empirical data that highlights the disconnect many Christians experience between their faith and work.[7] Complementing this, Miller incorporates David Bosch's seminal work, *Transforming Mission: Paradigm Shifts in Theology of Mission*,[8] particularly Bosch's classification of paradigms.

While this narrow dependency carries certain risks, it also allows Miller to bring remarkable clarity to the emergence and development of the Faith and Work movement. Like a cartographer, he employs these authors as trigonometric beacons to map an otherwise under-researched field with precision.

Miller, Millennialism, and the Birth of Faith and Work

Miller divides the Faith and Work movement into three distinct eras, each characterized by its own unique emphasis:

- The Social Gospel Era (ca. 1890–945)
- The Ministry of the Laity Era (ca. 1946–1985)
- The Faith at Work Era (ca. 1985–present)

Miller was unfortunate with his timing. Publishing in 2007, he narrowly missed the financial crisis of 2008. While this doesn't diminish the validity of his outline, it does mean that the world he describes differs

---

6. Miller, *God at Work*, 20.
7. Miller, *God at Work*, 100.
8. Bosch, *Transforming Mission*.

significantly from the one that emerged after the crisis. The pre-2008 landscape Miller depicts reflects a period of growing middle-class wealth, largely fueled by the housing boom in the United States.

Of course, we now know the sequel: the boom was unsustainable, propped up by fraudulent practices disguised as securitization. This collapse not only reshaped the economic landscape but also influenced the trajectory of the Faith and Work movement. In the post-2008 context, there was a notable shift toward an ethics-centered discourse, a trend that aligns with the argument advanced in this book.

Before moving on from Miller's omissions—again, largely a matter of timing—it is essential to address the 4IR. This revolution, significantly accelerated by the COVID-19 crisis, has brought profound changes to the nature of work and its relationship to faith. To leave this unexamined would render the chapter incomplete.

Referring to Miller's division of the eras as described above, two significant points emerge: (1) the movement is relatively young, and (2) it is responding to the rapidly changing nature of work in society. Understanding the contemporary Faith and Work movement requires an awareness of the movements that immediately preceded it. Miller's analysis contributes to our understanding of the classification of the respective genres and is well worth engaging.

Miller draws on Bosch's insights into millennialist paradigms, particularly Bosch's observation of "an intimate correlation between mission and millennial expectations."[9] While acknowledging that these paradigms have become increasingly irrelevant over time and are often regarded by contemporary theologians as "anachronistic and outdated," Miller nonetheless argues for their continued relevance. He contends: "However, a more extensive look at the premillennialist roots of evangelical Protestantism and the postmillennialist roots of mainstream Protestantism is a helpful method to illuminate and understand their respective orientations toward faith at work, particularly during waves one and two of the FAW movement."[10]

Miller is correct that millennialism now feels like a spent force. However, he captures our interest by emphasizing that it is the *roots* of millennialism that are significant. He identifies strands within premillennialism that focus on "personal salvation through Jesus Christ, ecstatic

---

9. Bosch, *Transforming Mission*, 341.
10. Miller, *God at Work*, 25.

experience, and the overcoming of personal sin."[11] Miller's argument is that the dominance of these premillennialist roots effectively sidelined the faith and work mission. To borrow Bosch's language, personal salvation was seen as the only reality requiring transformation, leaving the realm of work outside the focus of concern. In contrast, postmillennialists placed greater emphasis on structural change, which later influenced the move toward liberal Protestantism and ecumenical groups.

Econocentricity

Miller's focus is on the birth of a movement, not the origins of work or the social values that allowed this movement to emerge. As a preamble, it is necessary to review the transition to an *econocentric* society. This term describes a society centered on economics, but more specifically, on *ordinary* economics—an emphasis that becomes clearer when contrasted with earlier hierarchical structures supported by metaphysical centricity.

Chapter 3 introduced us to Taylor and his theory of ordinary life, which marks a transition to a view of life that many of us now take for granted. "Ordinary," in Taylor's terms, contrasts with "Higher" or "Extraordinary."[12] He writes, "The full human life is now defined in terms of labour and production, on the one hand, and marriage and family life, on the other. At the same time, the previous 'higher' activities come under vigorous criticism."[13] The key lies in Taylor's choice of words: "*The full human life*"—a concept that is deeply intertwined with identity.

Taylor's later work, *Modern Social Imaginaries*, expands on the ideas presented in *Sources of the Self*, exploring the impact of the economy on social structure. By the late nineteenth century, the locus of ordinary life was being significantly shaped by the market. This period saw what Taylor describes as the "promotion" of the economic component of society.

---

11. Miller, *God at Work*, 25.

12. It is worth reading Taylor's reference in full. "The rejection of the supposedly 'higher' activities, contemplation or citizen participation, or of 'higher' levels of dedication in the form of monastic asceticism, in favour of the ordinary life of marriage, children, work in a call conferred a higher dignity on what had previously been relegated to a lower status. This unleashed a powerful tendency in our civilisation, one which has taken ever new forms. Some of these involved turning against the very religious tradition which has inaugurated this tendency in our civilization and defending 'natural' desire and fulfilment against the demands of sanctification, now seen as specious and destructive" (Taylor, *Sources of the Self*, 70).

13. Taylor, *Sources of the Self*, 213.

Once occupying a supporting role, it increasingly came to be regarded as "the dominant end of society"[14]—a transition that began as early as the eighteenth century, well before the period Miller examines in his review.[15]

Taylor sums up this transition in the following excerpt: "And so perhaps the first big shift wrought by this new idea of order, both in theory and in social imaginary, consists in our coming to see our society as an economy, an interlocking set of activities of production, exchange, and consumption, which form a system with its own laws and its own dynamic."[16] The dynamic nature of this econocentricity is undeniable, but simply acknowledging its presence provides a sufficient foundation to proceed with Miller's division of Faith and Work into distinct eras.

Social Gospel Era (1890–1945)

Miller's designation of this period as the "Social Gospel" era is fitting. It was a time marked by significant technological advancements, where confidence often outpaced critical reflection. This era saw the emergence of transformative inventions such as commercial flight (1914), intercontinental telephone service (1927), and affordable motoring with the Model T (1908). Paraphrasing Wuthnow,[17] trust and hope in the economic realm were at an all-time high. The focus was on how these new industries could address some of society's greatest needs. Such was the emphasis on their potential to help that little space was given to consider how they might also harm.

Supporting the notion of a Social Gospel era, Miller highlights the formation of several significant special-purpose groups. These groups reflect Christians actively responding to societal changes. Notably, for perhaps one of the first times in history, there was a notable growth in Christian organizations that lacked specific denominational ties.[18]

---

14. Taylor, *Modern Social Imaginaries*, 74.
15. Taylor, *Modern Social Imaginaries*, 74.
16. Taylor, *Modern Social Imaginaries*, 77.
17. Wuthnow, *Poor Richard's Principle*.
18. Select examples from Miller are as follows:
- YMCA. Christian Associations at University (*God at Work*, 30).
- Samuel Shoemaker Faith at Work in New York (*God at Work*, 32).
- Lay founded and led groups like Gideons (*God at Work*, 32).
- Christian Businessmen's Committee (*God at Work*, 33).

Miller acknowledges that the Faith and Work movement during this era remained predominantly male, reflecting the prevailing social norms of the time. In terms of focus, he identifies a tension within the movement between individual and social transformation. He also notes that while much of the movement was clergy-dominated, there was a growing independence from ecclesial structures, hinting at the beginnings of a lay-led emphasis. This shift toward lay leadership ultimately became a key catalyst for the transition to the next era.

Although Miller does not explicitly link the Great Depression to a change of era, it can be argued that the significant welfare needs created by the Depression likely extended this period into the Second World War. However, the post-WWII period marked a clear turning point in the Faith and Work movement, signaling the beginning of a new era.

The Era of Lay Ministry (1946–1985)

A defining characteristic of post-war organizations was *coalition*. The unprecedented demands of war had necessitated the removal of many traditional boundaries, fostering a spirit of collaboration that extended into peacetime. As Miller observes:

> In virtually all spheres of life, new groups formed, including the military (the Allied Forces and later that North Atlantic Treaty Organisation), politics (United Nations), jurisprudence (international law courts), finance (the Bretton Woods system of the International Monetary Fund and the World Bank), trade (General Agreement on Tariffs and Trade and, later, the Word Trade Organisation), and religion (the World Council of Churches and the World Council of Reformed Churches).[19]

The influence of these coalitions extended into Christian organizations and ultimately shaped the Faith and Work movement.

Here, we can argue for some inverse parallels to the Reformation and the Thirty Years' War. This time, the outcome was reversed; instead of fostering division, war unified by dismantling social and ecclesial boundary walls. However, Miller interprets this differently. In his view, the stronger driver was not the removal of boundaries but rather the prevailing anti-institutional sentiment.[20] The cause merits further dis-

---

19. Miller, *God at Work*, 40.
20. Miller (*God at Work*, 40) writes: "By the 1960s, a mood of anti-institutionalism

cussion in the following section. For now, we acknowledge and support Miller's observation that this era is characterized by a newfound freedom to move away from the institutional church and toward an emphasis on the ministry of the laity.[21] This observation takes us to a comment made in an earlier section on the Faith and Work movement being both new and subject to change. Movements, like this era, emphasize shifts as more people apply themselves to the engagement between faith and work. Among the key internal drivers, Miller identifies strong leaders who, through their organizations and publications, made significant contributions to the development of the theology of the laity.

Compartmentalization

Miller's comments on leadership warrant two separate discussions, which will be addressed in the next sections. At this point, it is important to note that this era marked the rise of compartmentalization within the Faith and Work movement—or, more precisely, between work and faith. Drawing on insights from both Wuthnow and Bosch, Miller highlights three alternative responses of faith to work: harmonious, compartmentalized, and conflictual. Of these, Miller argues that the goal of a harmonious relationship between faith and work was "naïve and unrealistic."[22]

This is a crucial point for understanding Miller in greater detail, particularly because there is an argument to be made that a degree of compartmentalization—or perhaps more aptly termed a *shadow* of it—persists through to the conclusion of his book. It is essential to examine compartmentalization in conjunction with its relationship to conflict. As Miller himself notes: "Many found the paradigm of conflict—an unbridgeable chasm between faith and work—to be the only way to make sense of the tension between faith and work."[23]

---

and anti-establishmentarianism became the ethos of the baby boomers, with the result that many young people sought alternative forms of community and spiritual expression. There were also powerful centripetal forces at work in the church."

21. As is typical of Miller, he supports his argument with numerous examples of key publications and organizations that reflect this trend. In terms of publications, he cites Kraemer's *A Theology of the Laity*, Weber's *Salty Christians*, the WCC Evanston statement, and *Faith at Work* magazine. Regarding organizations, he mentions International Christian Leadership, Full Gospel Business Men's Fellowship International, and the Fellowship of Companies for Christ.

22. Miller, *God at Work*, 41.

23. Miller, *God at Work*, 41. Due to limited space, the writer briefly reflects on an

Miller's thesis asserts that compartmentalization gradually became untenable, giving rise to a new paradigm of integrating faith and work. While his observation of a paradigm shift in the mid-eighties is reasonable, the nature of this shift remains open to debate. What the reader should pay attention to is the presence of critical engagement. Without it, integration risks being a continuation of the compartmentalization paradigm rather than a genuine shift.

If we return to Wuthnow and Bosch's three options—*harmonious, conflictual*, and *compartmentalization*—it is the term "conflictual" that feels the most dated. The mid-twentieth-century sentiment suggesting that hopes for harmonious relations are naïve is understandable. However, viewing the alternatives as conflict or compartmentalization also carries a sense of naivete. These three positions offer little room for critical engagement and perhaps reveal their own antiquity. This theme will be explored later alongside Miller's "Integration Box" and revisited throughout the remainder of the chapter.

There are some additional comments from Miller on this era. While individualism is not a concept used directly in his book, he references it when discussing the decline of the millennialist paradigm: "Premillennialists moved to a hybrid position, gradually accepting the importance of saving society, as well as souls . . . postmillennialists moved toward a mode of amillennialism in which millennialist thought was no longer a central theological question or defining problem."[24] This quote provides context for the following statement: "By the end of wave two, the postmillennialist streams began to change, making an inward turn to focus on the soul and the therapeutic transformation of the self."[25] This quote captures our attention. Is the transformation driven by a maturing worldview, with the gradual unfolding of modernity making the tension between work and faith too great to ignore? Or is the change in era driven

---

interesting study of the parallel between "compartmentalism" and fundamentalism. Karen Armstrong has written extensively on this topic in her books, *Fields of Blood* and *The Battle for God*. The key parallel lies in the need for certainty and clarity, often at the expense of reality. The trend toward de-institutionalization could weaken this parallel, but it can be countered by the presence of strong charismatic lay figures. A more robust fundamentalism may have allowed it a longer existence. However, the conflict between its simplicity and the underlying complexity of reality ultimately causes this era to run its course.

24. Miller, *God at Work*, 41.
25. Miller, *God at Work*, 42.

by the growth of individualism—an inward bent that makes the tension between work and faith less intimidating?

Power

Miller's stance is predominantly driven by the outward focus of the church: how it engaged with society. These eras and their transitions are also influenced by internal forces, specifically the interplay of power and authority within ecclesial structures. The inward and outward aspects are linked—a connection not explicitly identified by Miller, but one that can be discerned by the reader through his writing. The writer noted that Miller believes compartmentalization to be a dominant theme of this era. This is supported by Miller's observation that the movement was lay-led, with minimal clergy participation or integration within mainstream ecclesial agendas. Notably, key books that contributed to the movement's popularization were written by and for laypeople.[26] Consequently, faith and work in this era "never became part of the cord of church life or a true mass movement."[27] Arguably, the compartmentalization of the Christian businessperson during this time may reflect the compartmentalization present in the movement's leadership.

Miller's commitment to providing an overview prevents him from lingering on this section, which is somewhat disappointing, as it suggests he has more to say. Nevertheless, he offers a brief but incisive observation: the church is "resistant to changes in the roles, functions, and expectations of its leaders and members. Behind such changes lies the subtler question of the transfer of power and authority."[28] This remark is particularly insightful, highlighting underlying dynamics within church structures.

A similar critique emerges later in the same chapter, again delivered with sensitivity: "When laity were involved, they were usually white males, reflecting the leadership patterns of society, with few women or people from racial or ethnic minorities."[29]

I find myself questioning Miller's intention. Is he intentionally refraining from expressing a viewpoint, or is his commitment to the Faith and Work ministry driving him to avoid contentious issues that might

---

26. Miller, *God at Work*, 57.
27. Miller, *God at Work*.
28. Miller, *God at Work*, 44.
29. Miller, *God at Work*, 59.

compel the reader to take a stance? This question feels especially relevant to his overview of the integration model, where I will argue that a critical element is notably missing.

The Faith at Work Era (1985–present)

The final era identified by Miller begins in 1985. "Work-related questions about meaning, purpose, ethics, and how to express one's faith at work began to drive the movement. And there appears to be an irrepressible urge in laity to live an integrated life. This manifest itself in a deep desire to connect faith and work, while hoping for both personal and social transformation."[30] For Miller, this era is more than just academic; he shares his own decision in 1995 to leave the field of private equity to enroll in theological seminaries.

External factors are important catalysts. Miller draws on economist Robert Fogel's *The Fourth Great Awakening and the Future of Egalitarianism* to capture the "constellation of social and economic variables" that undergirded this shift.[31] Fogel's awakening describes a perceived paradigm shift from material resources to an "egalitarian future."[32] This correlates with Taylor's thesis regarding the changing definition of "The Good Life."

---

30. Miller, *God at Work*, 61. Laura Nash's *Believers in Business* is a compelling example of the shift described by Miller. Nash's subtitle, "Resolving the tension between Christian faith, business ethics, competition, and our definitions of success," illustrates the early quest for integration. At the time of writing, Nash was an academic at Boston University. Her work is representative because it emerges from interviews with Christians in senior business positions. She identifies seven tensions experienced by over eighty-five Christian leaders, with a key emphasis on ethics. She notes that "not all Christians or even all evangelicals agree about what is the right thing to do" (*Believers in Business*, xiv). The book is aimed at those who are aware of the tension but unsure of how to respond.

Another more recent interview-based North American study is Lindsay's *Faith in Halls of Power*. The appendix provides a list of the 360 leaders interviewed on the topics of faith and work, as well as faith and politics. Reflecting on the period described by Miller, Lindsay writes: "Though the 1980s and the 1990s were generally good years for American commerce, many leaders I talked with said that their lives needed 'balance' or spiritual 'grounding,' now more than ever. Spiritual seekers were trying to integrate different parts of their life, renegotiating boundaries between personal faith and the workplace" (Lindsay, *Faith in the Halls of Power*, 162).

31. Miller, *God at Work*, 63.

32. Miller, *God at Work*, 65.

These external factors from the global stage all contributed to the broader social outlook. Politically, changes such as the collapse of communism and the end of apartheid in South Africa fostered global confidence while simultaneously creating an economic growth stimulus.

Miller overlooks some contemporary trends that have emerged since 2000. One significant example is the maturation of work beyond Taylorism, which focuses on work-life balance and employee wellness. The motivation behind this shift can be debated. Was it the growth of the knowledge sector combined with the third Industrial Revolution, or was it the gradual shift in power dynamics favoring employees over employers due to advancements in communication and mobility? More likely, technological advances played a significant role by removing or lowering many industry barriers to entry. This shift is marked by a reduced dominance of multinationals in favor of smaller, more agile start-ups, with the dot-com boom (and bust) serving as an iconic example.

Another perspective comes from Volf, who considers the crash of 1987 a transitional moment. For Volf, this event marks the shift of work from the periphery to the center of our outlook, driven particularly by the large-scale unemployment it caused.[33]

Clarity on the cause adds little to the debate. The writer agrees with Miller that there was a shift but enriches the discussion with insights from Volf.[34] There was a change in the nature of work that created an opportunity for the development of the Faith and Work movement. A more fitting description of the era might be "me at work," with faith serving as just a passenger. This scenario is arguably not too dissimilar to the impact of Pax Romana on the early spread of the gospel.

Where we can rely on Miller is in the documentation of how the growing faith and work era translated into organizations. Some of the more relevant examples are as follows:

- Up until 2003, the number of Faith and Work organizations doubled every decade.[35]

---

33. Volf, *Work in the Spirit*, 4.

34. It does seem odd to the reader that Miller and Volf could have been sitting in adjacent offices while Miller was writing. While Miller misses Volf's insight on the shift of work to the center, he draws the following from Wuthnow: "Americans have shifted from a spirituality of dwelling to a spirituality of seeking" (Wuthnow, *After Heaven*, 6, cited by Miller, *God at Work*, 72).

35. Miller, *God at Work*, 106.

- In 2003 Volf founded the Yale Center for Faith and Culture.[36] This marks a significant theological milestone. Although not mentioned in Miller's commentary, Volf is widely regarded as one of the pioneers of theological engagement with work and faith.
- Corporate chaplaincy emerged as a distinct practice.[37]
- Faith and Work journals were established, with Miller citing *Life@Work* and *Business Reform* as examples.[38]

Miller's Assessment of the Faith and Work Era

My primary interest in Miller lies in his outline of the eras and the classification model that follows. Between these two, he offers his assessment of the contemporary Faith and Work movement before moving on to share his ideas for its transformation. On these topics, I find Miller's views conservative and lacking in imagination. As a result, my recap here will be brief.

In summary, Miller's current outlook is critical, with "problem" being a more fitting descriptor than "opportunity." He identifies resistance from the workplace, rooted in social "taboos," and critiques the church for being uninterested, unaware, or unsure.[39] This assessment, however, overlooks significant opportunities. For instance, the social taboos he highlights become less daunting when viewed in relation to the rise of individualism. This perspective moderates the picture, suggesting that resistance is less about faith itself and more about the perceived autonomy of the individual and the intended neutrality of the workplace.

The gap Miller seeks to close is that of education. He observes, "Indeed, my research shows that there are many clergy and religious professionals who want to respond to the needs expressed by the FAW

---

36. Miller, *God at Work*, 96.
37. Miller, *God at Work*, 114.
38. Miller, *God at Work*, 122.

39. The church's position is reflected in the following quote: "Thus, despite some exceptions, the evidence strongly suggests that the church in general seems uninterested in, unaware of, or unsure of how to help the laity integrate their faith identities and teachings with their workplace occupations, problems, and possibilities" (Miller, *God at Work*, 81).

In relation to taboos, we read: "Faith at work appears to be one of the final taboos to be broken in the corporate world" (Miller, *God at Work*, 150).

movement but are unsure of how to do so."⁴⁰ His focus on clergy and religious professionals is surprising and unique among his peers. For Miller, it is this group, rather than the laity, who are to be the primary agents of change. To him, education means the education of the clergy: "A logical starting point for change is the place where the clergy are trained."⁴¹

However, Miller's application of this idea loses momentum. For instance, he suggests that clergy spend time in the workplace to gain perspective—a proposal that feels somewhat naïve, especially coming from a former investment banker. While it sounds reasonable in theory, one might question the practicality: what, exactly, would clergy do while the investment banker carries on with trades? Ironically, given his own professional background, one might have expected Miller to place greater hope in the investment banker navigating these challenges without the need for clergy support.

A quote from Miller's final page provides a concise summation of his work, highlighting his strong view of ecclesial responsibility. This is particularly evident in his choice of words such as "abandon" and "abdicate." The final sentence strongly supports the ethical bias proposed by this chapter's hypothesis:

> The church and the academy can offer theological resources and practical tools to equip those whose calling it is to serve in and through the marketplace. For the church to do anything less is to abandon millions of Christians for five-sevenths of their week, and to abdicate responsibility for and influence over this important sphere of society. Indeed, active participation in the transformation of individual employees, their workplaces, and the overall marketplace may be one of the most powerful means to help feed the hungry, clothe the naked, and welcome the stranger.⁴²

With an understanding of Miller's position in hand, the next section reviews his classification model.

---

40. Miller, *God at Work*, 93.
41. Miller, *God at Work*, 145.
42. Miller, *God at Work*, 153.

MILLER'S THEOLOGICAL TYPES

Miller refers to his classification tool as the "Integration Box."[43] He aims to identify patterns that help us understand how the Christian faith interacts with the market in its various forms. Earlier, I engaged with his outline of broad themes over time. While the term "Integration Box" may lack creativity, it is functionally effective. To borrow a colloquial expression, Miller is thinking "inside the box." In other words, the "Integration Box" is a framework focused solely on those aspects of the Christian faith that grapple with the question of integration. Perspectives rooted in opposition—which have many proponents—are deliberately excluded from Miller's scope. This approach aligns closely with my own focus and methodology.

Miller anticipates fluidity and movement within his process of classification, making two key observations in his introductory sections. First, he acknowledges the likelihood of a *dominant* type—a so-called "natural orientation or predisposition" toward one of the types. Second, he highlights the potential for *convergence*. Even with the dominance of a single type, manifestations of the others are expected to appear.

He explains:

> I increasingly find a more helpful image might be that of integration circles or spheres. Each of the Four E's can be visually imagined as a circle, yet the individual sphere might over time converge and overlap.[44]

Miller's four dominant "types" of integration can effectively be viewed as five. He concludes his discussion of each type by emphasizing the need for a balance among them. The writer suggests referring to this fifth type as "everything" to align with Miller's alliterative model. This is not a new concept, but rather a clearer packaging of what is already present. In addition, the writer introduces a sixth point called "excluded!" in which he will articulate dimensions that Miller has overlooked.

---

43. In relation to Miller's intent, he states, "The Integration Box offers a variable theoretical and practical framework and language for all four manifestations. Thereby enabling constructive analysis and critique of the key variable driving the movement and its participants" (Miller, *God at Work*, 128). This contribution sets Miller's work apart and makes it significant. Sure, others have made similar attempts to describe the engagement types, but few have been so explicit about "enabling constructive analysis and critique"—both of which are in short supply in the Faith and Work movement.

44. Miller, *God at Work*, 141.

Miller's "Integration Box" is intended by both him and the current writer to serve as a representative map of the work and faith genres. While the study has primarily focused on Miller's ideas, this is the appropriate moment to broaden the engagement. When Miller cites ethics as a genre, the perspectives of others can be included to authenticate its validity within the movement. Ethics is an easy sell. However, there will be more discussion regarding Miller's terms "experience" and "enrichment." His commitment to alliteration makes it less obvious where to categorize the more familiar genres of "vocation" and "service."

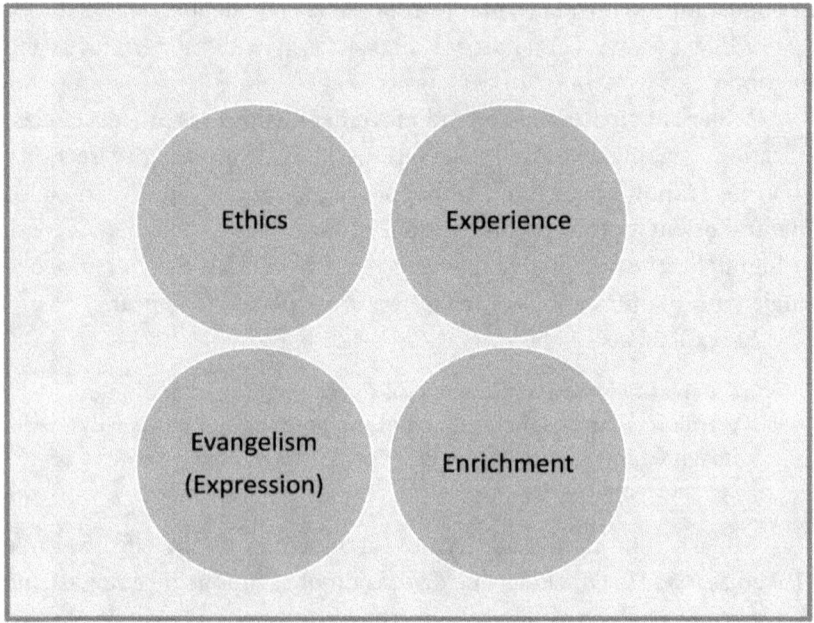

Figure 03: Miller's Graphic Depiction of the Integration Box

Once the review of the "Integration Box" is complete, the writer will follow with sections on representative theologians in the Work and Faith movement. Essentially, we take the "Integration Bo" and immediately apply it, assessing what Miller has missed. Does the tool maintain its integrity, or does the list of exclusions grow to the point that it is no longer a minority? It is important to note the dual commitment to Miller here. Not only does the writer view his review as built-for-purpose, but this perspective is also shared by Keller, who relied on it extensively in *Every*

Good Endeavor. If the "Integration Box" fails to be representative, it will remain in the study while the writer adjusts the starting position as he reviews Keller in the next chapter.

Type 1: Ethics

Ethics typically receives the most attention, and the discussion here will be no exception. The depth of the discussion directly correlates with the definition, which has several variants. The writer begins with Miller, who defines this type as "those whose primary mode of integrating faith and work is through attention to personal virtue, business ethics, and to broader questions of social and economic justice."[45] Just a year after this publication, the financial crisis of 2008 would thrust ethics into the spotlight of the market economy with a force that Miller could not have anticipated. This event led to a strong correlation between faith and work, along with a renewed ethical appetite within the market economy. The global crisis represented a series of failures in personal ethics to the extent that society began to question whether these ethics were truly personal after all. Indeed, it was almost as if a larger narrative was at play, gradually undermining capitalism from behind the curtain.

This brings us back to Miller's definition of ethics, which was already too narrow in 2007—a gap that has only widened over time. While he invites the reader into his dilemma regarding the positioning of ethics and briefly considers a broader approach, he ultimately settles on a constrained perspective.[46] Miller exhibits a tendency toward a justice bias, which detracts from his definition. While the term "ethics" is restrictive, Miller attempts to broaden it by referencing economic and social factors. Leaning on PEST analysis, we expect any model of social engagement to incorporate elements of political, economic, social, and technological factors.[47] We feel hopeful when we see the economic and social aspects in-

---

45. Miller, *God at Work*, 129.

46. "The issues of the FAW [Faith and Work] movement do not fit neatly into one seminary department or discipline and tend typically to span the areas of theology, ethics, biblical studies, ecclesiology, church history, mission, pastoral care, homiletics, and practical theology. The most logical place may well be ethics or practical theology, but then the workplace issues tend to be reduced solely to questions of ethics" (Miller, *God at Work*, 95).

47. Mind Tools, "PEST Analysis."

cluded in the definition, only to have them excluded by the word "justice" at the end. This confines ethics to "economic justice" and "social justice."

If this is to be the definition of this genre, then which genre addresses broader social and economic issues that extend beyond justice? What about the influence of politics and technology? These elements are certainly not fringe considerations in the dialogue of faith and work, and they do not clearly align with evangelism, experience, or enrichment. The answer is to incorporate them here and broaden the definition.

Miller argues that the popularity of ethics as a genre stems from its accessibility,[48] facilitated by its secular language that invites individuals from various faith backgrounds to participate in the discussion.[49] The popularity of ethics is not in question. In fact, this book hypothesizes that it has become too popular, overshadowing other, more important topics. The issue arises from the fact that this popularity has been driven by a narrow vision of what ethics entails, to which the majority of the Faith and Work movement has subscribed. Often, we could substitute "personal ethics" for ethics: an outcome of our rational self-electing its own virtue.

Macro and Micro Ethics

To further the discussion on the definition of ethics, it is essential to introduce the concepts of macro and micro ethics. Miller touches on these ideas only briefly, noting a tendency within micro ethics for conservative Christian engagement to lean heavily on extracting an ethical model from Scripture. While this approach may offer clarity in certain contexts, it often proves inadequate when addressing the complexities of the modern market economy.[50]

48. Miller, *God at Work*, 132.

49. Rosa (*Resonance*, 24–25) advances Miller's claim, demonstrating that ethics is a structural outcome rather than merely the lowest common denominator. "Precisely because the question of happiness and of the good life cannot be answered philosophically within the ethical horizon of modernity, in recent decades, debates in the fields of political and practical philosophy have focused largely, at times almost exclusively, on the questions of distributive justice. Whether the discussion centres on criteria of need, performance, or equality, or on an implicit assumption that any normative imperative should be calculated on the basis of the distribution of resources (not only material goods, but also rights and liberties, or, more generally, personal latitude and opportunities)—and that it is always better to have more resources than fewer" (Rosa, *Resonance*, 24–25).

50. "Generally speaking, those who are Christian and in the ET [ethics] type find

The levels as depicted by Miller are:

- *Micro level* (the personal). Miller sees evangelical, and theologically more conservative groups focusing here.
- *Mezzo level* (the corporate).
- *Macro level* (the societal). Miller sees the theologically more liberal groups focusing on the latter two.

Had Miller wanted to offer more commentary on macro ethics, he would not have had to look far. He was the executive director of the Center for Faith and Culture at Yale Divinity School, where Volf was a co-founder and remained on staff in 2007. Volf continues to be a central figure in the Faith and Work movement. Not only is he regarded as one of the founders of the movement in its current form, but he also provides balance through macro thinking and engagement with critical theory. He would likely be disappointed to be reviewed under the ethics section, as he wrote his seminal work, *Work in the Spirit*, with the hope of avoiding further contributions to the "flood of ethical theological literature on human work."[51]

Volf will receive focus in a separate section below, but for the purpose of the coverage on ethics he is the one who kept the macro agenda on the table. "Ethical questions about work can thus be properly addressed only in the context of a broad reflection on the anthropological, social, and cosmological dimensions of work: hence the need to interpret and evaluate work and its consequences from a dogmatic perspective."[52]

In hermeneutic terms, Volf suggests that the micro relates to the macro in the same way that Scripture relates to the canon. The former must be understood in the context of the latter. The attempted separation of micro and macro can be seen as a manifestation of individualism, where ethics becomes a personal subject detached from the macro environment. Volf understands this distinction more clearly than Miller. He argues that problems at the macro level shape the micro level, aligning with Einstein's dictum that problems cannot be solved at the level at which they were created.

---

ultimate ethical authority not in human constructs but in the biblical teachings and motifs. Yet the ethical choices that business people face are often highly complicated and laden with tradeoffs, where even biblical teaching seem to clash" (Miller, *God at Work*, 130).

51. Volf, *Work in the Spirit*, 75.
52. Volf, *Work in the Spirit*, 75.

Macro Ethics Expanded

The macro debate centers around the monetary system. At a theoretical level, it presents an argument for or against a decentralized monetary system. This debate typically revolves around the perspectives of Smith and Marx, as will be explored in the deeper discussion on Volf.

In the context of this overview, it is sufficient to note that both systems have faced criticism. The centralized economy of Marx has been challenged by Western ideals of autonomy and human agency. Conversely, capitalism has been criticized for the manner in which wealth is distributed, with Smith's invisible hand often absent in many instances. Capitalism's self-regulation was found lacking in 2008, when even regulators were complicit in the fraudulent representation of assets. Arthur Andersen's audit of Lehman Brothers and Standard & Poor's rating of housing bonds serve as notable examples.

In concluding an overview of this nature, it is important to recognize that if micro and macro belong together, then ethics is not the appropriate term. What researchers should consider is a descriptor like "evaluation," which encompasses all the interfaces that fall outside of evangelism and enrichment.

UnLocke-ing Ethics!

Arguably, the dominance of micro over macro is a manifestation of Western individualism—an outlook still constrained by Lockean rationalist influence, combined with the Cartesian perspective of placing the individual at the center of the universe. Taylor identifies another significant influence: Plato. He notes, "Plato's work should probably be seen as an important contribution to a long-developing process whereby an ethic of reason and reflection gains dominance over one of action and glory."[53] Chapter 3 addressed related matters of causation. The purpose of making this connection is to highlight that modern paradigms continue to operate within the framework established by these influential thinkers.

---

53. Taylor, *Sources of the Self*, 117.

Type 2: Expression/Evangelism or Mission

I return here to Miller's classification of types, focusing on his second type: *evangelism,* which he alternatively terms "expression." As Miller explains, "Christians place a high premium on the importance of introducing others to Jesus Christ as Lord."[54] A good example of this is Eldred's *God Is at Work,* which views business as a vehicle both for funding and for gaining access to mission fields.[55]

Under ethics, I previously noted that Miller's definition felt too narrow, and the same observation applies here. Evangelism belongs under the broader umbrella of *mission,* and mission encompasses far more than conversion. Van Duzer offers a helpful framework for understanding the wider scope of mission. Like Miller, he acknowledges various types of engagement but frames them as flowing out of mission itself: "A theology of business must be set, first and foremost, in the context of God's desire to restore this loving relationship."[56]

Van Duzer will be discussed in greater detail in a later section. However, to complete the definition here, I provide a summary of his views. Van Duzer uses the scriptural framework of Genesis to Revelation to articulate God's eschatological purposes in the present. Moving beyond the narrower view of mission as solely about conversion, he understands mission as participation in the stewardship of creation, emphasizing community and culture formation as central themes. Drawing from a conversation with Richard Niebuhr's *Christ and Culture,* Van Duzer develops a model of faith and work that complements Miller's framework.

54. Miller, *God at Work,* 132.

55. Eldred fits squarely within Miller's "evangelism" type, combining this with a perspective that views Christian business as both a gateway into new markets and a valuable source of financial support. This is evident in the following two references:

"I expect that Kingdom business will be a primary tool that revolutionizes missions in the twenty-first century by providing an economically self-sustaining vehicle that will enable an increasing number of missionary Christians to be welcome in any country" (Eldred, *God is at Work,* 46).

"The forces of the free market economy are winning over an ever-growing number of governments. These nascent economies are yearning for the business skills, technology and investment that are needed to propel them out of Third World status. The opportunity is ripe for Kingdom business" (Eldred, *God is at Work,* 53).

The above reference to "Third World status" reveals a pro-capitalist and pro-Western bias. "Like no other economic system in history of mankind, capitalism is producing needed goods and services and is improving the world's standard of living.... Unlike the modern examples of socialism, capitalism rests on the biblical principles of personal freedom and responsibility" (Eldred, *God is at Work,* 76).

56. Van Duzer, *Why Business Matters,* 27.

Rather than contradicting Miller, Van Duzer's model can be seen as an enhancement.[57]

We see some parallels here with the message of Gunton. Van Duzer introduces the topic of identity to his critical thinking, and has strong appreciation for diversity, or "particularity" as Gunton prefers to call it.

Type 3: Experience or Vocation

Miller's third type is *experience*. Here, his commitment to alliteration diminishes the clarity of his model. Both the "experience" and "enrichment" types lack immediate clarity. Readers familiar with the field are likely seeking commonly used terms like vocation and service. Fortunately, Miller's opening sentences provide the necessary clarity. He defines the experience quadrant/genre as follows: In the experience genre, the "primary means of integrating faith and work involves questions of vocation, calling, meaning and purpose in and through their marketplace professions. Their view of work is that it has both intrinsic and extrinsic meaning and purpose. That is, the particular work that someone does, in and of its own right, is of theological value."[58]

There appears to be a disconnect between Miller's definition and his subsequent treatment of Volf's work—an important relationship, given that Miller writes as the executive director of the institute Volf was instrumental in founding. Miller acknowledges Volf's contributions as "original and groundbreaking," particularly in articulating a new theology of work that "build[s] on biblical conceptions of charisms as an alternative to traditional Lutheran conceptions of vocation."[59] He further notes that *Work in the Spirit* was "a constructive move to introduce gifts of the Spirit to complement if not replace the traditional Lutheran concept of calling."[60] Reading this we are again confronted with the conclusion

---

57. The Faith and Work movement is a small ecosystem, evident in the many cross-references among leading scholars. It is therefore not surprising to find Miller's endorsement on the back cover of Van Duzer's book. Miller affirms both the "creation/mission" theme and the model that Van Duzer presents: "Van Duzer resists stereotyping and business bashing, opting instead for a careful theological treatment of the role of business in God's created order. . . . Van Duzer is to be applauded and his model should be carefully considered by those who choose to be in the world but not of it" (Van Duzer, *Why Business Matters*, back cover).

58. Miller, *God at Work*, 135.

59. Volf, *Work in the Spirit*, 100.

60. Miller, *God at Work*, 101.

that Miller's definition is too narrow. This can be resolved by breaking the type down further:

- *Called by natural gifting* (which can almost be classified as transactional).
- *Called in a mediated sense* (guided by God's Spirit). Volf would clearly place himself with the latter.

Volf's position, while compelling, carries a certain naivety. It seems to combine elements of socialism with an Augustinian inwardness. While this perspective may resonate with many, it lacks the robustness needed to address the broader context. Fundamentally, work is about provision.

Miller acknowledges the limitations of such positions, noting the risks involved: "Those who exclusively identify their work as a calling may be more likely to experience trauma and identity crises when faced with losing their jobs, whether through dismissal, retirement, or medical disability."[61]

This perspective can also foster elitism, much like Volf, who critiques the dominance of faith and work material written by executive white males. As Miller observes, "This view forgets that many in the workforce have limited career or occupational choices."[62] Agang supports this point in the recently published *African Public Theology*: "Those who are excluded from work feel it is an assault on their dignity and self-worth."[63] Notably, this is the only book referenced in this work that directly addresses the relationship between unemployment and dignity.[64] Writing from an African context characterized by high unemployment rates and a large unskilled workforce, Agang's insights underscore the elitism inherent in such perspectives.

Also, the notion of vocation "is not applicable to the increasingly mobile industrial and information society. Most people in these societies

---

61. Miller, *God at Work*, 136.
62. Miller, *God at Work*, 136.
63. Agang, "Work," 93.
64. Volf unsurprisingly gives unemployment a mention. He feels that his pneumatological theology of the Spirit combats the sense of uselessness experienced by the unemployed person. An unemployed person has not been deprived of charisms (*Work in the Spirit*, 156). Volf's pneumatology is beyond the scope of this book but is significant enough to warrant further studies. There is an irony in the point Volf makes here. The unemployed person is empowered, but there is no corresponding market opportunity to exercise the empowering.

do not keep a single job or employment for a lifetime, but often switch from one job to another in the course of their active life."[65]

I suspect that Miller would categorize servanthood under the vocational model. However, this is open to debate. Since Greenleaf's pioneering work, there has been sufficient focus on this genre to warrant its own distinct recognition.[66] Similar to ethics, its popularity might stem from its neutrality. Servanthood is a concept that seamlessly translates across various worldviews without provoking conflict.

Type 4: Enrichment or Individualism

The reference to *individualism* is not directly from Miller, as he is too diplomatic to frame it that explicitly. Instead, he describes this quadrant as "often personal and inward in nature, focusing on issues like healing, prayer, meditation, consciousness, transformation, and self-actualisation."[67]

Types in this quadrant include the prosperity gospel, exemplified by popular South African author Bruce Wilkinson and his *Prayer of Jabez*. Miller also highlights various religious hybrids, such as Christian Buddhists, that fall within this category.

Higginson offers a valuable critique of prosperity theologies, describing them as "distorted."[68] Wilkinson serves as a fitting example: his work is innocuous enough to be incorporated into the mainstream but is rooted in a highly individualistic interpretation of Christianity. Higginson's analysis goes further, providing examples where this distortion shifts from being merely harmless to genuinely harmful.

Type 5: Everything

For Miller, the ideal is a balance of the types: *something of everything*. "I increasingly find a more helpful image might be that of integration circles or spheres . . . [that might] converge or overlap."[69] While this does not introduce any new dimensions, it does acknowledge that his model is

---

65. Volf, *Work in the Spirit*, 109.
66. Greanleaf, *Power of Servant Leadership*.
67. Miller, *God at Work*, 137.
68. Higginson, *Faith, Hope and the Global Economy*, 24.
69. Miller, *God at Work*, 141.

simply a tool, and that the lines are sometimes blurred. What is not clear is whether the lines should be blurred.

Perhaps a better way to have an opinion is to open the discussion on what is excluded.

Missiology and Sociology

A review of Miller's sources offers a segue into a discussion about relationships with academic fields. Mission and sociology are dominant sources for Miller, but we will argue that this is insufficient. From a theological perspective, Miller contends that the Faith and Work movement belongs to mission. As Bosch reminds us, "Mission remains an indispensable dimension of the Christian faith and that, at its most profound level, its purpose is to transform reality around it."[70] Where Miller expands on Bosch is by guiding the reader to consider the inverse of Bosch's statement: the transforming impact of reality back onto Christian Faith. Miller builds on Bosch's argument but does not go far enough. In simple terms, missiology assumes that the recipe is right and that the gospel is ready for a production rollout. Here, the writer highlights one of the more significant points from previous chapters that will need to be woven into the conclusion of this chapter. There are theological presuppositions that inhibit and even damage our engagement with the world.

The inclusion of Wuthnow brings an important sociological perspective. The writer will support this addition and argue that Miller does not go far enough. Particularly as a North American author, Bellah et al. is a notable omission in Miller's work and could have helped him further along the path toward thinkers like Taylor and Gunton, who examine the long shadow of Plato through Augustine, Descartes, Locke, and the Reformers. If we consider this sentence alone, we see sociology, systematics, church history, and philosophy all playing a role in providing a more complete perspective on the present.

While we will only encounter Wuthnow through Miller, other contributors include engagement with sociological and economic perspectives through Marx and, by extension, critical theory. This is an important component, as we observe an element of grappling within the Faith and Work movement (as opposed to the Faith against Work movement). This sets the stage for later engagement with Rosa. Although Rosa does not

---

70. Bosch, *Transforming Mission*, xv.

write from a theological perspective, his work, *Resonance*, represents a comprehensive review of our relationship to society, along with proposals on how critical theory can be reconceived as a contributor.

In fairness to Miller, a lot has changed since 2007. The economic and technical landscape has evolved to the point where the boundaries between disciplines have become blurred. Although Miller's argument may be considered dated in light of these recent developments, his writing remains, arguably, the most comprehensive attempt to review the Faith and Work movement. It is still fit for purpose. As the writer examines this Faith and Work "movement" through the perspectives of Miller and others, he will do so with the arguments from chapter 3 in the rear-view mirror. The conclusion must reconcile both, assessing whether Gunton's perspective adds missing dimensions to this important field.

Type 6: Excluded!

Miller positions his model as a measure of integration. Perhaps he believes that a too-critical perspective would undermine the value of his work and possibly the very faculty he chairs at Yale. Regardless of the reason, his limited critical engagement is a clear omission. Engagement must include a critical component, and Miller needs to be pressed on this point.

There is, however, an interesting discussion in a short section where Miller addresses the inadequate coverage of theology. He writes that scholars "who have taken a constructive view of capitalist and nonstate-controlled marketplace economies have been in a minority for much of the twentieth century."[71] He goes on to elaborate on this: "Many of today's leading systematic theologians, ethicists, and clergy are heirs of Christian socialism, which was popular among many leading mainstream theologians, including to varying degrees Rauschenbusch, Tillich, Barth, and Reinhold Niebuhr." Miller identifies Marxist categories of analysis and resultant economic presuppositions, along with postmodern deconstructive methods, as the reasons why many clergy and theologians "failed to find and articulate a constructive doctrine of vocation or theology of work."[72]

Miller would benefit from reading scholars like Markovits, who concludes that Western elitism is self-perpetuating. It will be challenging

---

71. Miller, *God at Work*, 89.
72. Miller, *God at Work*, 90.

for Miller to dismiss this perspective as socialist or left wing, especially since it originates from the same academic institution he is associated with (Yale). The writer will review other examples below, which will further support the conclusion that Miller has not engaged critically enough with these ideas. Unfortunately, in this regard, Miller represents the broader Faith and Work movement.

Related to the omission of adequate critical thinking, the writer will consider the subject of this book: identity. Where should the writer place Gunton's arguments regarding ontology? While there is some debate about placing them under missiology, there is certainly little precedent for doing so.

Concluding Miller's Theological Types

Miller's historical overview is a commendable summary. Additionally, his attempt to synthesize this information into his "Integration Box" has provided this study with a useful schematic overview. However, graphically, Miller's tool has its shortcomings; his model would have been better served by a radar chart that allows for both a weighted and integrated view, as illustrated in the figure below.

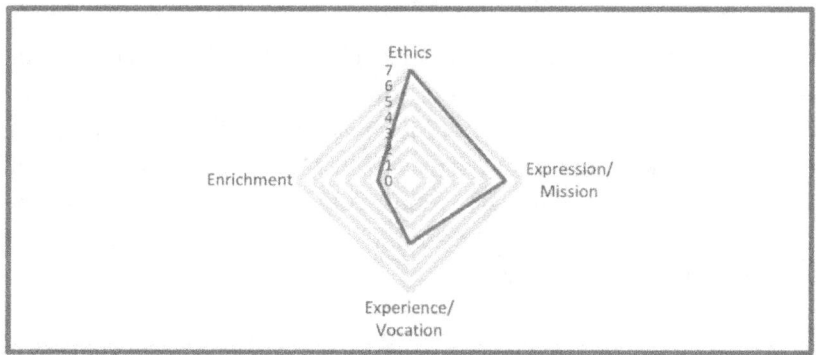

Figure 04. Radar Chart as an Alternative to Miller's Circles and Square Graphic

The irony in Miller's tool lies in the fact that "integration" is the opposite of "alienation," a term that is pivotal to Gunton. The reviewer is left to assume that Miller's commitment to an integration framework has hindered his critical perspective. There is no doubt that Miller's work is insufficiently critical to stand on its own, necessitating supplementation to achieve a more representative view.

Regarding the reference to alienation, it may be unfair to expect a detailed discussion from within the field of Faith and Work. For the most part, the movement aims to establish points of commonality, making references to alienation seem counterintuitive. To address this, the writer will need to look beyond the field of theology to other contemporary authors. However, there can be a bias toward reviewing any discussions on identity and individualism, both of which serve as connectors to the topic of this study.

Before proceeding, we need to further enrich the view of faith and work by consulting additional authors. Some of these authors have been referenced by Keller in his writing, *Every Good Endeavor*. This fulfills the dual task of balancing this chapter and assessing whether these authors have contributed to the necessary equilibrium within Keller's writings. The writer is reviewing some of Keller's sources and contemporaries to provide a platform for evaluating *Every Good Endeavor* in the following chapter.

INTRODUCING VOLF, VAN DUZER, HIGGINSON, AND OTHERS

Works by leading authors are discussed below, with each book presenting a familiar framework. The authors aim to understand the context, develop a theology of work, and outline a response. In these responses, the writer will look for diversity, overlaps with Miller's classification model, and indications of possible omissions. Additionally, he will revisit the conclusions of chapters 2 and 3 to find connections to the doctrine of God, identity, and individualism.

Volf and the Macro Context

Miroslav Volf preceded Miller at Yale and is regarded as one of the founders of the Faith and Work movement. The world of work he encountered when he wrote *Work in the Spirit* is very different from today's reality; however, his contributions to the Faith and Work movement solidify his position as a key figure. Volf's work encompasses ethics and vocation, among other topics, making it essential to consider his contributions as a whole.

From the perspective of this book, three key elements emerge from Volf's work that can enhance Miller's model. Although these points may not align precisely with what Volf would choose to emphasize, they certainly do not contradict the essence of his work.

- Validating alienation and critical macro engagement.
- Through appreciation of their work, validating Bellah et al. and Rosa.
- An openness to mediation through his view of working in the Spirit.

Validating Alienation and Critical Macro Engagement

Volf makes a significant contribution by critically engaging with the macro context,[73] particularly regarding work and its place in society.[74] Writing at the end of the twentieth century, he raises questions about relationships in the postindustrial and postmodern age. Although these questions may seem less fashionable in contemporary debates, this trend is more a result of distraction than resolution. This distraction pertains to the micro context: the individual's journey in faith and work, which has, in many ways, overshadowed the macro perspective. Volf's enduring contribution lies in maintaining focus on the macro context.

Volf's macro context is one of crisis—a strong term and a relatively rare perspective within the Faith and Work movement. While others acknowledge "distortions" in the nature of faith and work, few are willing to label it a crisis. This may reflect the fact that much of the scholarship originates from affluent sectors of society, where such crises are less visible and harder to diagnose.[75] The voices of the unemployed and undereducated remain largely unheard.

73. Volf, *Work in the Spirit*.

74. "Work is honest, purposeful, and methodologically specified social activity whose primary goal is the creation of products or states of affairs that can satisfy the needs of working individuals or their co-creators, or (if primarily and end in itself) activity that is necessary in order for acting individuals to satisfy their needs apart from the need for the activity itself" (Volf, *Work in the Spirit*, 11).

75. This is changing in more recent scholarship. Both Rosa and Markovits are key scholars in identifying the crisis amongst the affluent. They will be reviewed in detail later in the chapter.

To substantiate his conclusion of crisis, Volf first underscores the importance of work. His reasoning is straightforward: something insignificant could hardly warrant such a serious descriptor. Since the Industrial Revolution, work has become the primary means of sustenance and occupies a central role in our lives.[76] He eloquently refers to it as the "door to active participation in the home and the society at large."[77] While elegant, this definition is also revealing. The reference to *participation* encapsulates Volf's primary metric for evaluating work: its role in fostering self-determination. He extends this discussion to include a critique of market versus planned economies, expressing a strong view on the market's capacity to alienate individuals.[78]

An economic and theological critique can be made in response to Volf's agenda. Economically, while his examination of corruption within the market economy raises important issues, it does not necessarily substantiate his conclusions. For example, his argument that the market is "blind" to the future is unfair.[79] In truth, such shortsightedness is not unique to market economies—it is equally evident in both central and market economies. Both have post offices long after they are superfluous! Both systems, for example, have maintained outdated institutions like post offices long after their practical relevance has waned. Some allowance can be made for Volf's perspective given the timing of his publication. Written in 1991, his views likely predate the full collapse of socialist economies, which might have influenced his analysis. However, this is not the forum for an extended debate. The key point is that Volf's work invites and allows for critical engagement.

Volf's integration of the macro context closely mirrors the PEST framework, addressing political, economic, social, and technological factors.[80] At the heart of his approach is a deep conviction that private

---

76. The centrality of work: "After the industrial revolution, gainful employment become the main way of providing sustenance for the majority of the population and hence came to occupy a central place in the lives of individuals and their families" (Volf, *Work in the Spirit*, 9).

77. Volf, *Work in the Spirit*, 8.

78. "Traditional market economies put all the power in the hands of the owners and thus make the majority of the population unable to exert sufficient influence on the one dominant aspect of their lives, the economic aspect" (Volf, *Work in the Spirit*, 19).

79. Volf, *Work in the Spirit*, 20.

80. Volf, *Work in the Spirit*, 42. The PEST analysis refers to Political, Economic, Social, and Technological factors. Volf's focus, however, includes issues such as child labor, unemployment, discrimination, dehumanization, exploitation, and ecological crises (Volf, *Work in the Spirit*, 42).

and public theology are inseparably linked. His education under Moltmann and intellectual engagement with Marx uniquely equipped him for a leading role in public theology. Yet, the term "public theology" does not fully capture the breadth of his contribution. To appreciate the scope of his work, it is essential to incorporate critical theory, which can be understood in both broad and narrow terms.

Although Volf does not explicitly identify as a critical theorist, his application of Marx to explore the relationship between individuals and society situates him within the broader definition of critical theory. What sets Volf apart is his ability to navigate the intersection of Marxist critique and pneumatology, a synthesis that makes his work truly distinctive. In doing so, he ensures that faith and work is a debate that is part of the public theology domain and engaging with Marx certainly sits a lot lower on the controversy scale than taking a critical view of Augustine!

Volf argues that theologians often assess Marx primarily through his earlier writings—a pattern that, interestingly, Marx shares with Barth in this regard. These early works are favored for their philosophical and sociological insights, whereas Marx's later writings focus more heavily on economic analysis.[81] Central to Marx's thought is the alienation. While Volf adopts the term to describe the experiences of workers, he expands its scope, providing a definition that applies to both superordinates and subordinates. As he explains, "Alienation expresses itself basically in three interrelated ways: workers are powerless, they are exploited, and they become estranged from themselves."[82] It is the estrangement that is particularly relevant to this study on identity.

Both Marx and Volf write as products of the industrial age. While the factory floor still exists and debates around the division of labor remain relevant, the concept of "alienation" must be expanded to resonate with a broader audience as we navigate the 4IR.

Fortunately, Rosa has taken up the challenge of sustaining critical theory within this evolving discourse. Volf acknowledges this, as reflected in his endorsement of Rosa. However, it is Volf who deserves recognition for uniting discussions of alienation and pneumatology within a single volume. He also highlights the limitations of Miller's model, demonstrating the need for a broader, more critically engaged framework. Moreover, Volf's exploration of alienation creates a meaningful connection

---

81. Volf, *Work in the Spirit*, 56.
82. Volf, *Work in the Spirit*, 54.

to Gunton. While they approach the same context from different perspectives, their foundational concerns align. Both recognize the market as a significant driver of alienation, making their contributions deeply relevant to contemporary discussions.

Validating Bellah and Rosa

Volf's connection with Rosa serves as a crucial link for this book. His endorsement on the back cover of Rosa's recent work, *Resonance*, reads: "Affirmation of the ordinary life is a key feature of modernity, but alienation from the world is a persistent experience of modern men and women. . . . Rosa offers sketches of an alternative relation to the world and thereby a foundation for a sociology of a good life."[83] This endorsement reflects Volf's evolving understanding of "alienation" within a contemporary context. What may seem like a simple quote on a book cover becomes a significant bridge, connecting sociological and theological discourse in meaningful and impactful ways.

Volf's prominence in the field of faith and work lends significant weight to Rosa's contemporary contributions to social theory. Rosa's critique of society's relational dynamics aligns with and modernizes certain aspects of Gunton's message. His argument against alienation, as explored in *Resonance*, will be analyzed in greater depth below. For now, it is sufficient to note that Rosa's association with Volf enhances his credibility, making his inclusion not just valuable but essential.

Similarly, there is a clear alignment between Volf and Bellah et al. Not only does Volf reference Bellah et al., but their projects share a sociological focus: exploring the relationship between individuals and society. While both arrive at critical conclusions, Bellah et al. adopt a more moderate stance. The importance of Bellah et al. will be explored in the next chapter, where the writer examines Keller's interpretation of *Habits of the Heart*. Through Volf, the writer gains access to an additional critical perspective on Bellah et al., offering a useful comparison with Keller's conclusions. This comparative analysis will highlight what one theologian may have observed that the other overlooked, enriching the broader discussion.

---

83. Rosa, *Resonance*.

An Openness to Mediation

Volf's most significant contribution is his pneumatological approach, which he positions as an extension of the vocational genre. However, he prefers the term "heir" rather than "extension" to distinguish his theology from that of Luther.[84] He is also explicit in rejecting a vocational emphasis that excludes ethics, which he assessed to be in a poor state at the time of his writing. For Volf, both vocation and ethics are essential.[85] In other words, Volf suggests that traditional vocational theology risks remaining too detached from the messy realities of life. His critique of Luther, however, feels somewhat unfair and evokes echoes of Gunton's critique of Augustine. One could argue against Volf that Luther's economic engagement was overshadowed by his political genius. While this lies beyond the scope of this book, it remains an important topic for future research.

Volf acknowledges the significant influence of Moltmann's *Theology of Hope* by grounding his theological framework in eschatology.[86] Closely related to this, he critiques the Greek influence on Christian thought, leading to an affirmation of materiality and activity—or perhaps more accurately, creativity.[87] Once again, we see echoes of Gunton in

---

84. Volf captures his perspective succinctly: "The pneumatological understanding of work I am proposing is an heir to the vocational understanding of work" (*Work in the Spirit*, 105). He critiques Luther's view, arguing that it is "indifferent toward alienation in work" (*Work in the Spirit*, 107). However, this critique seems unnecessary, as it is unrealistic to expect a sixteenth-century Reformer to have developed a fully mature theology of work.

85. Here, Volf contributes to the widely held view that the relationship between work and faith is underrepresented in theological writings. As he states, "This book is an attempt to make a contribution to alleviation of that dire deficiency in Protestant social ethics" (*Work in the Spirit*, 107). He further observes, "Especially from Protestant pens, theologies of work are in short supply" (*Work in the Spirit*, 176).

86. Space does not allow for a full engagement with Volf's hermeneutic. In summary, he strongly advocates for a deductive approach: "The inductive approach to developing a theology of work is inadequate because of the scarcity of biblical materials, their limited relevance to the modern world of work, and their ambiguous nature. . . . We need to proceed deductively; we need to set up a theological framework in which we then can integrate the biblical statements of work" (*Work in the Spirit*, 78).
Volf proposes a "pneumatological theology of work cast within the framework of the concept of 'new creation'" (*Work in the Spirit*, 88). "The question of continuity or discontinuity between the present and future orders is a key issue in developing a theology of work" (*Work in the Spirit*, 89). This contrasts with prological theologies, which "tend to justify the status quo" (*Work in the Spirit*, 102).
For Volf, "Because of the eschatological continuity, the new creation is not simply a negation of the first creation but also its reaffirmation" (*Work in the Spirit*, 101).

87. In broad terms, Volf (*Work in the Spirit*, 103) is critical of what he sees as an

Volf's work: "The complete subordination of the *vita activa* to the *vita contemplativa* that has been basic to much of Christian theology through the centuries betrays an illegitimate intrusion of Greek anthropology into Christian theology."[88]

This affirmation forms the foundation of Volf's theology of the Spirit. In contrast to much of Christian theology, as Volf perceives it, God is actively transforming all of creation toward the eschaton. He writes, "The goal of the Holy Spirit in the church and in the world is the same; the Spirit strives to lead both the realm of nature (*regnum naturae*) and the realm of grace (*regnum gratiae*) toward their final glorification in the new creation (*regnum Gloria*). . . . Work is a cooperation with God in the eschatological transformation of the world! Work in the Spirit!"[89]

Here, we find only a loose connection to Gunton's concept of mediation. In Gunton's theology, soteriology is participatory, grounded in the mediation of the Spirit. Volf's understanding of mediation, while affirming God's active participation in creation, lacks the same explicitly Trinitarian foundation. Whereas Gunton's work emphasizes the affirmation of particularity, Volf's agenda seems more focused on affirming equality than particularity. "All human work, however complicated or simple, is made possible by the operation of the Spirit of God in the working person; and all work whose nature and results reflect the values of the new creation is accomplished under the instruction and inspiration of the Spirit of God."[90]

Volf's pneumatology does not fully align with his inclusion of the broader context. In his effort to be inclusive of all work, he seems to lack clarity on particularity. If the pneumatology becomes too arbitrary, it risks falling into the very critique Volf himself raises—where the means and ends are confused, and the nature of work becomes alienated from the blessing of the Spirit. Additionally, there is a sense in which the Spirit is presented as having a "centralized" function. The emphasis on the Spirit acting *through* humanity, rather than *with* humanity, risks undervaluing

---

"exclusion of the human body and materiality in general from the sphere of salvation in Protestant thought." "We need to look no further than the Gospels to see that the exclusion of materiality from the sphere of the present salvific activity of the Spirit is exegetically and theologically unacceptable" (*Work in the Spirit*, 104).

88. Volf, *Work in the Spirit*, 70.
89. Volf, *Work in the Spirit*, 119.
90. Volf, *Work in the Spirit*, 114.

both human particularity and the Spirit's transformative role in recreating us as "beings in communion."

Elevating Identity

While identity is not central to Volf's work, it is acknowledged as a significant topic within the integration of faith and work. There is little engagement with the concept of individualism, but Volf does address the recognition of a merit-based economy's influence on identity. He writes at a time when work was emerging as a dominant factor in identity formation, and his pneumatological approach aims to challenge this trend. As he asserts, "Since the presence of the Spirit is the key to human identity, there is no fear that by not working human beings may lose themselves."[91]

Concluding Volf

In this review, the writer highlighted aspects of Volf's work that contribute to the study of faith and work. Volf underscores the vulnerability of identity under market forces and provides tools for engaging with these forces critically. In a field prone to reducing engagement to individual choice, Volf ensures that attention remains anchored in the public sphere.

In summary, opportunities for further study of Volf's work are worth exploring. A particularly compelling avenue is the potential tension between his pneumatology and his critique of the free market. A deeper discussion could explore how these two aspects might be reconciled. If the Spirit empowers the worker, does this not lead to a market pneumatology?

A related area of study involves examining the connection between Volf's economics and his theology. Specifically, does his preference for a centralized economy influence his ecclesiology? His sharp criticism of the theological academy suggests an expectation that the center should drive direction.[92] But why should this be the case? An equally valid argument could be made that the laity has not done enough to empower itself in addressing this gap. This perspective finds support among those living with the legacy of the Reformation. Perhaps there is a reluctance to

---

91. Volf, *Work in the Spirit*, 133.
92. Volf, *Work in the Spirit*, 69.

acknowledge the role figures like King Henry VIII and Thomas Cromwell played in fostering theological transformation.

Van Duzer and the *Missio Dei*

Van Duzer's book, written during his tenure as dean of a business school, reflects his unique blend of academic and professional experience. After a twenty-year legal career, he became a professor of business law and ethics at Seattle Pacific University, a role he held alongside his deanship. The title, *Why Business Matters to God (And What Still Needs to Be Fixed)*, accurately reflects its content. Unlike Miller, who focuses on providing a historical overview of the Faith and Work movement, Van Duzer emphasizes constructing a theology of work rooted in mission. He proposes practical applications of this theology to foster a healthier relationship between faith and business, making his work complementary to Miller's. While Miller critiques the lack of clear teaching on the subject, Van Duzer addresses this gap by offering an application model for Christians in business.

The structure of this summary mirrors the analysis of Volf above. It includes a discussion of Van Duzer's key contributions and how these either support or challenge Miller's *types* model. Additionally, it offers a critique in light of the conclusions drawn from chapters 2 and 3. The discussion begins by identifying the central points in Van Duzer's work that enhance the review of Miller's model and the broader Faith and Work movement. These are:

- Affirmation of the importance of faith and work as a subject.
- A theology that seeks to engage at a macro level, offering a more market affirming perspective than Volf.
- An engagement with identity.
- An engagement model that talks to the character of engagement rather than content (as we saw in Miller).

Affirmation of the Importance of Faith and Work as a Subject

Van Duzer's quote from chapter 1 bears repeating: "In short, companies doing business will, in many ways, dictate the kind of world we live in. Thus, for Christians interested in advancing God's agenda of peace, justice and reconciliation, a focus on business and its role in society is critical."[93] The first sentence firmly establishes the significance of the subject. This point is clearly outlined in chapter 1. The second sentence provides insight into the nature of Van Duzer's response. His choice of the three words—*peace, justice, and reconciliation*—to encapsulate God's agenda sets the stage for meaningful engagement in public theology.

A Macro Engagement Through His Genesis-Revelation Model

We have already noted Van Duzer's dominance in the stewardship box—an intriguing outcome for a professor of business law and ethics. This emphasis on stewardship is not explicitly claimed by Van Duzer but is inferred from his theology, which views faith and work as integral to God's mission. This mission is not narrowly focused on personal salvation but encompasses a broader vision of God as Creator, working to transform all of creation. Humanity's role is to participate in God's plan to bring creation to its intended fulfillment. In essence, we are stewards of this divine mission.

The connection to the creation narrative signals to the reader that this is a book engaging with the macro issues at play: what are the overarching frameworks within which we operate? In many ways, this reflects a reactionary stance to what Van Duzer identifies as a theological vacuum. He observes, "We found a number of useful resources about personal ethics in the workplace but little or no work building the underlying framework for the discipline as a whole."[94]

Van Duzer's "creation" model begins by dividing Scripture into four movements: Creation, Fall, Redemption, and Consummation. He argues that any theology of business must be situated within the context of these movements, which he summarizes as "God's desire to restore his loving relationships."[95]

Genesis and Revelation serve as key texts, offering insight into God's purposes for creation and restoration. These texts provide the foundational "underlying framework" that Van Duzer identifies as lacking in the field. As he explains, "In an analogous way, all of humanity is charged with all of the Genesis tasks, but each individual and each individual

---

93. Van Duzer, *Why Business Matters*, 21.
94. Van Duzer, *Why Business Matters*, 16.
95. Van Duzer, *Why Business Matters*, 27.

institution is only one part of the body. Each institution has only a part to play in the whole."[96]

From his reading of Genesis, Van Duzer extracts critical principles that form the foundation of his model.

- "The material world matters to God."[97]
- "Human beings are called to steward God's creation."[98]
- "Made in the image of God." "Business must flow from relationship and be shaped so as to flow back to support the community."[99]
- "Humans are made to live within limits."[100]
- "God delights in variety."[101]
- "The Garden was incomplete."[102]

Comments on the above are too significant to wait for the conclusion. At first glance, there appear to be striking thematic parallels with Gunton: the anti-Platonic affirmation of the material, the placement of humanity within the context of creation, the relational nature of the image of God, and the celebration of variety. However, a deeper exploration of Van Duzer's model reveals a divergence between the two authors.

Notably, Van Duzer's extensive reliance on Genesis as a foundational text in his opening section exposes him to critique. As discussed in chapter 2, the incarnation stands as the ultimate affirmation of materiality. It is therefore surprising that Van Duzer introduces the incarnation much later in the book, and without a direct connection to this critical point.

Building on the critique of Van Duzer's treatment of the incarnation, it appears that his stewardship model lacks sufficient grounding in the doctrine of God. The separation of stewardship and the *imago Dei* is a departure from Gunton's approach and runs the risk of stewardship being open to a transactional exchange. While Van Duzer rightly emphasizes the need for humans to live within limits, the ultimate calling is to live in fellowship with the Trinity. So This theological distinction

---

96. Van Duzer, *Why Business Matters*, 41.
97. Van Duzer, *Why Business Matters*, 28.
98. Van Duzer, *Why Business Matters*, 29.
99. Van Duzer, *Why Business Matters*, 32.
100. Van Duzer, *Why Business Matters*, 33.
101. Van Duzer, *Why Business Matters*, 34.
102. Van Duzer, *Why Business Matters*, 35.

underscores the different foundations of their conclusions. While there are similarities between Gunton and Van Duzer's perspectives, Van Duzer's emphasis leans more heavily on activation, whereas Gunton focuses on participation.[103] This difference seems rooted in a Christology where the cross and resurrection eclipse the incarnation.

Despite its openness to critique, Van Duzer's Genesis-based model proves effective in facilitating a discussion on the continuity between the fall and the contemporary challenges of work. He approaches this with sensitivity, having already articulated his objections to demonizing the market. The discussion highlights two key emphases, which are grouped under the heading "Impact of the Fall" and are explored in the following section.

Impact of the Fall

The first point linking creation to the fall is the loss of abundance. Van Duzer refers to the economic principle of scarcity that governs the free market, writing: "It is a mechanism for allocating resources when there is not enough to go around for everyone. . . . Abundance, rather than scarcity, however, seems to have characterized God's original Garden design."[104] However, there is an issue of semantics here. While Van Duzer notes that the market economy *"assumes"* scarcity, he does not balance this with the observation that the market economy also "creates" scarcity. This critical nuance will be explored further below in the discussion of Rosa's concept of acceleration as a byproduct of economic growth.

The second point linking creation to the fall is the contrast between the merit-based principles of the market and the concept of grace.

> Similarly, participation in the market economy is limited to those who have something to sell that others want to buy. In effect the market values a participant based on what he or she can deliver. Payment is earned. This is the exact opposite of a grace or gift economy, and God is all about gifts. God's gracious character is revealed first in the Garden but continues to be

---

103. Van Duzer describes too core goals for the Christian businessperson:
   One goal for the Christian businessperson who is stewarding God's business is focused outward—providing goods and services that enhance the quality of life. One goal focusses inwards—creating opportunities for individuals within the company to express their vocation in the performance of God's glorifying work. (*Why Business Matters*, 42)
104. Van Duzer, *Why Business Matters*, 76.

evidenced through the Scriptures. God is in the business of giving people what they don't deserve.[105]

Van Duzer draws this contrast into focus, offering a critique of the market that is less severe than Volf's but still incisive. He portrays the market as neutral—neither inherently good nor evil. "Thus, the market system seems to have grown up after the Fall rather than having been inherent in God's original design. As such it can never lead us to salvation. It will not, left to its own devices, usher us back to the goodness of the Garden."[106] And similarly: "It simply will not suffice for Christians in business who are committed to the kingdom of God to always follow the market."[107]

Here, Van Duzer does not go far enough. Rather than merely being a mechanism to address scarcity, advanced capitalism actively manufactures it. The message of capitalism is unmistakable: "You are not enough!"

Revelation Completes Genesis

Revelation is seen as the completer of Genesis, depicting the ideal society we are called to work toward in the present. The conclusion of the model is that Revelation completes Genesis. Equipped with this insight, Van Duzer sees the role of the church as informing (perhaps transforming) culture. This engagement is not merely ethical, though ethical themes dominate; it also includes both vocational and relational dimensions, reflecting the comprehensive nature of Van Duzer's model.

Possible connections between Van Duzer's emphasis on relationality and Gunton's relational theology remain tenuous. This is evident in Van Duzer's interpretation of the city in Revelation, which he imbues with additional meaning: "God has entered into the very place of humanity's rebellion and adopted it as a means of grace."[108] Here, rebellion seems to overshadow communion in the symbolism—a reading inconsistent with Gunton's focus on relational communion.

Another reference to relationality comes through Van Duzer's discussion of the cross: "At the cross Jesus completed his identification with the human experience."[109] While much emphasis is placed on God's

---

105. Van Duzer, *Why Business Matters*, 77.
106. Van Duzer, *Why Business Matters*, 77.
107. Van Duzer, *Why Business Matters*, 79.
108. Van Duzer, *Why Business Matters*, 88.
109. Van Duzer, *Why Business Matters*, 108.

movement toward humanity through the cross, there is little focus on humanity's movement toward God. This is further validated by Van Duzer's post-Easter understanding of the Spirit's role as the enabler of ethical wisdom: "Thus one of the consequences of living post resurrection is that we have access to God's Spirit, who assists in discerning what is right and gives power to put right choices into action."[110] Unfortunately, there are no parallels with Gunton here.

Returning to Van Duzer's eschatological model, he calls Christians to use the tension between their eschatological hope and their present reality as a guide. He highlights the need to discern "tensions between their vocation as followers of Christ and their vocation as businesspersons," urging them to "work harder to uncover new possibilities consistent with both callings."[111] Despite echoes of relationality, the responsibility for this discernment and action rests primarily on the individual. While this does not necessarily support individualism, it also fails to recognize individualism as a key obstacle.

The vocational theme echoes his own experience. "I had lost my capacity to connect what I was spending so much of my time doing with anything that had a bigger meaning for me."[112] This is evidence that the new possibilities he calls for are not always found.

Work and Identity

The focus here is on identity, particularly in the context of work. Van Duzer acknowledges challenges similar to those highlighted by other authors, but his emphasis shifts toward the consumption of time rather than the deeper implications of how work shapes our self-understanding. He observes: "At a deep level the disruption of relations with God has also produced an identity crisis. Even as many of us search for a deeper sense of meaning in our work, work has become our identity. Increasingly many of us know ourselves primarily in terms of what we produce."[113] Rephrased, the threat to identity in Van Duzer's analysis arises more from displacement (the demands on our time) than from manipulation (distorted self-understandings). This interpretation is supported by his

---

110. Van Duzer, *Why Business Matters*, 112.
111. Van Duzer, *Why Business Matters*, 120.
112. Van Duzer, *Why Business Matters*, 101.
113. Van Duzer, *Why Business Matters*, 57.

critique of work being *"always on."* He notes that since World War II, an extra month has effectively been added to the working year.[114] Returning to the Genesis-Revelation model, he argues: "In the Garden, work was situated in a rhythm of activity and rest, work and leisure."[115] Van Duzer's classification of this busyness as idolatry rather than deception is revealing. He writes: "One of the manifestations of this servitude in business may be the frequent idolatry by Christians of market forces."[116] However, framing the issue as idolatry risks oversimplifying a complex phenomenon, offering an unhelpful conclusion that might obscure more nuanced understandings of the dynamics at play.

It is not that Van Duzer dismisses the possibility of manipulation in our relationships; he acknowledges it, particularly in the context of advertising aimed at children. However, he reflects the then-prevailing belief that adults are less susceptible to such manipulation.[117] Eleven years later, we are far more cognizant of the naivety of this position. This issue will be explored further in the engagement with Zuboff below.

Combining into a Model

The eschatological and ethical threads outlined above are woven by Van Duzer to create a model of engagement. Much like Miller, Van Duzer is developing a classification tool rather than a strategy of engagement. Where he departs from Miller is that he does not refer to the different types as preferences, but rather as outcomes of underlying beliefs. His model is presented as a table on two axes. He draws on his own emphasis on the image of God emerging from his creation/Genesis model and then maps these against a modified version of Niebuhr's descriptors.

H. Richard Niebuhr's 1951 *Christ and Culture* was, at the time, a thought leader in relation to paradigms and worldviews. Miller acknowledges that Niebuhr's work is subject to critique but believes it is still fit for purpose. However, he does not expand on the reasons for this critique, and by overlooking this, he compromises his model. Niebuhr's framework is dated and does not reflect the complexity of worldview construction as

114. Van Duzer, *Why Business Matters*, 71.
115. Van Duzer, *Why Business Matters*, 71.
116. Van Duzer, *Why Business Matters*, 146. "Have we somewhere along the line exchanged adventure and what really matters for something else, for comfort, for the opportunity to stay busy?" (Van Duzer, *Why Business Matters*, 198).
117. Van Duzer, *Why Business Matters*, 62.

we understand it today. For him, culture is identifiable to the extent that it is objectified. This position is markedly different from that of Gunton.

The cultural dimension exists on a continuum from Christ against culture to Christ transforming culture. This is juxtaposed with a continuum of continuity to discontinuity of God's image as God brings his creation to fulfillment.

Table 3. Van Duzer's Application of Niebuhr's Typologies.

	What happened at the fall?	Already/not yet tension	What happens at the end of time?
Christ Against Business	Image of God nearly erased	Not-yet emphasis	Radical discontinuity—all works burn up
Christ of Business	Image of God only slightly distorted	Already emphasis	No radical discontinuity—works building future kingdom
Christ Above Business	Image of God only slightly distorted	In balance	No radical discontinuity—works building future kingdom
Christ and Business in Paradox	Image of God seriously marred	In balance/"Save the Last Dance" model	Radical discontinuity—all works burn up
Christ the Transformer of Business	Image of God seriously marred	In balance/D-day model	No radical discontinuity—works building future kingdom

In commenting on an ideal stance, Van Duzer leaves the role of the church open, describing it as "life-affirming" rather than explicitly pro faith and work.[118] However, his words suggest that *Christ the Transformer* is a more accurate classification of his position. He writes, "First, it should seek to provide the goods and services that a community needs to flourish (an external focus). Second, it should seek to provide opportunities for individuals to express aspects of their God-given identities through meaningful and creative work (an internal focus)."[119] This model of engagement is closely tied to the ever-present ethical imperative in Van Duzer's framework. He

118. Van Duzer, *Why Business Matters*, 149.
119. Van Duzer, *Why Business Matters*, 152.

emphasizes the complementary roles of institutions, stating: "Business in the twenty-first century is well suited for certain responsibilities. Other institutions are better suited for other objectives. Together, however, they serve the common good. Or hearkening back to the discussion of powers, business is not the dike that holds back chaos. It is one part of a system of dikes that collectively does this work."[120]

Having reviewed the model above, I will now offer a brief conclusion.

Concluding Van Duzer

Van Duzer's affirmation of the material world is significant, but the Genesis model alone does not provide a sufficiently robust foundation. As previously argued, the incarnation is critical to fully grounding such a position, and this is an area where Van Duzer's treatment is notably light.

Van Duzer's concept of stewardship builds on Miller's perspective, adding depth to the vocational type. However, his articulation leans more toward transactional stewardship than participative stewardship, emphasizing God's commissioning but lacking Gunton's focus on the mediation of the Spirit.

The dominant model is that of ethics,[121] with the underlying issue identified as apathy rather than ignorance. "Christians in business need to train themselves through constant practices to discern right from wrong."[122] Similarly, he observes, "For many business leaders, their philosophy and approach to business may be much more thought out than their theology."[123] This highlights a significant gap with Gunton, whose critique of both theology and the philosophy of modernity forms the foundation of his arguments.

By focusing on ethics, Van Duzer misses an opportunity to offer a more substantial critique of business. His views on sustainability seem disconnected from the core principles of capitalism. This critique will be explored further when discussing Rosa's concept of dynamic stabilization—a theory that challenges Van Duzer's reliance on sustainability.[124]

120. Van Duzer, *Why Business Matters*, 163.

121. He might argue this point but gives it a strong punt. "While I emphatically deny that good ethics always translates into a profitable business, empirical evidence suggests that it often does so" (Van Duzer, *Why Business Matters*, 141).

122. Van Duzer, *Why Business Matters*, 189.

123. Van Duzer, *Why Business Matters*, 139.

124. Sustainability: "In the context of business, then, the pursuit of purpose should

Van Duzer's engagement with identity is weakened by his lack of reference to individualism. While his approach offers a somewhat sympathetic reading and adds depth to Miller's perspective, he ultimately falls short of providing a comprehensive view of why business matters to God and what needs to be fixed.

Higginson and Hope

Dr. Higginson's book, *Faith, Hope and the Global Economy*,[125] was written while he was teaching ethics at an evangelical theological college in the UK. It was part of the "Faith and Work" series edited by Mark Greene under the auspices of the London Institute for Contemporary Christianity. As part of a series on faith and work, Higginson's book does not aim to provide a comprehensive overview but focuses on exploring positive synergies between faith and the global economy, as reflected in its subtitle, *A Power for Good*. Higginson writes, "The Christian faith, rightly understood, can be an enormous power for good in the global economy. Much hangs on those words 'rightly understood.' The positive connection between faith and business does not always follow."[126] The book's emphasis on hope makes it a valuable addition to this review, as does its European perspective, which provides a refreshing contrast to the predominantly North American contributions in the field.[127]

Like Volf and Van Duzer, Higginson's *Hope* model is deeply rooted in eschatology. In Higginson's case, there is a shared influence of Moltmann, alongside the addition of N. T. Wright's *Surprised by Hope* as a key text. Higginson acknowledges that while neither author is specifically equipped to address a commercial context, both provide foundational concepts essential for developing a faith and work model.[128] Higginson's model, in essence, proposes that the integration of faith and work contributes to a partially realized eschatology. As Wright asserts: "All these things will last into God's future. . . . They are part of what we may call building for God's kingdom."[129]

---

be limited by the notion of sustainability. As a business pursues even godly objectives, it should do no harm" (Van Duzer, *Why Business Matters*, 158).

125. Higginson, *Faith, Hope and the Global Economy*.
126. Higginson, *Faith, Hope and the Global Economy*, 15.
127. That being said, neither Miller nor Volf are North American by birth.
128. Higginson, *Faith, Hope and the Global Economy*, 42.
129. Wright, *Surprised by Hope*, 205.

Higginson identified five key outputs from a positive engagement between faith and work. He consistently employs these as a litmus test for well-integrated theology. However, his commitment to creating an accessible and outcome-focused list seems to leave the underlying theological content largely assumed. If one is to critique faith and work for being theologically light, Higginson's work underscores the importance of revisiting and grounding such discussions in theological fundamentals.

Higginson's five outputs are as follows:

- Stimulating Enterprise
- Reducing Poverty
- Promoting Integrity
- Encouraging Sustainability
- Fostering Discipleship

In terms of classification, Higginson's work strongly emphasizes ethics and missional (expression) themes.[130] Does he ultimately contribute to the conversations initiated by Miller and Van Duzer? Yes, his positive outlook sets him apart as a differentiator. However, theologically, the book does not add significant new insights to the discussion. This observation is less a critique of Higginson and more a validation of Miller's comprehensive summary of the field. There are, however, three points from Higginson's work that warrant further elaboration:

- A focus on distorted theologies.
- The current crisis: Arrogance over design.
- Hope: Beyond integration to transformation. Practical application.

Distorted Theologies

Higginson stands out among those referenced for his critical stance toward distorted theologies within the Faith and Work space. Centering his book on the theme of hope, he navigates this critique while maintaining a

---

130. The Hope model supports the expression genre. However, the ethical theme is never far behind, coming through strongly again in the closing pages. "There is a very important place, then, for Christians working in big companies, winning respect by being effective at their jobs, and keeping corporate standards up to the mark or helping to improve them" (Higginson, *Faith, Hope and the Global Economy*, 221).

LIMITATIONS AND BLIND SPOTS IN FAITH AND WORK THEOLOGY 179

pro-business orientation. This approach often feels like a subtle disclaimer, aimed at avoiding alienation from theological camps whose positions might undermine the goal of hope. In essence, Higginson manages to be critical without crossing into condemnation. However, there are instances where his critique could have been more incisive.

The distortion of the prosperity gospel serves as Higginson's starting point. He highlights examples from the extreme end of the spectrum, where the "blessing"-driven ideology is easily identifiable. However, what is missing is an acknowledgment that no clear line distinguishes such distortions from more mainstream positions.[131] Eldred's *God Is at Work*, referenced earlier, provides a useful example. While it is a strongly pro-capitalist work that many would read uncritically, it demonstrates the issue Higginson hints at. Although Eldred meets all of Higginson's criteria, the book lacks meaningful dialogue between faith and work, as well as a critical engagement with the nature of capitalism itself.[132]

The question of the dividing line leads us to Higginson's discussion of the sacred-secular divide as a distorted theology.[133] Here, the line itself becomes the cause of distortion rather than a protector of orthodoxy. Higginson identifies the core issue as a "lack of theology rather than the imposition of a particular theology."[134] This observation aligns with a common point made by other writers referenced in this book. To reiterate the critique directed at Higginson, there is room to incorporate

---

131. Higginson, *Faith, Hope and the Global Economy*, 24.

132. Eldred sits squarely in Miller's "evangelism" type. He overlays this with a view of Christian business as a ticket into new markets as well as a valuable financial source. This is seen in the following two references:

"I expect that Kingdom business will be a primary tool that revolutionizes missions in the twenty-first century by providing an economically self-sustaining vehicle that will enable an increasing number of missionary Christians to be welcome in any country" (Eldred, *God at Work*, 46).

"The forces of the free market economy are winning over an ever-growing number of governments. These nascent economies are yearning for the business skills, technology and investment that are needed to propel them out of Third World status. The opportunity is ripe for Kingdom business" (Eldred, *God at Work*, 53).

The above reference to "Third World status" reveals a pro-capitalist and pro-Western bias. "Like no other economic system in history of mankind, capitalism is producing needed goods and services and is improving the world's standard of living. . . . Unlike the modern examples of socialism, capitalism rests on the biblical principles of personal freedom and responsibility" (Eldred, *God at Work*, 76).

133. The leading author here being Higginson's series editor, Mark Greene.

134. Higginson, *Faith, Hope and the Global Economy*, 37.

additional theological criteria into his existing checklist of five. Without this, it remains unclear where Eldred fits in.

Higginson's engagement with anti-capitalist theology proves far more constructive. He focuses on the writings of Timothy Gorringe, an English theologian strongly opposed to the market economy. Higginson's primary concern is Gorringe's outright condemnation of capitalism, where he believes a more balanced critique would be appropriate. He argues that such writings lack nuance: "The outspoken critics are not appreciative enough of the mainstream of business, the spirit of enterprise. This cannot simply be taken for granted; it needs nurturing."[135]

An example of a former powerhouse of anti-capitalist theology is liberation theology, a movement that has arguably lost much of its momentum. Higginson observes: "A generation later, what is the lasting impact of their work? Smaller than might have been expected."[136] However, this may not be a fair assessment in the South African context, where it could be argued that the contribution of liberation theology was significantly more impactful.

The Current Crisis: Arrogance over Design

In addressing the current context, Higginson highlights the familiar culprits of exploitation and greed, using this section to set the stage for his detailed discussion on hope. Central to his argument is the handling of responsibility for these forces, which he identifies as a key issue: "We seek to shift responsibility, because accepting it seems frighteningly costly."[137] Higginson provides a valuable analysis of the 2008 financial crisis, where the reader might expect an engagement with its root causes. In this regard, he identifies two cardinal virtues that were notably absent: "If we consider the behaviour that led to the financial crisis, two cardinal virtues were notably absent: moderation and prudence."[138] This analysis is supported by a unique and well-structured biblical narrative—the arrogance of Tyre leading to its destruction. Higginson links this theme of arrogance to the broader theological debate on annihilation and continuity, asserting that it is arrogance that will not continue. In summary, he

---

135. Higginson, *Faith, Hope and the Global Economy*, 33.
136. Higginson, *Faith, Hope and the Global Economy*, 34.
137. Higginson, *Faith, Hope and the Global Economy*, 64.
138. Higginson, *Faith, Hope and the Global Economy*, 77.

argues that moderation and prudence are essential virtues to counter the destructive force of arrogance.

Higginson highlights the issue of executive pay as particularly problematic. Uniquely among the works cited here, his analysis is informed by the research of Wilkinson and Pickett. He notes: "They show that on almost every index of quality of life, happiness or deprivation, a strong correlation exists between a country's level of economic inequality and its social outcomes."[139]

A Basis for Hope: Entrepreneurial and Eschatological over Ethical

Higginson expands on his conviction that Christians can and should strive for a more integrated relationship between their faith and work. This integration goes beyond merely addressing issues like arrogance; it also involves creating a positive and alternative vision for business outcomes. Business belongs under God's rule.[140]

Higginson's missional theme comes through key supporting Scriptures:

- Genesis 18:18–19 (a blessing to the nations).
- Isaiah 42:6 (a light to the nations).
- Psalm 67 (may your way be known).

Hope, in essence, is the result of aligning God's business with our business. Higginson identifies two key aspects of God's business. The first is entrepreneurship: "One role in the business world that captures God's character is that of the entrepreneur."[141] The second is the creation of community. Here, he draws on Wright: "Wright observes that God's purpose was to 'create a new community of people who in their social life would embody those qualities of righteousness, peace, justice and love that reflect God's own character and were God's original purpose for humanity.'"[142] This reflects an affirmation of the expression genre.

139. Higginson, *Faith, Hope and the Global Economy*, 157.
140. Higginson, *Faith, Hope and the Global Economy*, 211.
141. Higginson, *Faith, Hope and the Global Economy*, 49. There are parallels here between Higginson and Volf's pneumatology. God's entrepreneurial gifting may fall within the definition of Volf's view of "Working in the Spirit." Volf only gets a single reference in Higginson, and that was in relation to the doctrine of annihilation. It feels like he missed an opportunity here.
142. Higginson, *Faith, Hope and the Global Economy*, 91.

If Gunton were reading this, he might critique the utilitarian tone of the description. God's purpose in creating community was for community's sake, not merely for the sake of onlookers. Perhaps this vision of community would have been strengthened by linking it to the transformation of the ordinary through the Eucharist, as Higginson later describes: "This notion of God taking something ordinary that we offer and doing something extraordinary with it is found at the very heart of the Church's worship, the Eucharist."[143]

Higginson advances the familiar call to community through practical dimensions—or perhaps more accurately, extensions. One example is his appreciation for the role of the "toxic handler," someone who brings God's grace into places of discord: "They are individuals who absorb and soften emotional pain, voluntarily shouldering the sadness, frustration, bitterness and anger that are endemic to corporate life."[144]

He also references the Benedictine tradition to emphasize balance: "Benedict created a balance day in which prayer, work, private reading and time with one another will have their designated place."[145] The recurring theme of balance is unsurprising, yet the reader is left without a satisfactory explanation for why this balance is so often disrupted. The danger is that such teaching risks being perceived as aesthetic rather than as a genuine solution. Further insights into this phenomenon will be drawn from Rosa and Markovits in subsequent reflections.

Concluding Higginson

In conclusion, Higginson contributes to the expression and ethical dimensions of faith and work, emphasizing the hope of transformation through practical engagement. While his critique is thoughtful and measured, it does not go far enough. Following N. T. Wright closely, Higginson could have delved deeper into capitalism's inherent need for growth—or what Wright refers to as "the myth of progress."[146] Additionally, Higginson overlooks the restructuring of capitalism that has increasingly polarized the workforce, leaving skilled workers in positions where achieving balance becomes exceedingly difficult. Markovits's insights shed light on this

---

143. Higginson, *Faith, Hope and the Global Economy*, 198.
144. Higginson, *Faith, Hope and the Global Economy*, 165.
145. Higginson, *Faith, Hope and the Global Economy*, 188.
146. See Wright, *Surprised by Hope*, 93–100.

issue. In light of Markovits's hypothesis, Higginson's advocacy for a balanced life risks appearing somewhat naïve.

These observations can be summarized with the conclusion that Higginson ultimately misidentifies greed as a cause rather than a consequence. While this perspective aligns with many of his peers, it marks a key point of divergence between him and Gunton.

Other Authors

The dialogue above excludes some authors who have contributed significantly to the field of faith and work. For example, R. Paul Stevens,[147]

---

147. R. Paul Stevens has written widely on the field of Faith and Work. The three volumes reviewed for this book are: 1) *Doing God's Business: Meaning and Motivation for the Marketplace*; 2) *Work Matters: Lessons from Scripture*; and 3) The co-authored *Entrepreneurial Leadership: Finding your Calling, Making a Difference* (co-authored with Stevens and Goossen). *Doing God's Business* is positioned as a comprehensive review of faith and work, with *Entrepreneurial Leadership* providing an updated version of Stevens's Vocational Discernment model. The latter also includes twenty-nine tributes from other authors within the Faith and Work field—an impressive lineup!

Key drivers for Stevens are the vocational and community components of work, with ethics being a significant subset of the latter. "Good work is good for us, good for our neighbour, good for creation, and good for God" (*Doing God's Business*, 10). Simplistically, he offers an input/output model with guidelines for selecting your type of work (the input) followed by the output of glorifying God through the enjoyment of work. The guidelines for selection can be criticized as being biased towards skilled workers who have the luxury of mobility within the workforce. This is probably fair given his audience, just not representative of the entire workforce.

Vocation for Stevens is the antidote for finding meaning in a career. "The most significant challenge of the humanist model to Christian entrepreneurial leaders is that in it the individual looks for meaning in work itself. In the Christian model the entrepreneurial leader finds meaning in God through the context of the work" (*Entrepreneurial Leadership*, 77). Here Stevens draws from Calvin and Luther, particularly Luther's notion of a general calling. There are parallels here with Volf, although these parallels do not extend much beyond the notion of general vocation.

The importance of culture is linked to mission. Here Stevens offers a useful engagement with the homogenizing impact of globalization. The concept of "mission" flows into service, so while we see Stevens using the same genres of Miller, there is more fluidity between them.

Stevens addresses spirituality and briefly refers to *perichoresis*. Use of the term here is limited, and while there is some criticism of globalization, he does not go as far as using words like "alienation" or "crisis." Perichoresis demands more of a break with contemporary culture.

Arguably, Stevens's strongest contribution is his model on vocational discernment that brings his various threads together. It is rooted in the hope of integrating faith and work, offering an integrated picture of his vocational/ethics views.

a widely recognized scholar, is not included here because much of his perspectives are already reflected through other authors discussed.

Another category of contributors to consider is what can be termed "bridging authors." The pervasive nature of the market economy allows these authors to make important statements about the relationship between faith and work, or identity and work, even without a specific audience in mind. Bridging authors straddle two domains; they do not easily fit within the Faith and Work genre yet offer valuable insights. Like a bridge, they have feet in two camps, whereas the authors discussed above are firmly rooted in the Faith and Work camp.

The popular *leadership* camp includes authors such as Blanchard, Hybells, Lencioni, and Maxwell.[148] The *economics* camp features writers like Joerg Rieger.[149] A comprehensive engagement with these authors is neither possible nor necessary in this chapter.

---

148. A growing focus on leadership has been one of the byproducts of the Third Industrial Revolution, and Christian authors have followed suit. Notable examples include Blanchard and Hodges's *Lead Like Jesus* and Maxwell's *The 21 Irrefutable Laws of Leadership*. Many of these works fit into the "expression/mission" genre. While they often provide valuable sociological or leadership insights, they offer little in terms of theological engagement.

149. Rieger's work serves as an extension of the ethical genre. The title references Kennedy's interpretation of Adam Smith's invisible hand. In a comprehensive critique of macroeconomic policies, Rieger draws important connections between macroeconomic policy and macroeconomic experience. In summary, his view is that "big money equals big power in the current economic system" (*No Rising Tide*, 3).

While not focusing on the integration of faith and work, he makes the rare and important connection to individualism. "Myths like individualism are among the most important points of connection between religion and economics today. Individualism is one of the pillars on which both mainline theology and mainline economics rest" (*No Rising Tide*, 20). Particularly important for this book are his observations on identity: "During most of our waking hours, we are, therefore, more or less directly hooked up with the market economy" (*No Rising Tide*, 98). This relationship is portrayed as destructive: "What is commonly called 'consumerism' describes, thus, not a situation of freedom where people can do as they please, but a lack of freedom that is twofold: not only is desire produced in us and for us, but we are in a position to pursue our desires without impediment, we are even less free because we are really following someone else's script" (*No Rising Tide*, 105).

The important question is why relegate Rieger to a footnote and then argue that Christian engagement with the market economy is insufficient. The reason is simply that Rieger's sociological critique is more significant than his theological one. His observations are accurate, but he does not enable the reader to process them within a theological debate. He positions himself in the same contributing stream as Rosa, but, unfortunately, has less to offer.

CONCLUDING REFLECTIONS ON FAITH AND WORK LITERATURE

The next section transitions from authors writing specifically within the faith and work genre to introducing a broader group of contributors for consideration. This shift is driven by the gap between Gunton's theology and what is emphasized in the Faith and Work movement. There are too few connectors between the two. The key issues raised by Gunton do not receive the same level of attention within the Faith and Work movement. By casting the net wider, we are better positioned to evaluate the significance of Gunton's contribution. If this broader exploration reveals many more connectors, it may suggest that the Faith and Work movement is currently too narrow in its focus. Conversely, if the wider search uncovers little, it raises serious questions about the enduring value of Gunton's legacy. With the focus on identity, some summary remarks are provided below.

Miller's synopsis lays a valuable foundation for engaging the broader field, with his historical overview and type classification standing out as particularly useful. However, despite his focus on paradigms, Miller appears confined by several of his own. Theologically, he leans too heavily on Bosch's use of millennialism, while economically and sociologically, his reliance on a Marxist/capitalist dichotomy feels increasingly outdated over a decade after its publication. Moreover, Miller's work lacks direct engagement with individualism and omits any reference to Bellah et al., a cornerstone text in the North American context. Exploring the connections between the Puritanism articulated by Taylor and the individualism analyzed by Bellah et al. would add significant depth. As it stands, Miller's approach tends to critique without offering causation. This sharply contrasts with the bold and ambitious scope of Gunton's *The One, the Three, and the Many*, where no meaningful middle ground exists between the two.

It is precisely this missing middle ground that drives the need for a broader search. The contrast between Gunton and the Reformed writers reviewed here reveals a significant gap. It suggests that Gunton may be addressing an entirely different reality, prompting the writer to look beyond the current frameworks for answers.

CASTING THE NET WIDER: CONTEMPORARY VOICES ON IDENTITY AND ALIENATION

Alienation, according to Gunton, is the Enlightenment's enduring legacy to modernity—a powerful term made even more so by its prominence in Marxist scholarship. It serves as a vital link between Gunton's work and the theology of faith and work. Disappointingly, the term is seldom addressed in faith and work literature. While there is slightly more coverage among bridging authors, it remains insufficient to establish a meaningful continuity with Gunton's framework.

This gap necessitates a shift from theological engagement to the exploration of contemporary voices in sociology, technology, and economics. It falls to this section to justify why the marginalization of *alienation* is a significant omission. As a critical challenge to the Faith and Work movement and a central connection to Gunton's theology, this discussion may not offer the brevity some readers might expect.

A review of contemporary voices is central to the task of doing theology. The engagement that follows aligns with Ford's description of *Type 2* theology, which emphasizes that "Christianity itself needs continually to be rethought and that theology must engage seriously with the modern world in its quest for understanding."[150] Throughout this book, there are numerous examples of theologians engaging with the modern world. Gunton, for instance, draws on Taylor and Coleridge, while Keller references Ferry and Bellah et al. Similarly, Volf and Miller incorporate insights from Marx.

Properly ordered, theology must address identity as a first-order issue. Identity arises from our understanding of the doctrine of God and cannot be relegated to a lower priority. This section introduces four academic works, none of which have a theological purpose. They span three different genres, yet all place the topic of identity at their core. Moreover, these works engage with what is increasingly recognized as a growing crisis of alienation within the market economy. While the term alienation carries strong Marxist connotations, only two of the authors explicitly use it, and only one could be considered sympathetic to Marx.

Their socio-political ideologies are less relevant here than their commentary on present trends related to the nature of identity, making them similar to the bridge theologians discussed earlier. Markovits serves as an excellent example. Like Miller and Volf, he is a Yale academic, but

---

150. Ford, *Modern Theologians*, 2.

as a law professor writing into the field of behavioral economics, his book *The Meritocracy Trap* critiques the fallacy of meritocracy at the core of capitalist ideology.[151] What makes his critique particularly courageous is its self-directed nature. More specifically, it challenges the American education system from within one of its own elite institutions. Such an internal critique is exceedingly rare, making Markovits's work both unique and significant.

In terms of genre, Zuboff and Frischmann are closely aligned. Their respective works explore how market economies track personal information to influence behavior. While Rosa and Markovits are less aligned with Zuboff and Frischmann, they effectively address related issues—social acceleration and performance culture—albeit from different perspectives.

Before proceeding, it is important to recap the argument from chapter 3. At the core of modernity lies the elevation of the individual, or the self, as the center of all reality. The autonomous person stands as the ambassador of the modern worldview. However, what we are encountering today is a profound undermining of this central pillar. The relentless drive for progress and growth within market economies has led to the commodification and ultimate betrayal of their most prized ideal: the autonomous self.

Markovits

The market ideal claims to reward effort over station, but Markovits's book delivers a well-researched and scathing critique of this notion, arguing that the reality is far from the ideal. He writes, "Merit itself has become a counterfeit virtue, a false idol. And meritocracy—formerly benevolent and just—has become what it was invented to combat. A mechanism for the concentration and dynastic transmission of wealth and privilege across generations. A caste order that breeds rancour and division."[152] Markovits begins with these incendiary words—an unexpected critique from a Yale academic. This is not merely a commentary on a societal

---

151. Markovits, *Meritocracy Trap*.

152. "The conventional belief that meritocracy promotes meaningful work and widespread opportunity is misleading. Indeed, the common view gets things almost exactly backwards. Meritocracy's champions contend that meritocracy breaks the old link between inequality and poverty. But in fact, meritocratic inequality excludes everyone outside of an increasingly narrow elite" (Markovits, *Meritocracy Trap*, 30).

The Creation of an Elite

Markovits examines the impact of technology on the transformation of capitalism, observing that technology has not eliminated work but rather created a new demand for super-skilled elite labor.[154] He humorously connects this theme with Rosa's acceleration. "As every rich person knows, when an acquaintance asks 'How are you?' the correct answer is 'So busy.' The old leisure class would have thought this a humiliating admission. The working rich boast that they are in demand."[155]

Beneath the rise of this new elite labor lies the consequent decline of the middle class and a widening divide between the working and elite classes. In reviewing Markovits's work, I aim to examine his thesis on meritocracy and his perspectives on the socioeconomic polarization that has emerged.

Markovits's thesis is not that merit is being bypassed, but rather that access to merit is unequally distributed. As he explains, "The intensive training that rich parents give their children produces massive achievement gaps, so that meritocratic admissions themselves skew student bodies dramatically toward wealth, and the meritocratic elites can produce dynasties even without nepotism."[156] This perpetuates a self-reinforcing cycle.

Here, we see clear parallels with Rosa's concept of social acceleration driven by the need for growth. However, Markovits offers a different perspective. For him, the issue is less about the pursuit of growth and more about the nature of the responsibilities shouldered by the market's elite. He introduces the term "superordinate" and cites research indicating that many of those working over sixty hours per week would willingly trade income for increased leisure time.[157]

---

153. "Our anxieties concerning meritocracy and economic inequality are warranted, but they cannot be resolved by identifying villains or even righting clear wrongs. Rather, they reflect a deep and pervasive dysfunction in how we structure and reward training and work—how, in a basic and immediate way, we live our lives. This diagnosis attacks no one, but it should discomfort everybody" (Markovits, *Meritocracy Trap*, xxii).

154. Markovits, *Meritocracy Trap*, 4.

155. Markovits, *Meritocracy Trap*, 4.

156. Markovits, *Meritocracy Trap*, 17.

157. Markovits, *Meritocracy Trap*, 32. See also: "As an entire civilization centres its

The Nature of Alienation

This is where alienation emerges. Education is the commodity of the age, and the working class is effectively trapped in education poverty. Despite government support, a significant financial burden remains for those aiming to transition into super-skilled workers. This trap is exacerbated by the shrinking middle class, as work is restructured and increasingly flows upward to a small group of super-skilled elites.

The elite, however, are also ensnared by the transient nature of education—it dies with them. There is no automatic generational transfer, forcing them to work longer hours to sustain their positions in an ever more competitive landscape. As Markovits writes, "It is impossible to get rich off human capital except by exploiting yourself and impoverishing your inner life. . . . Meritocracy allows no route to domination besides through the destruction of the authentic self."[158]

Markovits draws a parallel with Marx, concluding that it is the elite who experience alienation.[159] Additionally, he argues that rising mistrust

---

economic life around an immense training and enormous industry of a tiny elite of its people, the weight that each superordinate worker must carry grows. Meritocracy concentrates production in an elite that is literally too narrow to shoulder the burden. This form of production exploits those who supply overburdened and alienated labour in order to enter and remain inside the meritocratic inner sanctum" (Markovits, *Meritocracy Trap*, 35).

And he circles back to the point again. "A brilliant vortex of training, skill, industry, and income holds elites in thrall, bending them from earliest childhood through to retirement to an unrelenting discipline of meritocratic production that alienates superordinate workers from their labour, so that they exploit rather than fulfill themselves and eventually lose authentic ambitions that they might ever fulfill" (Markovits, *Meritocracy Trap*, 71).

"American meritocracy has become precisely what it was invented to combat: a mechanism for the concentration and dynastic transmission of wealth, privilege, and caste across generations. A social and economic hierarchy with these comprehensive, dynastic, and self-referential qualities has a name: an aristocracy" (Markovits, *Meritocracy Trap*, 72).

158. Markovits, *Meritocracy Trap*, 285.

159. "Meritocratic production, by making elite workers rentiers whose income depend on exploiting their own human capital, renders work a site of suppression rather than expression of the superordinate worker's true self. This is, in fact, the same alienation that Karl Marx diagnosed in exploited proletarian labor in the nineteenth century. Indeed, as technological development render mid-skilled workers increasingly surplus to economic requirements, and at the same time place super-skilled labor at the very centre of productive life, meritocracy shifts the classic afflictions of capitalism up the class structure. The increasingly superfluous middle class assume the role once occupied by the lumpenproletariat, while alienated labor come home to roost in the elite" (Markovits, *Meritocracy Trap*, 40).

between classes, if left unchecked, can lead to conflict. While this perspective has merit, it falls short. The critique here is that his analysis does not go far enough. There are clear parallels with Archbishop Tutu's insights, as he often reminded us that both the oppressed and the oppressor are subjugated and repressed. Alienation, like oppression, is not an individual phenomenon; it is relational. We are not alienated from an idealized notion of "the good life." Rather, we are alienated from one another.

Useless and Used Up!

Another critical point is the absence of a technological perspective in Miller's account of the Faith and Work movement. How has the changing nature of work, driven by technological advancements, impacted the Faith and Work movement? Through the analyses of Markovits and Rosa on the growing polarization in the workforce, it becomes evident that work is no longer experienced uniformly. Addressing the widening divide between elite workers and the working class, Markovits observes, "Today, unskilled and skilled workers belong to separate tribes."[160] While both groups experience alienation, their experiences are fundamentally different. Markovits, with his characteristic punchy style, encapsulates this disparity in dramatic fashion, describing the two groups as "useless and used up"[161]—a portrayal that aligns closely with Rosa's diagnosis.[162]

---

160. Markovits, *Meritocracy Trap*, 205. "When mid-skilled and super-skilled—middle-class—and elite—workers are hired from distinct pools, chosen by different means, and segregated into separate firms and industries, the two classes inevitably come to embrace distinct and even competing cultures of work. Elite reverence and middle-class scepticism toward extreme ambition merely summarise or conclude pervasive differences in the life experience of work for the two groups" (Markovits, *Meritocracy Trap*, 205).

161. Markovits, *Meritocracy Trap*, 269.

162. Despite the alignment between Rosa and Markovits, the latter is a lot more dramatic in his conclusions. He is clearly fed up with the structure of society (particularly American!). "Meritocracy—include the immense skill, effort, and industry of superordinate workers—increasingly clearly serve's no one's interest. It renders the work and middle class who once occupied the charismatic centre of economic life surplus to economic requirements. It imposes idleness on the mass of citizens, whom it condemns to join a massive and growing lumpenproletariat. At the same time, meritocracy casts superordinate workers as rentiers of their own capital, which the mix with their alienated labor, and it subjects rich children to the rigors and affliction of ruthlessly instrumental elite education. Meritocratic inequality divides society into the useless and used up" (Markovits, *Meritocracy Trap*, 269).

Elite alienation may seem like an oxymoron, but it demands deeper engagement. Recognizing its existence is essential for understanding the role of identity in the Faith and Work movement. As Markovits notes, "Elite jobs subject superordinate workers to alienating and exploitative demands. But (partly on account their expansive intensity) these demands are framed in a language of fellowship rather than opposition, of collaboration rather than command."[163]

Elite alienation has significant implications for the Faith and Work movement, particularly in the growing emphasis on leadership. Just as MBA programs were developed to equip technical professionals for general management, the demand for leadership resources has risen to address the expanding responsibilities of elite workers. Leadership, like ethics, is a more neutral topic, making it accessible to a broader audience of Christian writers. Books like Blanchard's *Lead Like Jesus* coexist alongside his bestselling *One Minute Manager*. Similarly, the trend toward work-life integration is reflected in the popularity of works like Sharma's *The Monk who Sold His Ferrari* and *Leadership Without a Title*.

Two key observations emerge from this. First, it is increasingly difficult to discuss faith and work as a singular movement. There are, in effect, two distinct tribes integrating faith and work in markedly different ways: the elite and general workers. Second, while both groups face identity pressures and alienation, their experiences are profoundly different.[164] A review of the literature reveals a pronounced bias toward elite workers. While this focus is somewhat expected—given that this group is more likely to consume and produce related material—it remains problematic. The Work and Faith movement, in many ways, places greater demands on the "used up" while overlooking the "useless."

163. Markovits, *Meritocracy Trap*, 203.
164. There are some valuable supporting references from Markovits.
The first relates to the polar work experiences of the different levels of employees. Here we take particular note on the formative influence the respective experiences have on identity. "Non-elite workplaces adopt almost precisely the opposite approach along each of these dimensions. Not just the pay but also the culture of non-elite work increasingly reflects mid-skilled workers' subordinate status. Uniforms are common and serve to thwart self-expression and place workers in a hierarchy rather than to promote safe or efficient production (as craftsmen's technical work clothes once did). . . . Meritocracy flat-out banishes a large and growing class of subordinate persons from the status that work brings" (Markovits, *Meritocracy Trap*, 205–6).
Along the same theme, Markovits also comments on the parallel religious polarity. "Religions in the United States today are remarkably segregated by education and income" (Markovits, *Meritocracy Trap*, 211). The concern is that the Faith and Work literature has yet to develop the diversity and appreciation for both segments.

A second observation builds on this point. The creation of an elite through technological development aligns closely with modern definitions of identity. The emancipated self thrives on exercising complex skills in demanding environments. Ironically, these elite workers make high-stakes commercial decisions for their employers but struggle to apply similar value-driven decision-making in their personal lives. This paradigm, steeped in individualism, readily absorbs material—Christian or otherwise—that promises to enhance human capital.

The Link Between Markovits and Smith

Markovits builds on the concept of elite employees, providing a valuable connection to James K. A. Smith's *Desiring the Kingdom*. Smith offers a critical analysis of the formative—and alienating—nature of consumerism. It is formative because it is pervasive and often subliminal, shaping desires and behaviors. It is alienating because it presents an unattainable ideal. Markovits extends this perspective by highlighting the unique experiences of the elite worker.

> Where industry constitutes honor, meritocratic elites lack the time to cultivate the leisured habits that Veblen described, and (alongside conspicuously intense labour) luxury goods rather than exploit become the main avenue for establishing social and economic caste. The rich now consume conspicuously in order to shine rising inequality's light on their fortunes. Fine and expensive things become honour's physical manifestations: an embodiment of industry and of the elite's alienated personality: meritocratic virtue made flesh.[165]

Concluding Markovits

Markovits provides a striking example of the kind of critical engagement with social structures that is largely absent in contemporary discourse. Meritocracy, a foundational principle of the market economy, is placed under scrutiny. In this sense, Markovits acts as a whistle-blower—someone deeply embedded in the system (and as a Yale academic, he certainly

---

165. Markovits, *Meritocracy Trap*, 219–20. "Like the middle of the labor market, so the middle of the consumer market is literally being hallowed out as commerce shifts to the extremes of thrift and luxury" (Markovits, *Meritocracy Trap*, 222).

qualifies)—who exposes its destructive impact on society. His compelling blend of qualitative and quantitative research strengthens his critique.

More significant than the nature of his critique, however, is his prognosis: society is experiencing growing polarization, driven by the transition to a knowledge-based economy. Class distinctions are becoming more pronounced, not less. This conclusion should loom large on the agenda of the Faith and Work movement's leadership. If Thomas Kuhn were to read this book, might he not predict the emergence of another paradigm shift—or suggest that one is already underway?

In this work, Markovits aligns with Smith and others in affirming that individualism lies at the heart of society. Particularly striking is his analysis of individuals' responses to their children's education. Here, radical individualism, as observed by Markovits, is shown to falter—not delivering on its promises but instead defaulting to self-protection over the defense of a principle.

Rosa

Rosa, a contemporary sociologist, has made significant contributions to the field with his work on social acceleration. His focus lies in examining the market economy's impact on the relationship between life and work. In his more recent book, *Resonance: A Sociology of Our Relationship to the World*, Rosa grapples with providing an answer to the crisis identified in his earlier work. The central message of this book is that while modernity promises resonance, it ultimately delivers alienation.[166] In this regard, Rosa aligns closely with Gunton's thinking and would likely have been a compelling conversation partner for him in a post-2003 context.

---

166. Rosa, *Resonance*, 373. Matthew Crawford's widely read *Shop Class as Soulcraft: An Inquiry into the Value of Work* is not directly addressed in the body of the book but serves as a contemporary and accessible support for Rosa's hypothesis. Crawford's work responds to the heteronomous experience of the market, where, as he notes, "Both as workers and as consumers, we feel we move in channels that have been projected from afar by vast impersonal forces" (*Shop Class*, 7). Crawford is a PhD graduate who left his market research position to work as a bike mechanic. The book mixes biographical and sociological insights. As a consequence of heteronomy, he describes workers looking elsewhere for identity. "It is common today to locate one's 'true self' in one's leisure choices. Accordingly, good work is taken to be work that maximizes one's means for pursuing these activities, where life becomes meaningful" (*Shop Class*, 181). Crawford wants to combat this trend with re-imaging the vocational dimension of work, as well as the metrics used in measuring work.

Rosa's work resonates with the critical thinking of both Taylor and Volf, offering several key pillars that align with and support Gunton's conclusions:

- Rosa seeks to reposition critical theory as a tool for understanding our relationship with the world.
- Dynamic stabilization: One hand gives and the other takes away!

The Role of Critical Theory

Critical theory has evolved over time. Although its methods were "diverse, multifarious reflections," it was consistent in giving expression to "the concern that the modern relationship to the world could be quite problematic, misguided, even dire."[167] In his latest book, Rosa takes this concern further, moving beyond mere critique to propose a constructive framework. As he explains, "This book represents an effort to provide Critical Theory with a positive concept that will allow it to move beyond critique and embark on the search for a better form of being."[168]

Rosa's construct is not the primary focus here. What is particularly compelling is the critique he uses to lay its foundation. This critique serves as a valuable recontextualization of critical theory's roots, bringing them into a contemporary framework. Rosa, having the opportunity to refine and expand upon his original work, offers a sharp and incisive engagement with the market economy. His grounding in critical theory provides an advantage that many faith and work theologians lack. These theologians often write from within the market economy and address an audience also situated within it, creating a closed system. Rosa, by contrast, operates from outside this framework. He does not face the same pressures to appear sympathetic or to temper his critique. Identifying with the critical theory tradition positions him as an outsider whose audience is drawn to the strength and insight of his observations alone. The hurdle is far higher for him, which demands a critique of exceptional depth and relevance.

Another important point is that the critique and the construct are not a package deal. One can accept Rosa's critique without necessarily subscribing to his solution. This distinction is valuable for both the

---

167. Rosa, *Resonance*, 26.
168. Rosa, *Resonance*, 444.

reader and Rosa himself. In the case of the latter, his critique is far more significant than his construct and is best appreciated in isolation.

One Hand Gives and the Other Takes Away

The heading above is a paraphrase, of course—simple language is not Rosa's forte. In his own way, however, he masterfully depicts the give-and-take dynamic in the modern relationship with the world. Rosa presents a picture of circularity that few have articulated with his level of clarity. While Wright touches on the myth of progress, Rosa brings the notion of circularity to the forefront. Oddly enough, this emphasis on circularity does not appear to be central to Rosa's own argument. Perhaps it holds less significance for him.

For this body of work, however, Rosa's perspective echoes *The One and the Many*, Gunton's diagnosis of the tension within modernity. Rosa's approach is distinct: he revisits the centrality of autonomy in the market economy, a condition he describes as "radically open." He then layers on the consequences, which manifest as dynamic stabilization and, ultimately, self-alienation. His analysis offers significant parallels to Markovits's arguments, albeit with a stronger economic articulation.

RADICALLY OPEN: A SELF-DETERMINED WAY OF LIFE

We are well-acquainted with the demand for autonomy at the core of the modern identity. Rosa's terminology of "radically open" not only encapsulates this concept but also validates the eschatological focus prominent in thinkers like Moltmann and his followers. Their effort seeks to restore the end from which humanity has been alienated. As Rosa states:

> Modern Western societies are defined by an ineluctable ethical pluralism and individualism. In contrast to antiquity, the Middle Ages, marked by Christian scholasticism, and even most known premodern cultures, modern Western societies, at the level of their constitutive theoretical and practical self-interpretation, have radically abandoned the idea of the human being as creature designed with a particular purpose in life, a telos. We instead understand the human being as an animal equipped with certain propensities and capabilities, needs and desires, on that—when it comes to the question of what it will do with said equipment, which needs or capabilities it will develop and

for what, which desires it will cultivate and pursue—must be regarded as radically open.[169]

Dynamic Stabilization

Writing within a tradition deeply attuned to the ownership of capital, Rosa identifies money as the key link to the prized autonomy.[170] While the connection between money and autonomy is not new, it becomes the gateway to circularity through Rosa's concept of "dynamic stabilization." His theory posits that the contemporary market economy achieves stability only through perpetual growth. As Rosa explains,

> One of the basic premises of this book is that modern societies are capable only of dynamic stabilization. Structurally, they are geared toward continuous progress by means of growth, acceleration, and innovation. And this not only creates temporal and spatial, technological and economic tendency toward escalation that consistently pushes back the horizons of the possible, but also ensures that the kinetic or transformational energy of society remains high.[171]

---

169. Rosa, *Resonance*, 18.

170. "The promise of autonomy . . . lies at the root of the modern appeal of money; the more money subjects have at their disposal, the more latitude they have to shape their lives. Money grants us the ability to materially determine, independent of the circumstances and opinions of others, where we live, what we eat and wear, where we want to travel, etc. Money and rights have this become the basic media for securing the modern autonomy" (Rosa, *Resonance*, 19).

171. Rosa, *Resonance*, 21. If we interpret Rosa as highlighting a structural rather than a cultural driver, a parallel emerges between his observations and Volf's views from thirty years earlier. Volf challenges the notion that the rhythm of work is dictated by the mechanics of the Protestant work ethic. In response to this ethic, he writes,

> But there is very little that is either specifically Protestant (religious) or ethical about the contemporary drive for work. This is not to deny the historical contribution of the Protestant work ethic to modern workaholism. But after Western civilisation has climbed up the ladder of the Protestant work ethic to a state in which incessant work has become one of its main features, it has pushed this ladder aside but continued to work even more frantically. Work through today more on the insatiable hunger for self-realisation than on the Protestant work ethic. In their own eyes and in the eyes of their contemporaries, modern human beings are what they do. The kind of work they do and what the accomplish or acquire through work provides a basic key to their identity. (Volf, *Work in the Spirit*, 129)

This raises the question: how does this requirement for growth impact the identity of its consumers?

> Since they cannot say with any certainty what a good life is, what concept of happiness they wish to pursue, or what their inner core or internal standard is, they are all but forced to concentrate instead on their level of resources. . . . Under the conditions of dynamic stabilization, however, devoting one's energies to accumulating resources becomes nothing less than a categorical imperative if one hopes to have even a chance of a self-determined life.[172]

The consequence of this shift is alienation, as our very identity is reduced to a resource for competition in the market economy.[173] As Rosa explains, "Also part of our nature, and for the same reason; is the fact that we as subjects become alienated from our body as a thing. We then no longer feel comfortable in our own skin; our body becomes foreign to us or even uncanny. What is specifically modern, however, is the ongoing shift in our relation to the body from a more instrumental to a more resource-oriented mode."[174]

Rosa's critique could be seen as overly focused on economic factors and therefore too narrow in scope. While this is a valid criticism, it does

---

172. Rosa, *Resonance*, 22.

173. "As a stroll through any shopping mall anywhere in the world immediately makes it plain, the commodification desires of late modern subjects are directed toward the body—and notably primarily towards one's own body—to an extent perhaps unparalleled in history" (Rosa, *Resonance*, 123). One could easily remove Rosa's reference here and substitute Smith, as both articulate the same idea. However, Rosa adds an important emphasis on the dynamic nature of this phenomenon. Today's offer is never sufficient for tomorrow. "This means that individuals must invest ever more energy into maintaining their own competitiveness and resource levels in order to keep their place and thus reproduce the status quo" (Rosa, *Resonance*, 104).

174. Rosa, *Resonance*, 104. Capturing the depth of Rosa's commentary on alienation in just a few paragraphs is a challenge. He paints a bleak picture of public spaces—where we spend much of our lives—as environments in which we feel profoundly foreign. The following sentences encapsulate his sentiment:

- "My proposal is therefore to define alienation as a mode of relating to the world in which the subject encounters the subjective; objective, and/or social worlds as either indifferent or repulsive" (Rosa, *Resonance*, 178–79).
- "Alienation has thus become the basic mode of relating to the world, against which escaping to the resonant oases of fragrant bathrooms, movie theatres, or wellness resorts seems like a panic reaction" (Rosa, *Resonance*, 377).
- "By increasing one's attractiveness, fitness, health, creativity, and performance capability (physical capital), the radius of what is attainable is likewise expanded" (Rosa, *Resonance*, 417).

not diminish the observed tendency toward self-commodification in a resource-driven environment. When combined with Markovits's analysis of the polarization of marketable skills, the likelihood of many participants in a market economy experiencing alienation becomes significant. They may genuinely enjoy their work, utilizing the gifts they have received (*Work in the Spirit*), yet the relentless pace demanded of them clashes with their natural rhythm. This creates a sense of entrapment, as they find themselves caught in a cycle with no viable options for a gradual or gentle exit.

The connection to Gunton lies specifically in *The One, the Three, and the Many*. The pursuit of autonomy has paradoxically resulted in heteronomy, reducing *The One* to merely one among many. This insight has profound implications, as it directly challenges many of the conclusions drawn by the Faith and Work movement. The issue these authors face is not merely structural but deeply philosophical—or, as Gunton would describe it, ontological. The solution is not found in a Benedictine balance or additional teaching, particularly not more of the same. This is precisely Rosa's point: we are ensnared in an economic and philosophical circularity. "The desire to increase our share of the world so dominates the cultural imagination and the relationship to the world of late modernity that reform proposals currently under discussion almost always move within this framework."[175]

No Cognitive Exit

Rosa's proposed antidote is not the primary focus here and, indeed, may seem disappointingly naïve to those in the developing world. What is noteworthy, however, is his assertion that humanity lacks the capacity to devise a cognitive exit plan. Could it be that theology is ensnared in its own version of Gladwell's "Cockpit Culture,"[176] circling the runway while no one dares to acknowledge that we are running out of fuel? Disturbingly, Rosa observes that even fundamental behaviors, such as forgiveness, are being eroded. "In a society whose dominant mode of interaction is competition, and whose subjects consequently are subjected to pressures of optimization

---

175. Rosa, *Resonance*, 435.
176. Gladwell, *Outliers*.

in nearly all spheres of life, the concept of forgiveness (along with the resulting possibility of new beginning) tends to lose all meaning)."[177]

His conclusion provides little encouragement for those striving to integrate faith and work. He contends that competition is fundamentally incompatible with social concord, stating, "Competition and resonance are thus two incompatible attitudes to the world."[178]

Conclusion

Rosa argues that we are radically open, while Gunton maintains that we are radically closed. Despite this divergence, both agree that our contemporary relationship with the world is profoundly alienating. They share the conviction that modernity, with its dismantling of relationality, is at the core of the problem.[179] Yet, both also extend a message of transformation and hope.

The contribution to this project is not merely an affirmation of Gunton's critique. Rather, like Markovits, Rosa exemplifies critical social engagement that far surpasses anything encountered in the faith and work literature reviewed for this study. It is evident that this was not "business as usual" for Rosa; his work reflects a deliberate effort to transform critical theory into a framework offering a constructive response. Regarding the nature of work, Rosa's theory of dynamic stabilization presents a macro-level challenge to the future of the market economy. Concepts such as "dynamic stabilization" demand far more than "an institution mediating grace to the individual."[180] Rosa calls for structural reform that directly confronts the distortion of human identity caused by living at odds with its environment. This is an uncomfortable message for faith and work integrators but an invaluable challenge to ground theology in sufficiently broad and critical thinking.

---

177. Rosa, *Resonance*, 214.

178. Rosa, *Resonance*, 417.

179. "The sociology of human relationships to the world presented here aims not to recapitulate this theoretical aporia, but to overcome it by radicalizing the very idea of relationship. It precisely does not assume that subjects encounter a preformed world, but instead posits that both sides—subject and world—are first formed, shaped and in fact constituted in and through their mutual relatedness" (Rosa, *Resonance*, 33).

180. Gunton, *Promise*, 51.

Zuboff

Shoshana Zuboff, a professor emeritus at Harvard Law School, is widely regarded as a leading critic of surveillance capitalism. While her work may seem far removed from theology, her insights into identity and its manipulation within a market economy speak directly to the concerns raised by Gunton and highlight the vulnerability of identity in such an environment. Her book's subtitle, *The Fight for a Human Future at the New Frontier of Power*, is particularly poignant. This book engages with her work for several compelling reasons.

- There is a contrast between her level of critique with that found in the Faith and Work literature.
- There is an affirmation of Gunton's concerns about the alienation of identity.
- Her theory reviews how in the current threat to identity, the ideals of autonomy are being undermined.
- The writer disagrees with her starting position. For Zuboff, the modern ideal of autonomy is the position to protect.

The core of Zuboff's argument centers on the erosion of modernist ideals of autonomy, driven by what she terms "surveillance capitalism." In her view, certain segments of the market economy have shifted from merely reviewing and predicting human behavior to actively shaping it using the data we generate.[181] Shaping behavior is not a new concept, but Zuboff introduces the term "behavioral surplus" to argue that the Fourth Industrial Revolution has enabled an unprecedented form of human engineering. While the term "Fourth Industrial Revolution" is not her own, she would likely not object to its use in this context. Behavioral surplus refers to the vast accumulation of data—or "cookies"—generated by our online activities. With the decreasing cost of data storage and the increasing power of search engines, this surplus has become a valuable resource for those seeking to analyze and influence behavioral preferences. An apt analogy is the mining companies that reprocess waste dumps to extract gold overlooked by earlier, less advanced techniques.

Zuboff delivers a stark warning about the crisis facing identity, revealing the extent to which our behavior is recorded and how this data is used to influence us. While her primary focus is on consumption,

---

181. Zuboff, *Age of Surveillance Capitalism*, 338.

she highlights that the same mechanisms underpin the spread of fake news designed to sway political decisions. Tactfully, she avoids referencing specific presidential elections, opting instead to revive the words of Karl Polanyi, reinterpreting them for the modern era. According to her, Polanyi might now assert: "If industrial civilisation flourished at the expense of nature and now threatens to cost us the Earth, an information civilisation shaped by surveillance capitalism will thrive at the expense of human nature and threatens to cost us our humanity."[182] What we are discussing here is heteronomy masquerading as autonomy. At this point, the contrast between Zuboff's depth of critique and that of the Faith and Work movement becomes striking. While Zuboff is not beyond critique herself, her work demonstrates a level of research into causal factors that is notably absent from much of the Faith and Work literature. This depth of critique is comparable to that attributed to Gunton, despite his acknowledged blind spots. The result in the faith and work writings is a recognition that identity is under pressure. However, this recognition largely focuses on symptoms, falling short of conveying the full gravity of the situation or providing the tools necessary to address and, where possible, mitigate these underlying causes.

Woven into Zuboff's analysis is a compelling division of modernity into two distinct stages. While both stages are familiar, her delineation offers a helpful framework for understanding their progression. The first stage introduces individualization and an open-ended view of personal formation.[183] The second stage reflects the transformative power of wealth, which elevates the self to a position of dominance.[184] She captures this transition powerfully, stating, "The first modernity suppressed the

---

182. Zuboff, *Age of Surveillance Capitalism*, 346.

183. "Around two hundred years ago, we embarked upon the first modern road where life was no longer handed down one generation to the next according to the traditions of village and clan. This 'first modernity' marks the time when love became 'individualised' for great numbers of people as they separated from traditional norms, meanings and rules. That meant that each life became an open ended reality to be discovered rather than a certainty to be enacted" (Zuboff, *Age of Surveillance Capitalism*, 33).

184. "Industrialisation modernity and the practices of mass production capitalism as its core produced more wealth than had even been imagined possible.... Hundreds of millions of people gained access to experiences that had once been the preserve of a tiny elite: university education, travel, improved life expectancy, disposable income, rising standards of living, broad access to consumer goods, varied communication and information flows, and specialized, intellectually demanding work" (Zuboff, *Age of Surveillance Capitalism*, 35).

growth and expression of the self in favour of collective solutions, but by the second modernity, the self is all we have."[185]

Gunton may not have been familiar with the concept of behavioral surplus, but he would likely not have been surprised by its implications. Rewriting the foreword to *The One, the Three, and the Many* to address this contemporary manifestation would be a small task, as it represents an extension of the modernity Gunton engaged. The threat to has simply been intensified. Where Gunton may challenge Zuboff is on the originality of this manipulation. He would argue that what we see today is not the origination of manipulation but rather its customization. As discussed in chapter 3, the roots of this manipulation can be traced back through the Reformation and the Enlightenment to Augustine. While Zuboff presents it as something new and critical, Gunton's argument emphasizes that the crisis is not novel but an ongoing issue.

Controversially, Zuboff conducts a comparative analysis of totalitarianism and instrumentalism in their application of power. She meticulously charts their similarities and differences across various forms of social behavior. Of particular interest to this study is her discussion of social patterning: totalitarianism seeks radical isolation, while instrumentalism aims for radical connection.[186] The danger of radical connection lies in its potential to act as an anesthetic, numbing awareness of deeper, growing issues.

Zuboff's references to totalitarianism evoke historical interventions like the *Barmen Declaration*, a moment when so few theologians were willing to recognize National Socialism as a crisis. Among the theologians considered here, Volf stands out as one who identifies such crises. Zuboff's work issues a challenge to theologians, urging them to elevate the standard of both critique and response.

Frischmann and Selinger

Frischmann, a professor of law, business, and economics at Villanova University, and Selinger, a professor of philosophy, collaborated on the 2018 book *Re-Engineering Humanity*, published by Cambridge University Press. This engaging volume is the product of crossdisciplinary research. Their message aligns closely with Zuboff's, though it is tailored

---

185. Zuboff, *Age of Surveillance Capitalism*, 36.
186. Zuboff, *Age of Surveillance Capitalism*, 397.

for a more technical and academic audience, with a focus on themes such as contractualism, extended cognition, big data, and predictive analytics. Like Zuboff, their conclusion conveys a profound sense of urgency.

> It's difficult to appreciate how powerfully the tools we develop shape us. One of the most important ways is by shaping our imagined reality, our very beliefs about ourselves, and our preferences and values. If the ends worth pursuing are determined by our tools, but their constructed reality (the contours and contents of the lit space under the lamp-post), then nothing less that our very humanity may be at risk of being whittled away. Our imagination could be bounded by the constraints embedded in the tools and logics they perpetuate. We are not there, at least not yet.[187]

Frischmann and Selinger's title signals what they perceive as the death of autonomy: humanity is increasingly being shaped as an engineered product rather than as the result of independent, individual choice. Their use of the term "engineering" also reflects their perspective on Taylorism, which they identify as the foundational building block for contemporary methods of social conditioning.[188]

Central to Frischmann and Selinger's theory is the concept of "extended cognition," a process in which decision-making is increasingly supported by technology. They explain, "The dynamic interplay between human minds and the constructed socio-technical environment is the main link connecting extended mind theory with our analysis of techno-social engineering."[189] This point is vividly illustrated through the example of programming autonomous cars and the ethical dilemmas posed by their default responses to potential accident scenarios.[190] How does this debate intersect with Gunton's work and his analysis of identity in the market economy? Part of the answer lies in the substance of Frischmann and Selinger's critique; the other part resides in what remains unsaid. Attention will first be given to these omissions.

---

187. Frischmann and Selinger, *Re-engineering Humanity*, 51.
188. Frischmann and Selinger, *Re-engineering Humanity*, 72.
189. Frischmann and Selinger, *Re-engineering Humanity*, 92.

190. "Who should decide how autonomous vehicles will perform when difficult situations arise? Should it be politicians? Automotive executives? Or should people be allowed to customize the moral dashboard of their cars so that their vehicles execute moral decisions that are in line with their own preferences?" (Frischmann and Selinger, *Re-engineering Humanity*, 135).

Both Zuboff and Frischmann consistently sound the alarm about the demise of autonomy, arguing that the marketplace has become the dominant driver of the prevailing worldview. This is where their analysis invites critique and connects to the conclusions of chapter 3. They operate under the assumption that autonomy once existed and is now being replaced. However, as discussed in chapter 3, an alternative perspective suggests that the concept of autonomy itself is an engineered product. While it may not have originated from "behavioral surplus," there is substantial evidence to support its roots in an earlier form of "extended cognition." What we may be witnessing is not the birth of social engineering but rather the culmination of a power shift—from state and academy to the market.

If this critique holds true, then what is framed as a crisis may, in fact, present an opportunity—particularly for identity. As one form of identity transitions to another, there arises a moment for pause and reflection on what identity truly means to us. Subtle hints of this perspective emerge within the text, such as the reference to humanity as a shared resource. "Our description of humanity's techno-social dilemma implies that humanity is a shared resource and our humanity can be lost. Many have said that humanity can be taken away. . . . We need to better understand our humanity if we are to preserve, protect, and sustain it for ourselves and future generations."[191]

This critique provides a fitting transition to the conclusion. Both Zuboff and Frischmann highlight how impressionable humanity truly is, revealing that the autonomous rationality of the individual offers little defence against the relentless accumulation of data "cookies." While their level of critique and analysis of social trends deserves commendation, we are not bound to accept all their underlying assumptions. Instead, we can view this moment as a transition—an opportunity to reconsider human identity at its most fundamental levels. The market economy is poised to remain a dominant force in shaping human identity for the foreseeable future, making this rethinking all the more urgent.

CONCLUSION AND TRANSITION: ADDRESSING THE GAPS IN FAITH AND WORK LITERATURE

This concluding section serves as a preliminary step. From here, the discussion moves to dhapter 5, which provides a detailed review of Timothy

---

191. Frischmann and Selinger, *Re-engineering Humanity*, 245.

Keller's work, applying the same balance between intra-theological and extra-theological writings. By crafting these two summary statements, the writer aims to facilitate a more streamlined and (hopefully) insightful analysis in dhapter 5.

The initial intention for chapter 4 was to focus on the dominance of ethics and evangelism within the field of Faith and Work. To this end, Miller's classifications were chosen as the backbone of the chapter's content. The underlying hypothesis anticipated a theological problem to be explored from a Trinitarian perspective. However, this approach encountered challenges, beginning with the engagement of Taylor in chapter 3 and continuing with Volf in this chapter.

Volf serves as a signpost in this discussion. His account stands out for its use of terms such as "crisis" and "powerful structural forces," which signal deeper issues. While his elaboration is limited, he directs readers to further studies. Criticizing Volf for providing only an entry point feels misplaced, as he was writing at the early stages of the Faith and Work movement with a constructive response in mind rather than a purely critical one. Moreover, Volf's primary aim was to offer a pneumatological perspective, with his sociological insights emerging as a secondary by-product of his broader exploration.

Volf's challenge prompted a broader reading beyond Christian literature, revealing both a complexity and an extent of influence on identity that had not been anticipated, nor adequately represented in theological accounts. Consequently, this led to a disproportionately longer section aimed at balancing Faith and Work writings with the complexities they had overlooked. Incorporating these additional insights alongside the original focus on ethics and evangelism, the two concluding statements are as follows:

- Faith and Work literature has a dominant (but not exclusive) focus on personal ethics and evangelism.
- Faith and Work literature does not grasp the impact of the market economy on identity.

What elevates these points from mere observation to meaningful contribution is the recognition of circularity. An epistemic and autonomous bias underpins the dominance of ethics and evangelism, restricting much of the discourse to the micro-context of individual experience. Superficially, one could argue that these biases reflect the standard tendencies of

Reformed public theology. However, what emerges is not the product of genuine engagement with the broader context but rather an adaptation of familiar concepts set to a new tune. The wider issues are not entirely ignored but are overshadowed, reflecting a "curious blindness" reminiscent of the discussion in chapter 3. This also recalls Gunton's critique of classical theology in chapter 2, where he argued that it lacked awareness of its own presuppositions and foundations.

Our examination of the antidote proposed by Reformed theology highlights its limited grasp of the broader issues. The most common explanation for this gap in the literature has been ignorance—an issue presumed to be easily addressed through education. The literary contributions examined here appear to stem from this conviction. Volf, Miller, and Van Duzer advocate a shared message: the field of Faith and Work literature lacks the depth of theological investment evident in other areas. They assume they have accurately apprehended the reality and focus on providing resources to convey this understanding to others.

Their response reflects an epistemic bias and an individual bias, making it inadequate for addressing the magnitude of the challenges being faced. The issue at the heart of the relationship between faith and work extends far beyond ethics—it speaks directly to our very identity.

Chapter 3 explored the transition of the individual to the center of society. In this chapter, the focus shifted to the transition of work to the center of the individual. In today's context, we grapple with defining ourselves apart from our work—what we do constitutes a substantial part of our identity. Consequently, it is no exaggeration to claim that work has become the most dominant and influential institution in contemporary society.

The recognition of formation is a given, as evidenced by the contributions of faith and work authors, who clearly demonstrate their conviction in its importance. Additional evidence can be seen in the substantial investments made by organizations in shaping their employees. These efforts are not limited to technical skill development but frequently extend to cultural formation, aiming to align employees with the organization's values.

Markovits reminds us that this is the generation of human capital. We invest significantly in our own formation and that of our children to enhance or protect our status in a knowledge economy. This kind of investment is in continuity with the modern ideal of an autonomous individual, but what then do we make of Zuboff's "behavioral surplus" and Frischmann's "extended cognitions" where influence takes a heteronomous turn?

Adding to the infringement of influence are the alienating effects of workforce polarization highlighted by Markovits—a phenomenon likely to intensify under Rosa's theory of dynamic stabilization. These realities pose significant challenges to the concept of integrating faith and work, challenges for which the Faith and Work literature is insufficiently equipped. Chapter 5 builds on these concluding arguments, further validating them through a detailed examination of Tim Keller's contributions.

5

Tim Keller's Cartesian Conversion

INTRODUCTION: KELLER'S THEOLOGY AND THE CHALLENGE OF IDENTITY IN FAITH AND WORK

THE PURPOSE OF THIS chapter is to critically review Keller's theology and evaluate the claims made in previous chapters. The opening chapter of this book summarized Keller's soteriology with the phrase *"Try Harder,"* arguing that his theology is primarily logical rather than relational. Unlike *perichoresis,* where love is the essence of the image of God, Keller's perspective frames love as an outflow of the image rather than its core. These are significant assertions, and this chapter examines them in depth through Keller's treatment of faith and work in *Every Good Endeavor.*[1]

This chapter lays the groundwork for chapter 6, where the focus shifts to the role of theology in shaping identity within the market economy, particularly through a dialogue between Gunton and Keller. Although this chapter references Gunton, the detailed engagement with his ideas is reserved for the next chapter.

Central to this discussion is the classification of Keller's theology using Miller's typology. By analyzing the interplay between Keller's doctrine of God and soteriology, his understanding of identity is unpacked. Moreover, Keller's application of public theology to the market economy comes under scrutiny. Central to this critique is the concept of "curious

---

1. Hereinafter referred to as *Endeavor.*

blindness"—a term borrowed from Charles Taylor and explored in chapter 3 before being applied to faith and work in chapter 4. It highlights the failure to recognize or engage with critical issues raised by contemporary philosophy and sociology regarding humanity's relationship to work.

Faith and Work Thought Leaders: Tim Keller and Katherine Alsdorf

Keller stands apart from other writers and thinkers in the field of Faith and Work due to the extent of his influence. He embodies what many Reformed theologians aspire to be. There is something iconic about a pastor founding a church in New York and growing it into a hub for both national and international ministry. Moreover, he is a leader who addresses contemporary issues relevant to many Christians through the establishment of the Center for Faith and Work. Keller's contributions are not merely theoretical; they are substantiated by tangible, on-the-ground engagement at the epicenter of the wealthiest city in the world's largest economy. In this context, Keller rises head and shoulders above his peers.

An exalted position from humble beginnings! Keller was born and raised in Pennsylvania, pursuing his education at Bucknell University, Gordon-Conwell Theological Seminary, and Westminster Theological Seminary.[2] At Westminster, Keller completed his DMin under Harvie Conn, the professor of missions at the time. Hart notes that Conn's theory and practice of urban ministry profoundly influenced Keller, especially in the areas of church planting and city-based mission.[3]

At the time of writing *Endeavor*, Keller was serving as senior pastor of Redeemer Presbyterian Church, which he founded in 1989.[4] Keller has consistently been productive, publishing, preaching, and teaching extensively. His works span genres such as Bible commentaries, family, marriage, apologetics, and faith and work, offering ample material to analyze his theology. A common thread across these works is his commitment to integrating the Christian faith into both the public and private spheres of society. Unlike Gunton, there is no clear evidence of theological shifts in

---

2. Keller and Alsdorf, *Every Good Endeavor*, 303.
3. Hart, "Looking for Communion," 158.
4. Hart, "Looking for Communion," 161.

Keller's career. If anything, his later works, including *Endeavor*, reflect a deeper commitment to public theology.[5]

The relationship between Keller and Luther is addressed briefly in this section through Keller's use of the concept of "idolatry." This limited focus is not reflective of Luther's overall significance to Keller but rather constrained by the specific lens of our engagement with Keller on identity. While the scope here is necessarily narrow, further exploration of Luther's influence on Keller would make for an important and worthwhile study.

Katherine Alsdorf co-authors *Endeavor* with Keller. According to her LinkedIn profile, she is the founder and director emeritus of the Redeemer Center for Faith and Work, established in 2002. Before this role, Alsdorf held senior executive positions in Europe and America. She completed her undergraduate studies at Wittenberg University and earned an MBA before joining Redeemer. She also credits seminary courses at Regent College in Vancouver for shaping her perspective. In 2002, Redeemer identified Faith and Work as one of its key initiatives, appointing Alsdorf as its executive head.

Critics

The notable differences between Keller and Gunton lie in the nature and volume of critiques they receive. In academic settings, rigorous debate is encouraged, as evidenced by Gunton, where even close colleagues openly highlight shortcomings. In contrast, the pastoral environment is more contained. While pastors often receive widespread appreciation from their community, critiques tend to come infrequently and primarily from within their tradition. Such critiques are usually limited in scope and not widely circulated, leaving much of the reflective critique to be self-navigated. David Gay's book, *A Case of Mistaken Identity*, is a short, self-published work responding to Keller. Surprisingly clear, concise, and even witty, it provides valuable confirmation of the findings on Keller. In contrast, *Engaging with Keller* is more substantial but less impactful. It was authored by some of Keller's European counterparts as a critique of what they perceived to be deviations from Presbyterian doctrine.

---

5. Hart talks to the founding of the Redeemer Center for Faith and Work as a pivotal point for Keller's theology of the city. Here, Keller is thought to have drawn on the writings of his mentor, Conn, on the "redemptive-historical significance of the city" (Hart, "Looking for Communion," 161).

Additionally, Keller's invited critics, featured in *Shaped by the Gospel*, offer further perspectives. While this engagement feels somewhat staged, it nonetheless provides some useful insights.

INTRODUCING *EVERY GOOD ENDEAVOR*

Audience and Genre

Not all the cited authors share the same audience. Many of Keller's peers write from an academic perspective, addressing either fellow academics or Christians engaged in faith and work. Keller, however, focuses solely on the latter. Additionally, p. 257 of *Endeavor* highlights that many at Redeemer are new to their faith but are notably well-educated.[6] The range of conversation partners in *Endeavor* is diverse, assuming a well-read audience.

Keller has engaged with Miller's work and concurs with his assessment of the current literature landscape. In essence, Miller identifies a dichotomy: an ecumenical movement focused on social justice and an evangelical emphasis on evangelism. Keller summarizes this dynamic succinctly in the endnotes:

> The mainline church understood the relationship of faith to work primarily as an effort to apply just social ethics to capitalism—which was viewed with suspicion. Many conservative evangelicals were by contrast much more individualistic in their understanding of faith. They were more positive toward market capitalism and so did not put their reform emphasis there. Instead their greatest concern was the need for personal decision and salvation. Therefore, to be a Christian at work meant primarily to evangelise your co-workers.[7]

Keller's diagnosis aligns with the hypothesis of this study. As we have seen through Gunton, the failure to hold these two foci in tension often stems from the underlying theology that supports them. The question, then, is whether Keller can move beyond the parameters he has set for himself. The conclusion of this section will revisit the quote and present a verdict.

While Keller is aligned with Miller on the problem of ignorance, *Endeavor* represents a different solution strategy. Miller, as we recall,

---

6. Keller and Alsdorf, *Every Good Endeavor*, 257.
7. Keller and Alsdorf, *Every Good Endeavor*, 305.

believed that the "logical starting place" was with the training of clergy.[8] Keller's book approaches the solution from a different angle. The Redeemer imprint describes itself as "dedicated to books that address the spiritual and social issues of the day in a way that speaks both to the core Christian audience and to seekers and sceptics alike."[9] The genre is clearly constructive, wanting to make a contribution to what we have argued to be an important field.

While not aimed at an academic audience, Keller guides his readers through complex and diverse intellectual territory, examining the influence of ancient Greek thought, the Enlightenment, modernity, and the postmodernity debate. His choice of sources reflects common patterns among faith and work authors, drawing on theology, sociology, and philosophy. With reference to thinkers such as Nietzsche, Ferry, Thiselton, MacIntyre, and Bellah et al., Keller invites his readers to engage critically with social structures and norms.

However, as argued in the concluding section of chapter 4, the Faith and Work literature often lacks sufficient critical depth. Despite Keller's inclusion of critical sources, it is evident here that his analysis does not advance critical thinking beyond the contributions of his peers.

In terms of theological positioning, the book operates on several assumptions. It is not feasible to revisit all key theological positions while also providing a comprehensive engagement with the subject of work. To engage with Gunton's theological critique, this chapter will draw insights from *Endeavor* and supplement them with observations from Keller's broader body of work.

For consistency, I refer to Miller's categorization types introduced in the previous chapter. This chapter argues that the ethical theme is the strongest, with expression as a close second—a claim that will be substantiated through the content of this chapter.

Authorship deserves attention at this point. In a co-authored book, the key question is whether the content accurately reflects Keller's perspective. While this can only be speculative, the writing style and discontinuity with Keller's other works suggest that the first half of the book

---

8. Miller's recommendation is to start with training clergy. "A logical starting place for change is the place where clergy are trained. Seminaries and divinity schools should recognize anew the theological, practical, and pastoral importance of the workplace with a view toward training pastors to minister more intentionally and effectively to their parishioners in the business world and other workplaces" (Miller, *God at Work*, 144).

9. Keller and Alsdorf, *Every Good Endeavor*, 267.

leans heavily toward Alsdorf, while the latter half aligns more closely with Keller's established writing. Although this cannot be definitively validated, situating the critique within the context of Keller's broader works helps address this uncertainty.

Structural Overview of the Book

Keller's structure aligns with that of his peers, presenting the material in three parts:

1. **God's plan for work**—This section establishes the ideological foundation. Keller adopts an apologetic tone, likely anticipating that many readers might view the title as an oxymoron, assuming work was never part of God's plan.

2. **Our problems with work**—Building on the foundation, this section addresses the challenges and obstacles to fulfilling God's plan for work, aptly titled to reflect these difficulties.

3. **Living out the plan**—The final section focuses on application, exploring how to live out God's plan for work while navigating the challenges presented in the previous section.

Key Themes and Initial Responses

The value of Keller's work lies in its themes rather than its structure. While the structure, as previously noted, is generic, the underlying themes reveal Keller's specific theological perspective. This section identifies three key themes underpinning the book: (1) The concept of worldview; (2) The dignity of work; and (3) Soteriology and idolatry. These themes are restated here to highlight their linear relationship. The concept of perception/worldview provides the foundation for a coherent structure. The argument progresses as follows: Work is intrinsically valuable and dignified → this dignity has been lost/distorted through problems → these problems can be rectified through education and application.

The division of the book's structure might seem like a matter of semantics, but framing the discussion around themes provides a sharper and more focused analysis. This section will identify the key themes and initiate a response to them. While the themes themselves are appreciated, the common critique is that the book demonstrates a limited depth of structural analysis and a weak engagement with social complexity. These shortcomings will be explored in greater detail in a subsequent section.

Theme 1: The Concept of "Worldview"

The concept of "worldviews" is central to Keller's book. He acknowledges their pervasiveness and power, stating: "All Christians live in cultures and work in vocational fields that operate by powerful master narratives that are sharply different from the gospel's account of things."[10] His response to worldviews can be summarized as "disclose to disarm." This concept is further developed in his book *Center Church*, originally published the same year as *Endeavor* and republished in 2016 under the title *Shaped by the Gospel*. Keller views the articulation of worldview as part of a broader process of reframing cultural contexts through a "theological vision." He cites Lints: "A theological vision allows [people] to see their culture in a way different than they had ever been able to see it before. . . . Those who are empowered by the theological vision do not simply stand against the mainstream impulses of the culture but take the initiative both to understand and speak to that culture from the framework of the scriptures."[11] This idea ties directly to the third part of *Endeavor*, where Keller focuses on reframing the worldview of work.

The term "worldview" is widely used, making it essential to understand how Keller employs it. The concept gained prominence during the postmodernity debates of the 1990s, emerging from a specific historical context. Postmodernity turned modernity's rationalism inward, rejecting the confidence of modern thought without offering a clear alternative framework.

While this debate was significant at the time, it no longer holds the same prominence or enthusiasm today. The postmodern critique carried a sense of confident criticism that, in hindsight, appears somewhat naïve. For instance, the mantra *"No More Metanarratives!"* is paradoxical, as it functions as a metanarrative in itself.

The term "worldview" comes with certain baggage, as it is perceived to encompass some elements while excluding others. This is evident in the subsequent developments in philosophy. While confidence may have

---

10. Keller and Alsdorf, *Every Good Endeavor*, 183.
11. Lints, *Fabric of Theology*, 315–16, cited by Keller, *Shaped by the Gospel*, 14.

waned, the underlying concepts remain intact. We are still left with the self at the center of the equation. In fact, we have heightened the autonomy of the individual through the addition of pluralism, allowing the rational self a wider array of choices.

How does this relate to Keller? The key point is that there are differing opinions on the scope of a worldview. The argument that follows will demonstrate that Keller's worldview is narrower than Gunton's. Keller lacks Gunton's extensive reach of causation. His conception resembles a group photo where the photographer has accidentally missed the smiling face of the tallest family member, leaving the viewer focused solely on the torso. Keller's view is too limited, and as a result, his confidence in its transformation is misplaced.

In arguing for Keller's reduced concept, we don't need to leave much to speculation. Keller outlines his framework in *Shaped by the Gospel*. Here, he employs the computing analogy of hardware, middleware, and software. According to Keller, the worldview functions as the "middleware" in his theological framework. He explains this concept in detail:

> I am no computer expert, but my computer-savvy friends tell me that the middleware is a software layer that lies between the hardware and the operating system and the various software applications being deployed by the computer's user. In the same way, between one's doctrinal beliefs and ministry practices should be a well-conceived vision for how to bring the gospel to bear on a particular cultural setting and historical moment.[12]

Essentially, *Endeavor* is an effort to upgrade the middleware.

There are some problems with this conception when contrasted with both Gunton and some contemporary writings. Continuing with the analogy, while I do not claim a superior technological background to Keller, middleware is relatively easy to change. Gunton addresses something that is more entrenched than middleware. Arguably, Gunton offers an even more enduring view of concepts than Kuhn does. He posits that these concepts are even more than a paradigm; our conceptions of homogeneity and diversity seem hardcoded. They have become the instruction set that comes pre-coded on our processor. To extend this analogy geographically, these views are like the ancient footpaths and bridle paths that gave way to the somewhat arbitrary road configuration of contemporary London.

12. Keller, *Shaped by the Gospel*, 13.

Keller's perspective on the ability to transform our views is far more simplistic. Analogously, his approach reflects a hermeneutic of only two horizons. Once the farther horizon is explained in terms of the present, a bridge is built between the two. This optimism comes through in Keller's writing. Of course, common sense tells us to cease analysis when we have uncovered a problem. The challenge here is that Keller has stopped too soon. In this sense, the contemporary use (or perhaps even abuse) of the term *worldview* has diluted it of its value. As will be argued below, there comes a point beyond which Keller will not proceed. This limitation reduces his vision. Regarding criticism, Professor Jeremy Begbie often reminded his students that "the best view of the landscape is when you have your toes over the edge of the cliff."[13] This is the best view, but not the safest. Take a few steps back, and the view is already obscured by the ground in front of you. For Keller, any theological or structural criticism is off the agenda. He has opted for what he sees as a safer position but has lost some of the view. As a result, Keller will achieve some of the change he desires, but not the change we need.

The criticism of Keller's understanding of worldview is important here, linking back to the earlier section titled "These Choices [Identity] Are Not as Rational as We Once Believed." Keller's engagement with Smith below will develop this point further.

Theme 2: The Dignity of Work

The second theme explores the negative perceptions of work, with Keller emphasizing that work in the marketplace carries *"no less dignity and nobility"* than work in Christian ministry.[14] He firmly rejects the notion of a sacred-secular divide. Interestingly, Keller attributes the need for this affirmation to the lingering influence of Greek disdain for materiality. As a corrective, he draws on scriptural references from Genesis, affirming that work is something God himself does: "While the Greek thinkers saw ordinary work, especially manual labour, as relegating human beings to the animal level, the Bible sees all work as distinguishing human beings from animals and elevating them to a place of dignity."[15]

---

13. Begbie made these remarks in a 1996 course entitled Christian Theology offered in 1996 through the Cambridge Theological Federation.

14. Keller and Alsdorf, *Every Good Endeavor*, 40.

15. Keller and Alsdorf, *Every Good Endeavor*, 36.

Keller's engagement with Greek thought will be revisited later, but this particular chapter holds limited relevance for this study. Its primary function is to prepare readers of *Endeavor* for the positive theology of work that follows. The discussion notably parallels themes we have already encountered in Higginson's work.

Theme 3: Soteriology and Idolatry

Drawing from Ferry, Keller emphasizes that everyone operates with a form of soteriology, whether religious or philosophical. He uses this concept to challenge readers, asserting that faith and work cannot always coexist harmoniously;[16] there are moments when they compete for the same ultimate goal. Recognizing that one of the primary challenges in the Faith and Work movement is the absence of effective "connectors," Keller undertakes the task of bridging these two domains. His chosen bridge is the concept of soteriology, which serves as the common currency to integrate faith and work.

With soteriology established as common ground, Keller introduces the concept of idolatry, revitalizing a term often associated with antiquated contexts and making it relevant for contemporary readers. Drawing on a quote from Luther, Keller observes: "Luther argues that when we fail to believe that God accepts us fully in Christ, and look to some other way to justify or prove ourselves, we commit idolatry."[17] Keller makes it clear that idolatry is a pervasive and powerful problem.[18] This, in Keller's view, is the central crisis facing Christians in the workplace. Building on the concept of worldview, he argues: "Modern societies turned away from the authorities of religion and tradition, and replace them with the authorities of reason and individual freedom."[19] With this clarity in hand,

---

16. Keller begins his chapter "Work Reveals Our Idols" with a story that effectively sets the stage for the ideas he later unpacks. He then addresses the relative unfamiliarity of the term *idol*, linking it to the biblical context of the Ten Commandments. This provides a foundation for his argument. Keller introduces his first reference to Ferry's discussion on salvation, found in the introduction (pp. 3–12), observing, "Ferry, himself a nonbeliever in God, likewise argues that everyone seeks 'some way to face like with confidence, and death without fear and regret.' All of us look to something to assure ourselves we have spent our lives well. . . . Whatever it is we seek, Ferry says, it is a form of salvation" (Keller and Alsdorf, *Every Good Endeavor*, 128).

17. Keller and Alsdorf, *Every Good Endeavor*, 129.
18. Keller and Alsdorf, *Every Good Endeavor*, 130.
19. Keller and Alsdorf, *Every Good Endeavor*, 133.

it is valuable to move from a review of *Endeavor* to an engagement with idolatry across Keller's wider writings.

The concept of idolatry is not only a central theme in *Endeavor* but also a central theme in all of Keller's writing. If anything, the handling of this theme in *Endeavor* is sensitized for those who are just being introduced to the concept. The reality is that for Keller, idolatry is not just a significant problem; it is the only problem. This is a bold claim and, therefore, important to substantiate. Fortunately, Keller has articulated his underlying theological views in *Shaped by the Gospel*.[20] This book provides an explanation of his methodology rather than being the fruit of its application.

Regarding the importance of idolatry, we read: "One of the most important biblical and practical ways to help people come to see how they fail to believe the gospel is by instructing them on the nature of idolatry."[21] There are two elements to this quote. The first is the centrality of idolatry. The second, which is valuable for responding to Keller, is the conviction that instruction serves as the active illuminator. To use a loaded term, there is a rational pathway that can guide us out of difficulty. We will continue to build on this response in the following section.

On Keller's interpretation of Luther as foundational, he writes:

> Luther's teaching is this: Anything we look to more than we look to Christ for our sense of acceptability, joy, significance, hope, and security is by definition our god—something we adore, serve, and rely on with our whole life and heart. In general, idols can be good things (family, achievement, work and career, romance, talent, etc.—even gospel ministry) that we turn into ultimate things to give us the significance and joy we need. Then they drive us to ground because we must have them. A sure sign of the presence of idolatry is inordinate anxiety, anger, or discouragement when our idols are thwarted . . . Luther also concludes from his study of the commandments that we never break one of the commandments unless we are also breaking the first. We do not lie, commit adultery, or steal unless we first

---

20. Another source that illustrates the pervasiveness of the idolatry model is Keller's commentary on the book of Romans. In the appendix, he provides a list of twenty contemporary idolatries. Here are the prefixes he uses: Power, Approval, Comfort, Image, Control, Helping, Dependence, Independence, Work, Achievement, Materialism, Religion, Individual, Irreligion, Racial/Cultural, Relationship, Belonging, Family, Suffering, Ideology (Keller, *Romans 1–7*, 191–92).

21. Keller, *Shaped by the Gospel*, 126.

make something else more fundamental to our hope and joy and identity than God.[22]

The extended reference to Keller above is justified, as idolatry is a pivotal concept in his theology. It is crucial to understand how he has developed this idea from a perceived commitment to his Reformed roots. The centrality of idolatry for Keller is underscored by Campbell, who states: "For Keller, idolatry is not simply one expression of sin, but the root out of which every sin arises."[23]

Idolatry Is Binary

First, it is important to understand that, for Keller, idolatry is binary: we either score a 0 or a 1. This perspective is supported by his conclusion to the discussion cited earlier: "So if the root of every sin is idolatry, and idolatry is a failure to look to Jesus for our salvation and justification, the root of every sin is a failure to believe that gospel message of Jesus, and Jesus alone, is our justification, righteousness, and redemption."[24] Here, the limitations of Keller's reduced concept of worldview begin to emerge. The core issue with Keller's line of reasoning is precisely that—it relies too heavily on reasoning. It appears as though Keller has adopted a framework rooted in the concepts of reason and freedom, suggesting that idolatry is merely the result of a reversible decision or action. This perspective oversimplifies idolatry, portraying it as something we can abandon as easily as we might discard a bad habit.

It is easy to see how this is possible when it is introduced through a reference to the Ten Commandments. To be fair, Keller's position does offer recognition that the type of influence is complex (*"Idolatry has power over our action because it has power over our hearts."*)[25] However,

22. Keller, *Shaped by the Gospel*, 127. Gay supports this conclusion on Keller. "In other words, the unregenerate are seeking their sense of self-worth in some experience, job, possession, whatever. Keller, latching onto that desire tries to make sure that his hearers know they will never get that self-worth by pursuing such ends. But if they are prepared to receive the sense of self-esteem or happiness that is offered them in Jesus, they will get it. That, for Keller, is what regeneration and conversion are all about. Tragic" (Gay, *Case of Mistaken Identity*, 57).

23. Campbell, "Keller on 'Rebranding,'" 32. Campbell's thesis is that Keller aims to shift his readers away from viewing sin merely as the act of breaking divine rules, and instead to understand it as anything we use to replace God ("Keller on 'Rebranding,'" 28).

24. Keller, *Shaped by the Gospel*, 127.

25. Keller and Alsdorf, *Every Good Endeavor*, 130.

the recognition is not enough. Keller's hermeneutic fails to bridge the gap between the two horizons and the challenge is thrown back to the conscience of the Christian.[26]

Individualism as Idolatry

Having explored the complex and varied path to individualism in chapter 3, Keller's simplified view stands in stark contrast. For Keller, individualism is categorized under the broader concept of idolatry. He begins with a promising engagement, drawing on Ferry to highlight the modern tendency to absolutize the individual:[27] "Modern societies no longer saw the world as containing binding moral norms of truth to which all people must submit. Rather, they insisted that there was no standard higher than the right of the individual to choose the life he or she wanted to live." However, the complexity of this issue is quickly pared down as Keller connects this shift to the replacement of God: "In other words, the human self had replaced God."[28] This replacement, by definition, is labeled idolatry. By extension, work in the modern world becomes a potential replacement for God, particularly as a vehicle for self-expression. Keller asserts: "So the modern idol of individualism has tended to raise work from being a good thing to being nearly a form *of salvation*."[29] The semantics of this point need further discussion.

In unpacking the above statement, we are able to map Keller's diagnosis and cure for idolatry in contemporary society:

- Individualism is an idol.

- Individualism has raised work from performing a good function to performing a soteriological function.

---

26. The role of Christian conscience can be seen in the following: "Christians seeking to work faithfully and well must discern the shape of the idols functioning in their professions and industries so as to both affirm the beneficial aspects and offset the excesses and distortions" (Keller and Alsdorf, *Every Good Endeavor*, 135).

Keller's position is recognized in the comment of Michael Horton. "Keller rightly emphasizes that idolatry is the common denominator of these sins. Yes, the first work that needs to be done here is penetrating and soul-searching 'first use' of the law—to expose our sin and show our need for Christ. The law reveals our idolatry, and the gospel proclaims freedom from its condemnation and power" (Horton, "Reflections," 89).

27. Keller and Alsdorf, *Every Good Endeavor*, 138.
28. Keller and Alsdorf, *Every Good Endeavor*, 138.
29. Keller and Alsdorf, *Every Good Endeavor*, 139.

- Understanding the above is the key to preventing individualism and the subsequent soteriological nature of work.

There is much to engage with here. Starting with individualism, it is clear that Keller has relied on Ferry to help formulate his position. However, Ferry's insights are not consistent with Keller's conclusions, leading us to conclude that Keller has misinterpreted him. Ferry discusses a paradigm or view of reality that extends far beyond individual will. For Ferry, individualism represents the global transition of the self to the center of reality. He is not referring to a conscious individual experience or choice. Instead, for Ferry, this paradigm predetermines our actions through "the concealed and unconscious logic which imprisons us without our knowledge."[30] The relationship between the conscious and the unconscious is where Ferry and Keller diverge. This is an important distinction that we will continue to explore in this chapter.

Take the analogy of a flooded house. Water has an ability to permeate everything. It seeps into the motors of electrical appliances, infiltrates plug sockets, and travels through conduits. It carries dirt that permanently stains carpets. Much of the damage goes unseen. Ferry understands this well; Keller, less so.

On this point, Gunton and Keller come head-to-head. While this will be primarily explored in the following chapter, it is worth recalling Gunton's[31] lament about the church as "an institution mediating grace to the individual rather than a community formed on the analogy of the Trinity's interpersonal relationships." Gunton's argument is that individualism has permeated our theology, and it will take more than a mere articulation of a worldview to disempower it. Simply put, individualism is beyond the power of the individual. Keller does not recognize this, and we have reason to be disappointed. His reading of Ferry could have led him there. From Ferry, we find, "Today's world of globalised capital places all human activities in a state of perpetual and unending competition, history is moving beyond the will of men."[32] A failure to acknowledge Ferry's critique is significant and warrants a separate discussion below.

Keller argues that individualism is responsible for elevating work to a soteriology. While there is some validity to this, it must be balanced with context. For example, consider the technological changes outlined by

---

30. Ferry, *Brief History*, 203.
31. Gunton, *Promise*, 51.
32. Ferry, *Brief History*, 206.

Markovits, which have led to workforce polarization and emphasized the importance of intellectual capital. These are structural realities that impact the nature of work. Keller views the overworked executive as idolatrous and overlooks the time pressures faced by elite knowledge workers.

Race and Progress as Idolatry

The pervasiveness of the idolatry model for Keller has been introduced above. Engaging with all the forms of idolatry he lists would be tedious. However, two forms worth singling out in this context are "race" and "progress." "Race" is critical to Keller's context and presents an important opportunity to affirm diversity (Gunton's particularity). We are looking for evidence that Keller has a theology of identity that supports particularity. Unfortunately, there is little to be found. Keller's treatment of this issue is superficial, making it difficult to discern what underlies his perspective. "The idolatries of more traditional places and cultures also affect our work. The idol of race can mean that many businesses are close to people and ideas from culturally and racially different backgrounds—to the overall detriment of the company's competitiveness and the community's health."[33]

Progress is a familiar topic, particularly in relation to Rosa's theory of dynamic stabilization: the idea that Western capitalism requires growth to remain stable. Rosa argues that capitalism, in its current form, cannot exist without growth. While Keller engages with capitalism, he does not appear to make the same connection between progress and stabilization. This is evident in two specific references.

First, he frames progress as an ideal without linking it to economic mechanisms: "The modern value of 'reason' includes several elements. One is the ideal of progress."[34] Second, he argues that capitalism has become an idol: "modern capitalism is no longer simply a useful instrument for the distribution of goods and services, but has become a near-absolute idolatry."[35] Here, we assume that Keller is addressing certain behaviors within capitalism rather than capitalist principles themselves. The assumption is that the heteronomous decisions of a centralized economy are far more susceptible to idolatry than those of a command economy.

---

33. Keller and Alsdorf, *Every Good Endeavor*, 136.
34. Keller and Alsdorf, *Every Good Endeavor*, 137.
35. Keller and Alsdorf, *Every Good Endeavor*, 143.

Reviewing Keller's narrow application of idolatry and noting the lack of clarity in certain aspects of his engagement highlights the need for a more detailed examination of his critique of social structures. This call for critical engagement was introduced in chapter 3 and subsequently applied to the Faith and Work movement in chapter 4. It began with a reference to Taylor and the pervasiveness of a "curious blindness" to the contemporary understanding of the individual. As Taylor[36] observes: "The mistake of moderns is to take this understanding of the individual so much for granted that it is taken to be our first-off self-understanding." This will be the focus of the following sections, where we will examine Keller's strong reliance on Cartesian thinking alongside a noticeable lack of complexity and critical engagement.

THE CARTESIAN CONVERSION: KELLER'S CONTRADICTION

A hypothesis of this study is that Christian writing related to work tends to focus on evangelism and ethics. Here, the writer examines how this classification applies to Keller, particularly in *Endeavor*. Additionally, he highlights the contradiction at the center of Keller's theology.

Keller's introductory pages reference vocation; however, this message is inconsistent with the content that follows, which is more clearly centered on evangelism and ethics. The two concepts are closely related in Keller's idolatry model. When combined with the study's chapter on the journey from Augustine to Adidas, a more accurate summary for Keller is the notion of a "Cartesian conversion." This term reflects Keller's conviction that rational, autonomous thinking leads to the awakening of the conscience and behavioral modification. We can summarize this process as follows: changed thinking → changed behavior → changed impact. The thinking is almost utilitarian, where changed behavior leads to changed impact, which is the ultimate goal. Of course, these two terms can be substituted with ethics (behavior) and impact (evangelism).

This position is clearly articulated by Keller: "This is because biblical Christian faith gives us significant resources not present in other worldviews, which, if lived out, will differentiate believers in the workplace."[37] He further addresses market plurality, stating, "But contemporary

---

36. Taylor, *Modern Social Imaginaries*, 64.
37. Keller and Alsdorf, *Every Good Endeavor*, 209.

capitalism increasingly has the power to eliminate the intimacy and accountability of human relationships. So, in the marketplace, as in every field, there is an urgent need for those with a powerful compass."[38]

Beyond *Endeavor*, this position finds further validation in *Shaped by the Gospel*, where Keller quotes his friend and peer Don Carson at length:

> It does not take much to think through how the gospel must also transform the business practices and priorities of Christians in commerce, the priorities of young men steeped in indecisive but relentless narcissism, the lonely anguish and often guilty pleasures of single folk who pursue pleasure but who cannot find happiness, the tired despair of those living on the margins, and much more. And this must be done, not by attempting to abstract social principles from the gospel, still less by endless focus on the periphery in a vain effort to sound prophetic, but precisely by preaching and teaching and living out in our churches the glorious gospel of our blessed Redeemer.[39]

There is also a particularly strong link to the Cartesian paradigm found in *The King's Cross*.

"Gospel renewal is a life-changing recovery of the gospel. Personal gospel renewal means the gospel doctrines of sin and grace are actually experienced. Not just known intellectually. This personal renewal includes an awareness and conviction of one's own sin and alienation from God and comes from seeing in ourselves deeper layers of self-justification, unbelief, and self-righteousness than we have ever seen before."[40]

---

38. Keller and Alsdorf, *Every Good Endeavor*, 231.

39. Keller, *Shaped by the Gospel*, 62.

40. Keller, *King's Cross*, 101. The title of "Cartesian conversion" refers to a self-medication in relation to idolatry. We see it referenced again in the commentary on Romans. "What idols could be, or are already jostling for position with my Creator in my heart and life?" (Keller, *Romans 1–7*, 37).

"Sin can only dupe you if you can't see if for what it is, or don't care about what it is" (Keller, *Romans 1–7*, 145).

"We need to realize that we are not to be stoics when it comes to sin: Just say No! Paul is showing us here that sinning comes not so much from a lack of willpower, as from a lack of understanding our position and a lack of reflection and rejoicing" (Keller, *Romans 1–7*, 147).

"We must remember that idols create a 'delusional field' around themselves. We have deified them and inflated them cognitively and emotionally" (Keller, *Romans 1–7*, 195).

"Your life is shaped by whatever preoccupies your mind. The overcoming of sin in our lives begins in our minds; and victory over sin is only ever the result of having minds set on the Spirit" (Keller, *Romans 8–16*, 17).

The Cartesian conversion lies at the heart of the contradiction within Keller's theology. When crudely paraphrased, it could be summarized as: "Saving yourself, from yourself, by yourself!" This highlights the centrality of rationalism and autonomous self-determination in Keller's model. Keller appears unaware of his own reliance on Cartesian principles. Gay makes a similar observation in *A Case of Mistaken Identity*: "In other words, the greatest idol of them all—self—is not only left intact, it is exalted."[41] Having emphatically established the contradictory, the transition is to considering the complex and the critical.

THE ABSENCE OF THE COMPLEX AND THE CRITICAL

Concerns have been raised about the simplicity of Keller's definition and treatment of idolatry. For some readers, it may appear that Keller is equipped with a hammer and sees everything as a nail. These concerns about simplicity echo the findings of chapter 4, which indicate that contemporary Christian writings often fall short in terms of critical engagement. However, these preliminary conclusions do not always reflect Keller's views accurately. The simplicity of his perspective on idolatry is sometimes interspersed with references to a more nuanced understanding of reality. With complexity comes critical engagement. In this section, the writer will attempt to provide a clearer picture of Keller's critique of current social structures, reviewing three of Keller's sources in more detail.

---

41. Gay, *Case of Mistaken Identity*, 74. Gay's quote is best appreciated with the dry British humor of the preceding sentences: "In Keller's model, the unregenerate are silly, but in regeneration they are made sensible; having been previously misguided, mistaken, off course, off target, they are put on the right road; formerly confused, they are straightened out—'reordered'; having been living in a fog, they are brought into sunlight. And it's all about finding the right way to get self-esteem! In other words, the greatest idol of them all self—is not only left intact, it is exalted" (Gay, *A Case of Mistaken Identity*, 74).

Elsewhere, Gay makes a similar point that is worth capturing: "Keller, though he talks of 'saving,' is in fact appealing to the sinner's desire for happiness, self-esteem, self-worth, and telling him he will find them in Christ" (*Case of Mistaken Identity*, 69).

Robert Bellah: Fear of Acknowledging Structures of Power

The very first words in Keller's book *Endeavor* read as follows: "Robert Bellah's landmark book, *Habits of the Heart*, helped many people name the thing that was (and still is) eating away at the cohesiveness of our culture—'expressive individualism.'"[42] Both the words and their positioning are high praise for Bellah, which is not unexpected given the similarities between the two authors. At its core, Bellah et al.'s seminal book on individualism analyzes the American worldview, a subject to which Keller devotes considerable attention. The surprise, however, is that this is the only sentence from Bellah et al. that is referenced.[43] This situation is analogous to discovering a room full of treasure and selecting only a single coin before leaving. It can also be argued that even this one sentence is taken out of context. Is this all Keller could glean from his reading? Is he merely sermonizing by using authorities to make an entrance? Or does Bellah et al.'s critique extend too far for Keller, or at least for his perception of his audience's appetite?

To substantiate such a strong opinion, it is first necessary to review Keller's specific reference to Bellah et al. Following this, an analysis of Bellah et al. and the thread of their argument leading to this conclusion will be conducted. This framework will highlight, first, the omission in Keller's engagement and, second, the questionable hermeneutic employed.

As noted above, Bellah et al.'s opening sentence pins the blame on expressive individualism, and the ten chapters that follow outline its sources, manifestations, and consequences. Keller's singular reference to this book comes from the concluding chapter entitled "Transforming American Culture." For want of a better word, Bellah et al. articulate something of an "antidote" for individualism. The quote reads: "To make a real difference . . . [there] would have to be a reappropriation of the idea

---

42. Keller and Alsdorf, *Every Good Endeavor*, 1.

43. The bibliography only contains selected works of Keller. Selective, but not insignificant, they represent some of his more influential writings and provide a comprehensive exposure to his theology. While both Bellah et al. and Ferry are used to support this text, they are not mentioned in any of the other cited books. Is the subject of faith and work really that different that they are not applicable in other contexts? The likelihood of this is small. Another possibility is that these contributors to Alsdorf are trying to bring a more informed external engagement to Keller.

of vocation or calling, a return to the idea of work as a contribution to the good of all and not merely a means to one's own advancement."[44]

When reviewing the quote in its context, it seems that Keller and Bellah et al. do not have the same understanding of vocation. There is a tendency in Christian writing to frame vocation as an extension of individualism, emphasizing personal gifts and God's calling to the individual. This echoes the core quote of this book regarding Gunton's view of Christianity as focused on the mediation of grace to the individual. Calling and vocation can fall within this framework. One way to determine the underlying meaning is to assess the level of macro engagement in the surrounding texts. Do we observe a narrow focus on the individual, or is there engagement with broader social structures?

What Bellah et al. write about is the latter. Their previous chapters have given a contemporary façade to the familiar concept of alienation: the separation of the means and ends of labor. In the concluding chapter, they discuss a shift away from the individual as the center of the equation. They assert that there is something fundamentally wrong with the structure of power in society. To appreciate this emphasis, we need to draw more from the preceding chapters.

As a start, the very sentence before the one quoted reads: "Reducing the inordinate rewards of ambition and our inordinate fears of ending up as losers would offer the possibility of a greater chance in the meaning of work in our society and all that would go with such a change."[45] Stating the obvious, Bellah et al.'s quote comes with structural conditions attached. We can see early traces of Rosa's argument here, even though the two authors are separated by thirty-four years. Bellah et al.'s book is more critical and radical than Keller suggests. Work needs reform, not simply a readjustment of worldview. The discussion will support this through a broader review of the book.

Bellah et al.'s purpose is sociological. They position their study as a follow-up to Alexis de Tocqueville's *Democracy in America*, written in the

---

44. Bellah et al., *Habits of the Heart*, 287–88.

45. Bellah et al., *Habits of the Heart*, 287. Bellah et al. are critical of the notion of the career as something that has served to de-value work satisfaction. "What the new idea of middle class meant to individuals was summed up in another new term that only gained currency in the middle and later nineteenth century: career, in the sense of 'a course of professional life or employment, that offers advancement or honor.' Profession is an old word, but it took on new meanings when it was disconnected with the idea of a 'calling' and came to express the new conception of a career" (Bellah et al., *Habits of the Heart*, 119).

1830s. Bellah et al. recount how de Tocqueville was the first to identify individualism as a condition that would progressively isolate Americans and eventually undermine the conditions of freedom.[46] This aligns with Keller's opening sentences. Bellah et al.'s project expands on this notion, arguing that this very idea of freedom is unsustainable and undermines the fabric of society.[47]

Bellah et al.'s argument coalesces in the sixth chapter, where he summarizes the Enlightenment roots of individualism. Here, we observe strong parallels to Taylor and Gunton, with a key role assigned to Locke and the priority of the individual. "The essence of the Lockean position is an almost ontological individualism. The individual is prior to society, which comes into existence only through the voluntary contract of individuals trying to maximize their own self-interest."[48] We are already familiar with this notion of priority. Bellah et al. further develops the argument by layering in the uncertainty and ambiguity that manifest through social norms. "Middle-class individuals are thus motivated to enter a highly autonomous and demanding quest for achievement and are left with no standard against which achievement is to be measured except the income and consumption levels of their neighbours, exhibiting anew the clash between autonomy and conformity that seems to be the fate of American individualism."[49]

The above text presents a broader sociological observation that Bellah et al. translate into a work context, bringing the discussion closer to their understanding of vocation. "We insist, perhaps more than ever before, on finding our true selves independent of any cultural or social influence, being responsible to that self alone, and making its fulfilment the very meaning of our lives. Yet we spend much of our time navigating through immense and bureaucratic structures—multiversities, corporations, government agencies—manipulating and being manipulated by others."[50]

In conclusion, there is some acknowledgment of overlap between Keller and Bellah et al. However, this overlap is insufficient to support Keller's reference. Bellah et al.'s notion of vocation rests on a social critique that Keller does not engage with. For example, in addition to a superficial handling of social structures, there is no mention of gender or

---

46. Bellah et al., *Habits of the Heart*, viii.
47. Bellah et al., *Habits of the Heart*, 143.
48. Bellah et al., *Habits of the Heart*, 143.
49. Bellah et al., *Habits of the Heart*, 149.
50. Bellah et al., *Habits of the Heart*, 150.

race issues in Keller's book. After all, these, like materialism, are simply other manifestations of individualism: a blindness to particularity. In contrast, Bellah et al. write, "For all the lip service given to respect for cultural differences, Americans seem to lack the resources to think about the relationship between groups that are culturally, socially, or economically quite different."[51]

This quote leads to the final point, which is more significant than merely demonstrating a poor fit between Bellah et al. and Keller. Ignorance or caution may be potential reasons for Keller's omission. Bellah et al. present their own perspective, to which they refer repeatedly. Avoidance appears to be a condition commonly found among North Americans, not just theologians. Bellah et al. state: "A conception of society as a whole composed of widely different, but interdependent, groups might generate a language of the common good that could adjudicate between conflicting wants and interests, thus taking the pressure off the overstrained logic of individual rights. But such a conception would require coming to terms with the invisible complexity that Americans prefer to avoid."[52] If only one reference to Bellah et al. is necessary, this should be it. Keller's intention has been to pull back the curtain on the true nature of society. In this task, he has not come close to Bellah et al.

Luc Ferry

Luc Ferry, a contemporary French philosopher, explored key ideas in his 2011 work *Brief History of Thought*, which aims to "give an account of everything that I consider to be truly indispensable in the history of thought."[53] An apt counterpart for Keller, Ferry addresses an audience with a general interest in philosophy and its practical application to life. He asserts: "There is in philosophy the wherewithal to conquer the fears which can paralyze us in life, and it is an error to believe that modern psychology, for example, can substitute for this."[54] Ferry is referenced seven times in *Endeavor*, with these references falling into distinct groupings. Notably, Ferry has been instrumental in helping Keller articulate the contemporary worldview—a connection that is both clear and straightforward.

51. Bellah et al., *Habits of the Heart*, 206.
52. Bellah et al., *Habits of the Heart*, 207.
53. Ferry, *Brief History*, xii.
54. Ferry, *Brief History*, xiv.

However, there are instances where the relationship with Ferry is less clear. Ferry introduces a conflicting message on Greek influence that requires further discussion. In adopting this view, Keller's position drifts further apart from that of Gunton. There is also evidence of a selective reading of Ferry. As noted in Keller's reading of Bellah et al., Ferry offers a contemporary critique that either goes unrecognized by Keller or is consciously omitted. As argued in chapter 4, this lack of critique ultimately weakens his position.

Questions on Greek Influence

Ferry devotes two chapters to Greek influence: the first addresses the dominant emergence of Greek thinking, while the second discusses what he calls "The Victory of Christianity over Greek Philosophy."[55] This position contradicts the Gunton/Taylor view of Greek influence and appears to create a contradiction in Keller's argument.

Ferry asserts that "Christian thought gained the upper hand over Greek thought and dominated Europe until the Renaissance."[56] He not only acknowledges this "upper hand" but also considers it central to the history of thought. While not a Christian himself, Ferry makes a notable effort to provide a fair account of Christianity. However, he falls short in linking a worldview to the concept of salvation discussed earlier. Thus, when he describes Christianity as offering an alternative *telos*, this must be interpreted as a victory.

As established earlier in chapter 2, Gunton's position is radically different. He contends that the Christian gospel has been constrained and fundamentally derailed by the influence of Greek dualism. Keller addresses this in his chapter, "A New Compass for Work." Drawing from Ferry, he states, "Before Christianity, both Western and Eastern cultures conceived of salvation as entrance into an impersonal and anonymous state. There was no concept that we came from divine love and could return to experience it. But Christianity understood ultimate reality to be rooted in a personal God who created out of love."[57]

Keller makes a second reference to Greek influence, this time guided by Hardy in his chapter on "The Dignity of Work." While Ferry's

---

55. Ferry, *Brief History*, 17–92.
56. Ferry, *Brief History*, 58.
57. Keller and Alsdorf, *Every Good Endeavor*, 210.

message conveyed a sense of Greek defeat by the paradigms of Christianity, Keller cites a different message of victory from Hardy.[58] Questioning the consistency between these two messages is not pedantic; rather, it helps determine whether the dialogue with Greek influence represents a serious attempt at redaction or is merely an embellishment on a predetermined point.

In Keller's chapter on "The Dignity of Work," we encounter references to both Plato and Epictetus. "Plato in his dialogue Phaedo argues that being in the body distorts and hampers the soul in the quest for the truth. In this life, the person who develops spiritual insight and purity must do so by ignoring the body as much as possible. . . . To be most human was to be the least involved and the least invested in the material world."[59] Keller believes that this view has too much influence in contemporary perceptions and feels compelled to argue against it.[60] Against a Platonized legacy, he contends that work has dignity, a view affirmed by the Christian gospel. "We are both body and soul, and the biblical ideal of shalom includes both physical thriving as well as spiritual."[61]

Are these contradictory views? The answer is both yes and no. Yes, Ferry is correct that Christianity offered a soteriological alternative. However, he views Christianity from only one perspective and overlooks the impact of Greek thought on Christian doctrine. Keller does not address these two views, so his position remains unclear. In short, this appears to be an important subject that has been insufficiently engaged. If Greek influence held significant weight in Keller's intellectual arsenal, he would have identified the discrepancy or at least helped the reader understand the very different usages. This point is crucial when considering the centrality of Greek influence on Gunton's thought. If Keller perceives any negative impact of Greek philosophy on Christianity, he does not express it in any way.

---

58. This latter message is more consistent with Keller's reference to Greek thought elsewhere. This is seen in his commentary on Romans: "In Greek thought, the physical was bad, to be rejected and hopefully one day left behind; the spiritual was good, to be embraced" (Keller, *Romans 8–16*, 21).

59. Keller and Alsdorf, *Every Good Endeavor*, 33.

60. Keller quotes Hardy as saying, "'Greek attitude toward work and its place in human life was largely preserved in both the thought and practice of the Christian church' through the centuries, and still holds a great deal of influence today in our culture. What has come down to us is a set of persuasive ideas" (Hardy, *Fabric of This World*, 16, quoted in Keller and Alsdorf, *Every Good Endeavor*, 34).

61. Keller and Alsdorf, *Every Good Endeavor*, 40.

Complacent Synthesis!

On the cover of Ferry's work, Crawford states, "Ferry does not offer a slack pluralism, or complacent synthesis; rather, he invites us to enter into those arguments."[62] Although directed at Ferry, the term "complacent synthesis" aptly describes the very condition Keller is targeting. Keller's view of idolatry as a good thing that becomes the ultimate thing aligns with this critique. The significance of Crawford's quote lies in the pairing of these words with the concept of arguments; these arguments serve as a countercurrent to complacency. I agree with Crawford that these arguments are evident in Ferry's work, but they are less visible in Keller's. This is not to say that Keller is uncritical; rather, his criticism is perceived as behavioral rather than structural. Ferry delivers strong cautionary messages, emphasizing that contemporary challenges require more than just honest and caring citizens. In contrast, Keller's approach tends toward avoidance. Like the priest and the Levite in the Parable of the Good Samaritan, he passes by on the other side of the road. This represents a strong criticism that needs to be substantiated with specific points.

- In his opening chapters, Keller provides a critique that clearly resonates with the workforce polarity identified by Markovits. "Western societies are increasingly divided between the highly remunerated 'knowledge classes' and the more poorly remunerated 'service sector,' and most of us accept and perpetuate the value judgements that attach to these categories."[63] This polarization is a significant indicator of structural distortions—an issue Keller reduces to a value judgment before moving on.

- To reiterate, the point made here is that Keller encountered strong social and structural insights in Ferry's work but chose not to use them. While various angles could be explored, perhaps the most pertinent is Ferry's notion that society and its trajectory are moving "beyond the will of men."[64] Keller's autonomous ideals are not always realistic.

---

62. Ferry, *Brief History*.
63. Keller and Alsdorf, *Every Good Endeavor*, 34–35.
64. "In this sense, we could say that in today's world of globalized capital which placed human activities in a state of perpetual and unending competition, history is moving beyond the will of men. Competition is becoming not only a form of destiny, but, what is more, there is nothing to suggest that it is moving in the direction of what is better" (Ferry, *Brief History*, 207).

In a book on faith and work, readers reasonably expect an engagement with structural injustice and an acknowledgment of the significant challenges posed by capitalism. Ferry addresses these issues in several places, references Keller would have undoubtedly encountered but ultimately chose not to engage.

- "The difficulty is not so much that globalization supposedly impoverishes the poor in order to engorge the rich, as ecologists and alter-globalists suggest, but that it dispossesses us all of any purchase on history, and divests history itself of all purpose."[65]

- "The modern economy functions like Darwinian natural selection; within the logic of globalized competition, a business which does not 'progress' each day is quite simply doomed to extinction. But this advance has no other end than itself—to stay in the race with the other competitors."[66]

- "Hence the fearsome and incessant development of technology, tethered to and largely financed by economic growth, and the fact that the increase of human power over nature has become completely automatic, uncontrollable and blind, because it everywhere exceeds the conscious will of the individual. And this is, quite simply, the inevitable result of competition."[67]

- "Hence the Enlightenment ideal gives way to a diffuse and multiform anxiety, always ready to focus upon this or that particular threat, in such a way that fear is slowly becoming the characteristic of democratic emotion."[68]

- "However, by smashing all our idols with his hammer, and delivering us—in the guise of clear sightedness—bound and gagged to the world of whatever is the case, Nietzsche's thought serves however unintentionally the incessant flux, the hither and thither of modern capitalism."[69]

There is no evidence that Keller would have held back in protecting his readers from the likes of Nietzsche. Keller has either read Ferry selectively

65. Ferry, *Brief History*, 207.
66. Ferry, *Brief History*, 213.
67. Ferry, *Brief History*, 213.
68. Ferry, *Brief History*, 216.
69. Ferry, *Brief History*, 217.

or failed to engage with the important critiques outlined above. While the former seems more plausible, this remains speculative. Regardless, it constitutes a notable omission on Keller's part.

James K. Smith

The final source of Keller to engage with is James K. Smith. Smith's insights into identity were key to the opening chapter of this book, particularly his assertion that identity choices are becoming far less rational than traditionally assumed. This perspective draws heavily on Taylor's *Modern Social Imaginaries*. Smith not only appreciates Taylor's work but also seeks to build on it, integrating a more explicitly soteriological lens to complement Taylor's sociological framework.[70]

The reference to Smith in *Endeavor* is easy to overlook, as it is tucked away in note 149. However, the depth and substance of the comments in this note make it deserving of closer attention. Smith's importance lies in his intellectual proximity to Gunton. While the two scholars did not engage directly, both sought to translate Charles Taylor's insights into a contemporary theological context, bridging sociological analysis with theological reflection.

The argument here is that Keller has misread Smith, or perhaps not read him at all. This section leans toward the latter. Keller's objective in using Smith was to support the centrality of a worldview. However, the two writers could not be further apart. They differ on both the extent of market influence on identity and the nature of that influence. Smith presents a significantly more critical view of the market and its influence, emphasizing the non-cognitive. This contrasts with Keller, who, as discussed, has an approach to "identify in order to disarm" (my words, not Keller's). This is achieved by empowering people through theological vision. "Those who are empowered by the theological vision do not simply stand against the mainstream impulses of the culture but take the initiative both to understand and speak to that culture from the framework of the Scriptures."[71] Smith opposes this, arguing that the shaping of our fundamental wants and desires often occurs through subconscious messages.[72]

---

70. Smith's appreciation for Taylor is best witnessed through his book *How Not to Be Secular*, a commentary on Taylor's *Secular Age*.

71. Lints, *Fabric of Theology*, 315–16, quoted in Keller, *Shaped by the Gospel*, 14.

72. Smith, *Desiring the Kingdom*, 205.

It is essential to begin by outlining Keller's position before addressing the inconsistencies with Smith. What is the purpose of this engagement? The goal is to gain sufficient insight into Smith's perspective to challenge Keller on two fronts: his Cartesian bias and his insufficient critique of the market.

This analysis begins with a quote from note 149, with added emphasis to facilitate engagement.

> [Smith] argues that most people conceive of "worldview" today in terms that are too cognitive. *He argues that your worldview is not merely a set of doctrinal and philosophical beliefs, which are completely formed by reason and information.* It also compromises a set of hopes and loves—"tacit" knowledge and heart attitudes—which are not all adopted consciously and deliberately. Worldview formation then does not happen through argument or mainly through politics. Rather, it is the result of the narratives we embrace, especially those that give us a compelling and desirable picture of human flourishing that captures our heart and imagination. Those narratives are presented to us not only (or even mainly) in the classrooms but through the stories we see, hear and read from various cultural sources.[73]

Keller's summary of Smith here is diluted but reasonable. The phrase "not merely" downplays Smith's emphasis on the non-cognitive narratives that surround us. However, this is not the main reason for critiquing Keller. The critique lies in the disconnect between Keller's own methodology and what he has referenced from Smith. It is Smith's distinction between non-cognitive and cognitive narratives that is at play. Throughout this chapter, we have highlighted a Cartesian bias in Keller: the conviction that a rational grasp of reality serves as the antidote to idolatry. In other words, people can be empowered through rational analysis. Furthermore, the writer has criticized the simplicity of Keller's critique as a one-size-fits-all analysis of contemporary life. At the core of Smith's book is a rebuttal of the idea that identity can be constructed rationally and of the oversimplification of market influence. Smith contends that identities are caught, not taught.[74]

---

73. Keller and Alsdorf, *Every Good Endeavor*, 286n149 (emphasis added).

74. "An education, then, is a constellation of practices, rituals, and routines that inculcates a particular vision of the good life by inscribing of infusing that vision onto the heart (the gut) by means of material, embodied practices" (Smith, *Desiring the Kingdom*, 209).

Smith argues that, regardless of the market's message, it is a much more convincing teacher than Keller—not because of the message itself, but due to the manner in which it is delivered. "Because our hearts are oriented primarily by desire, by what we love, and because those desires are shaped and moulded by habit-forming practices in which we participate, it is the rituals and practices of the mall—the liturgies of mall and market—that shape our imagination and how we orient ourselves to the world."[75]

Keller and Smith share common ground on many points regarding the market's negative influence and the belief in the transformative power of education. However, their approaches to education diverge significantly. For Smith, education is liturgical rather than purely intellectual. This contrast is clear, as Smith emphasizes throughout his work. He articulates this perspective in the following quote: "It's not so much that we're intellectually convinced and then muster the willpower to pursue what we ought; rather, at a precognitive level, we are attracted to a vision of the good life that has been painted for us in stories and myths, images and icons."[76]

---

75. Smith, *Desiring the Kingdom*, 25. The same sentiment expressed in other words: "We are what we love, and our love is shaped, primed, and aimed by liturgical practices that take hold of our gut and aim out heart to certain ends" (Smith, *Desiring the Kingdom*, 40).

76. Smith, *Desiring the Kingdom*, 54. Smith's engagement with the market is framed through the narrative of the mall. For Smith, the mall serves as the market's place of worship, where we see the manifestation of the market's character and values. Understanding this context makes the references to the mall easier to grasp.

The purpose of citing multiple Smith references below is to emphasize that Keller cannot be excused for missing the point unless he was blind to it. Smith, of course, is not beyond critique; objections can be raised against some of these perspectives. However, his critique of the market and his recognition of the non-cognitive (or, to align more closely with Gunton, the "pre-cognitive") positions us in a much stronger place than Keller does.

"The pedagogy of the mall does not primarily take hold of the head so to speak; it aims for the heart, for our guts, our kardia" (Smith, *Desiring the Kingdom*, 24).

"We are what we love, and our love is shaped, primed, and aimed by liturgical practices that take hold of our gut and aim our heart to certain ends" (Smith, *Desiring the Kingdom*, 40).

"I'm suggesting that the sort of orientation that has commonly been described as a 'worldview' is actually, for the most part, operative on this nonconscious level" (Smith, *Desiring the Kingdom*, 63).

"Several times I have suggested that the model of the human person as lover shifts the centre of gravity of human identity away from fixation on thinking, ideas, and doctrines and locates it lower, as it were, in the region of our effective, nonconscious operations" (Smith, *Desiring the Kingdom*, 63).

The conclusion drawn from note 149 is highly significant. Keller's problematic reading of Smith highlights two key issues:

1. It provides additional evidence that Keller is avoiding a more critical and nuanced engagement with contemporary culture.

2. It underscores the severe limitations of his rational, overly intellectualized approach to faith and work.

The model presented by Keller is aptly described as a "Cartesian conversion," reflecting his reliance on reason and individual autonomy as the primary means of transformation.

Prozac/Adidas and Other Idolatry: Concluding Comments and Critique

It is important to draw some preliminary conclusions about Keller. In *Shaped by the Gospel*, there is a chapter on Keller written by Horton. Horton's criticism in this chapter is somewhat measured but still present. Keller addresses one of the key points: "One of Horton's most important criticisms to reflect on is that some of my rhetoric may be 'giving folks the impression that every rough patch in their lives can be solved simply by a better grasp of the gospel.'"[77] Keller disagrees with Horton, believing that his theology presents a healthy balance of realized and unrealized eschatology. This leaves us wondering where Prozac fits into Keller's theological framework. If the Greek influence was misguided and materiality does matter, then there are conditions beyond our control that can impact our identity and overall mental health. Identity choices are much less rational than Keller believes. At some point, even Keller's preaching may not be sufficient. Prozac has a place.

"It's not so much that we're intellectually convinced and then muster the willpower to pursue what we ought; rather, at precognitive level, we are attracted to a vision of the good life that has been painted for us in stories and myths, images and icons. It is not primarily our minds that are captivated but rather our imaginations that are capture" (Smith, *Desiring the Kingdom*, 54).
On the critique of a more cognitive bias:
"In particular, both these models remain focused on the cognitive aspect of our nature and tend to reduce us to that aspect (whether in terms of thoughts or beliefs). As a result, significant part of who we are—in particular, our non-cognitive ways of being-in-the-world that are more closely tethered to our embodiment or animality—tend to drop off the radar or are treated as non-essential" (Smith, *Desiring the Kingdom*, 46).

77. Keller, *Shaped by the Gospel*, 94.

Chapter 3 noted that there is room for a stronger social and structural analysis in the theological writings on faith and work. Unfortunately, Keller's work falls short compared to his peers, making this gap even larger. The limited engagement by Keller with his peers is notable. In his use of Miller, the review primarily focuses on Miller's historical overview with little else. We know Keller has read some of Volf, as evidenced by a reference in *Shaped by the Gospel*, but there is no mention of an important work like *Work in the Spirit*. The examples cited in this section demonstrate that Keller had ample opportunity to engage more critically with social structures—opportunities he appears to have avoided.

The reasoning behind Keller's unusual pairing of broad referencing with very shallow engagement is left to speculation. Campbell's[78] hypothesis suggests that Keller enjoys "trawling contemporary culture to expose its emptiness." This implies that the engagements lack integrity and merely serve to highlight the emptiness of the gospel's alternatives. This characterization presents a bleaker view of Keller and is difficult to uphold without more detailed support. For the purposes of this discussion, it is sufficient to acknowledge the omission and leave the cause to speculation.

At this point, the discussion needs to transition away from Keller's sources and toward his theology, which is the fuel that drives his public theology. The aim is to provide a qualitative framing that explores the nature of Keller's engagement with core doctrines. The purpose here is not to conduct an exhaustive review of Keller's systematic theology but to selectively engage with those doctrines that are relevant to this study.

EXPLICIT AND IMPLICIT REFERENCES TO THE TRINITY

The selected doctrinal topics below fall under the umbrella of explicit and implicit references to the Trinity. A review of Gunton reveals how his doctrine of the Trinity informs and is informed by the doctrines of revelation, creation, *imago Dei*, incarnation, atonement, mediation, and particularity. Unlike Gunton, Keller's purpose is not to articulate Christian doctrine. However, we can assess his doctrine of the Trinity by examining how it informs his soteriology and influences his public theology.

---

78. Campbell, "Keller on 'Rebranding,'" 44.

The starting point is the explicit references to the Trinity, most clearly seen in the *imago Dei*.

Imago Dei: For Keller the Individual Is Prior to Community

Gunton's lament addresses the influence of Greek thinking on the doctrine of the *imago Dei*. The issue is not merely its analogous application in theology; rather, the nature of the analogy closely resembles Platonic forms. As a result of this influence, the image becomes an attribute—something we can possess as individuals.

Keller's interpretation aligns with the attribution view that Gunton critiques. By considering these attributes as representative of the image, the connection between the image and work and creativity becomes central in *Endeavor*. Essentially, Keller suggests that we reflect God's identity through our work. This is an attribute that we can possess as individuals.

The following three references support this:

- "It was part of God's perfect design for human life, because we are made in God's image, and part of his glory and happiness is that he works, as does the Son of God, who said, 'My Father is always at his work to this very day, and I too am working' (John 5:17)."[79]
- "If we are to be God's image-bearers with regard to creation, then we will carry on his pattern of work."[80]
- "God is Creator of the world, and our work mirrors his creative work when we create culture that conforms to his will and vision for human beings—when it matches up with the biblical story line."[81]

Elsewhere we see the attribute of suffering as a sign of likeness: "As we bear the family likeness of suffering, we become more and more like the Son, and our Father, in our characters and attitudes. This is how the Christian looks at persecution and counts it as a privilege.... We get to be like him!"[82] Like the above, this is another non-relational reference. That

---

79. Keller and Alsdorf, *Every Good Endeavor*, 23.
80. Keller and Alsdorf, *Every Good Endeavor*, 47.
81. Keller and Alsdorf, *Every Good Endeavor*, 186.
82. Keller, *Romans 8–16*, 33. An additional attribute reference that falls outside the "work" or "suffering" reference. "Humans are uniquely made in the image of God, made to relate to him in his world and reflect his nature and goodness to the world" (Keller,

being said, there are some relational references in Keller. Two of these are found in the *King's Cross*. The first is vague and not suitable for drawing conclusions: "If this world was made by a triune God, relationships of love are what life is really all about."[83] The second points more clearly to relationality. Where Gunton would differ is the reference to the dance that we are "made for" as opposed to "made through": "So why would he create us? There's only one answer. He must have created us not to get joy but to give it. He must have created us to invite us into the dance, to say: If you glorify me, if you centre your entire life on me, if you find me beautiful for who I am in myself, then you will step into the dance, which is what you are made for."[84]

Bidwell mounts a lengthy and critical response to Keller's use of the "divine dance" as an explanation for the Trinity.[85] The reader gets the impression that Bidwell has put more thought into it than Keller. While there are clear shortcomings in Keller's analogy, it is important to note that many Trinitarian scholars have utilized Rublev's icon as an illustration without progressing to describe the Trinity as the Divine Dinner. When used in isolation from proper theological engagement, Keller's analogy risks being interpreted in multiple ways. At best, it reflects a shift away from a transactional soteriology toward a relational one. Oddly enough, Bidwell does not address the conditional nature of the dance. The word "if" appears three times in Keller's text, indicating conditions for entering the dance and implying a theology of works.

However, in interpreting Keller's notion of the divine dance, the key point is that the creation of community is ultimately a secondary act or enhancement to the main event: the salvation of the individual. In *Endeavor*, there is a reference to the rejection of a soteriology focused on "mere individuals" as opposed to the notion that God "also wants . . . society." The sentence reads as follows: "We get the sense that God does not want merely more individuals of human species, he also wants the world to be filled with a human society."[86] The deduction here is that

---

Romans 1–7, 28).

83. Keller, *King's Cross*, 9. Another example of a relational reference where a conclusion is unclear can be seen in Romans. "Even the Christian doctrine of God as triune, consisting of three persons who have known and loved one another from all eternity, demonstrates that relationships of love are the building blocks of all reality (Keller and Alsdorf, *Every Good Endeavor*, 210).

84. Keller, *King's Cross*, 10.

85. Bidwell, "Losing the Dance."

86. Keller and Alsdorf, *Every Good Endeavor*, 44.

Keller's soteriology prioritizes the individual over society. This concept is also evident in his commentary on Romans, where the building of community is portrayed as the task of the individual: "Are we creating a community that is the fulfilment of what God had called Old Testament Israel to be? Would a devout Jew look at our church and be aroused to envy, and give the gospel a hearing?"[87]

The conclusion is clear: Keller's position on the logical priority of the individual over the community is significantly different from Gunton's use of being-in-communion. To understand this, Keller's reasoning is speculative; however, it is probable that his doctrine of God is informed by his soteriology. This will be expanded upon below.

Incarnation and a Transactional Atonement

For Trinitarians, the identity of God informs their soteriology. This is evident in Gunton's emphasis on mediation, participation, and particularity. In contrast, the remainder of the Reformed tradition seems to prioritize *a* transactional view of atonement, particularly the movement from the Son to the Father on the cross, which risks overshadowing other relations within the Trinity.

This tendency can be seen as a hallmark of modernist theology, as it begins with the self and works outward. Regardless of its accuracy, the crucial point is that we must examine Keller's soteriology to gain a deeper understanding of his doctrines of God and soteriology, particularly his commitment to a transactional view of atonement. Here, James Torrance directs our attention to Bonhoeffer's diagnosis, arguing that, for Keller, the "What" takes precedence over the "Who."[88]

Gunton's own *Actuality of Atonement* was written earlier in his career, yet the beginnings of his Trinitarian theology are evident. While affirming substitutionary atonement, he strongly criticizes penal substitution as unbalanced. Penal substitution is the form of transactional atonement that Keller subscribes to. "Sin always entails a penalty. Guilt

---

87. Keller, *Romans 8–16*, 91.

88. "He [Bonhoeffer] pleaded for following the biblical pattern of giving priority to the question of who over what and how—that we interpret the atonement and personal faith in terms of the incarnation (the triune God of grace) and not the other way round. The pragmatic problem-centred preoccupation with the question of how in our Western culture can so easily reduce the gospel to a category of means and ends" (Torrance, *Persons in Communion*, 17).

can't be dealt with unless someone pays. The only way God can pardon us and not judge us is to go to the cross and absorb it into himself."[89] Like an accountant balancing the books, sin is a debit that requires a matching credit. There is little or no room for understanding sin as an orientation. The following are further references from Keller regarding the transactional/legal nature of sin:

- "To be 'under sin' is a legal term; we are citizens of sin. It is as though we all have a spiritual passport, which shows our legal citizenship. It is either stamped Under Sin or Under Grace."[90]

- "God does not set his justice aside; he turns it on himself. The cross does not represent a compromise between God's wrath and his love; it does not satisfy each halfway. Rather, it satisfies each fully and in the very same action."[91]

- "To be 'justified' is to be pronounced and treated by God as legally righteous and blameless because of the work of Christ in his life and death."[92]

The implications for the theology of the Trinity are significant. In a transactional theology, Christ's position in the Trinity provides him with "bargaining power"—a pearl of great price rather than the gate of glory! This means that an understanding of the Trinity, Christ's incarnation, original sin, and sin in general is essential. If we do not grasp, for example, that Jesus was not just a good man but the second person of the Trinity, or if we fail to understand what the "wrath of God" entails, it becomes impossible to comprehend what Jesus accomplished on the cross.[93]

The "representative" nature of Christ is articulated in Keller's commentary on Romans under the terminology of "Federal Headship." He writes:

> We are highly individualistic in the west, each man is an island—interconnected, but rising or falling, succeeding or failing according to our own actions and decisions and abilities. . . . The Bible takes a radically different approach—that of human solidarity. . . . The idea of solidarity is that you can have a legitimate

---

89. Keller, *King's Cross*, 101.
90. Keller, *Romans 1–7*, 66.
91. Keller, *Romans 1–7*, 83.
92. Keller, *Romans 8–16*, 51.
93. Keller, *Shaped by the Gospel*, 33.

relationship with a person so that whatever that person achieves or loses, you achieve or lose.[94]

Surprisingly, Keller turns to the concept of covenant rather than to atonement. "The word 'federal' comes from the Latin *foedus*, or 'covenant.' A federal head is a person who, through a covenant relationship, represents or stands in for someone else."[95]

This is Keller's theology at its weakest, and it falls on the logic of priority. In Keller's Christology, there is an *a priori* conception of covenant into which Christ is assumed. This is the route he chooses ahead of the incarnation. In so doing, he reinforces a transactional view of the atonement and downgrades the humanity of Christ as a qualification for the final exam. The participatory nature of the life of Christ is lost on Keller.

Pneumatology and Mediation

By the time the examination shifts to Keller's doctrine of pneumatology and mediation, expectations have significantly diminished. The coverage is predictably sparse. In a model of transactional atonement, there is little room for mediation. The Spirit's role is not to present us "in Christ" to participate in the perichoretic relationship of the Trinity. Instead, in Keller's view, the Spirit's role seems to echo the "extended cognitions" of Frischmann and Selinger. Keller writes, "In other words, we are led to hate the things the Spirit hates (sin) and love the things he loves (Christ). We are thus led by the Spirit."[96] We are compelled to conclude that, for Keller, there is no room for ontological mediation.

A DISCONNECTED HERMENEUTIC

In *Intellect and Action*, Gunton succinctly defines the task of systematic theology as "to examine the coherence of different dogmatic expressions not only with Scripture but with one another."[97] This commitment to coherence is evident in Gunton's focus on epistemology and his attempt to eliminate foundationalism with its *a priori* assumptions. Systematic theology shares this skill with biblical hermeneutics, as scholars bring various

---

94. Keller, *Romans 1–7*, 126.
95. Keller, *Romans 1–7*, 126.
96. Keller, *Romans 8–16*, 27.
97. Gunton, *Intellect and Action*, 12.

horizons to bear on the present. However, this commitment to coherence and logical priority is not a strong area for Keller. While he makes some important connections, ultimately, they are not sufficient. For example, Keller affirms the material but does not conduct further investigations to determine whether other Greek legacies are subconsciously influencing our choices. Additionally, there is no cross-check to ensure that all his references to Greek influence lead to the same conclusion.

While this is not an engagement with Keller's biblical interpretation, it is very much an engagement with his hermeneutic. His use of Scripture illustrates how he employs other sources.

As a preacher, Keller has a deep appreciation for narrative. The best illustration of this is his use of the book of Esther in *Endeavor*. He recounts how Esther uses her position to protect her people. Ultimately, at great risk to herself, Esther confronts the king about his injustice. Keller's application of this passage draws a parallel between Esther and the contemporary businessperson. Predictably, the focus is on ethical behavior, with Esther serving as a type for the contemporary businessperson. Keller identifies selfishness as the core of the message: "Even the most loving, morally beautiful people fall prey to motivations of self-interest, fear, and glory seeking."[98] Esther is the one who overcomes, putting duty before self. Keller phrases this response as follows: "Unless you use your clout, your credentials, and your money in service to the people outside the palace, the palace is a prison."[99]

There are two ways in which the use of this narrative creates dissonance. Firstly, Keller's modern view of the "palace" seems to equate it with the modern corporation. Here, he appears to conflate the corporation with the system in which it operates. If we overlay Esther's story, would it not be a call for courage directed at the whistleblower rather than a call to be selfless? If it were the latter, Keller would do well to note that selfishness is equally problematic in cathedrals as in corporate headquarters. Thomas Cranmer, once a resident of a palace, would have been the first to agree. This interpretation is disappointingly narrow. What about the people inside the palace? Here, Keller could learn from Patrick Lencioni, who opts for a positive teaching on trust rather than the idolatry of selfishness.[100]

---

98. Keller and Alsdorf, *Every Good Endeavor*, 113.
99. Keller and Alsdorf, *Every Good Endeavor*, 119.
100. Lencioni, *Five Dysfunctions*.

The second point of disconnect is Keller's Old Testament bias. In *Endeavor*, his use of the Old Testament is almost exclusive, with minimal reference to the New Testament. Keller appears so focused on the narrative that he neglects to connect all the theological dots. This critique is not new; he has encountered it before from Michael Horton, whose words he was willing to have published alongside his own in *Shaped by the Gospel*. Horton writes:

> Yet here is also my first area of disagreement with Keller. I'm not quite persuaded by his statement that "the narrative approach poses the questions, and the propositional approach supplies the answers." In scripture we find that doctrinal propositions arise out of the narrative itself.... What Keller wishes to overcome is a reductionism that creates a false choice between the personal and global implications of the gospel.[101]

Horton's use of "reductionism" effectively summarizes this chapter's critique of Keller. An initial reading of Keller presents a broader and more engaging discourse, but subsequent revisions reveal a rapid narrowing of scope.

Keller courageously responds to Horton: "I think his critique hits home. He gives me credit for later seeing the ultimate compatibility of biblical theology and systematic theology, but he thinks that at some points I drive too much of a wedge between propositional and the narrative. I think he's right."[102] However, the writer is uncertain whether Keller has fully grasped Horton's argument.

CONCLUSION: ONE SMALL STEP FOR REFORMED THEOLOGY!

Keller now needs to be summarized to allow the following chapter to focus exclusively on the key points of both his theology and Reformed faith and work theology in general. In the opening sections of this chapter, Keller was quoted as being critical of other faith and work authors. He wrote,

> The mainline church understood the relationship of faith to work primarily as an effort to apply just social ethics to capitalism—which was viewed with suspicion. Many conservative evangelicals were by contrast much more individualistic in their

---

101. Horton, "Reflections on Gospel Theology," 80.
102. Keller, *Shaped by the Gospel*, 92.

understanding of faith. They were more positive toward market capitalism and so did not put their reform emphasis there. Instead their greatest concern was the need for personal decision and salvation. Therefore, to be a Christian at work meant primarily to evangelise your coworkers.[103]

The purpose of this section is to evaluate Keller's effectiveness in delivering a theology that extends beyond the paradigms he has established with these words.

Initial remarks on Keller must begin with affirmation. *Endeavor* represents an attempt to bring theology into the public sphere. The establishment of The Center for Faith and Work is central to this effort. Here is a church that has invested considerable resources into engaging and equipping its congregation and the wider church for ministry in the workplace. Although commerce is not an area of expertise for Keller, he has prepared by studying the subject to deliver a resource, in the form of *Endeavor*, to pastors and commercial Christians around the globe. When it comes to assessing a need, Keller is on target.

In summary, Keller's objective was to provide a more holistic response—not just for evangelism, but for the evangelized as well. It is not primarily a guide on the Great Commission, but a book that enables Christians to navigate the different realities of work and faith in a more constructive way. In this sense, he has sought to advance the cause of integration. In the table below, Keller outlines the movement he intends to initiate.

Table 4: Keller's Summary of Theology Shift.[104]

Change From	Change to
1. Individual salvation	The gospel changes everything (hearts, community, and world)
2. Being good	Being saved
3. Cheap grace	Costly grace (awareness of our sin)
4. Heaven is "up there"	Christ will come again—to this earth
5. God is value add to us	In God's providence we should contribute to his work on earth
6. Idols of this world	Living for God

103. Keller and Alsdorf, *Every Good Endeavor*, 267.
104. Source: Keller and Alsdorf, *Every Good Endeavor*, 254.

Change From	Change to
7. Disdain of this world	Engaged in this world
8. "Bowling alone"	Accepting community
9. People matter	Institutions matter
10. Christian superiority	God can work through whomever he wants (common grace)

Yes, Keller has succeeded in creating a more integrated view. It is quite possible that he has put the teaching of faith and work into the hands of more Christians—both pastors and workers—than any other leader or teacher before him. He has not taken an easy path, and his attempt to make the concept of paradigms accessible to contemporary readers is a clever move.

Keller's success has been aided by opportune timing. Globally, there has been a growing trend toward physical and mental health in the workplace. Future scholars may regard this as a paradigm shift driven by the transformation of Taylorism into a knowledge economy. Robin Sharma's *The Monk Who Sold His Ferrari* comes to mind as a book reflecting this epoch. It was published in 1997 and has sold more than three million copies, which is significant for a book that many find disappointing and conflicted. After all, not many people have a Ferrari to sell to fund their newfound asceticism. *Endeavor* essentially appeals to the Christian member of this target market.

While this chapter has criticized his monistic use of the concept of idolatry, he deserves commendation for not shying away from an unpopular term. Other Christian writers have taken an "indirect" route to teach Christian principles without using Christian jargon. We see this in the works of Blanchard, Buford, Lencioni, and movements like the Global Leadership Summit. It is also important to note that since the crash of 2008 and several high-profile ethical disasters, capitalism has had to develop a stronger appetite for critical self-reflection.

In response to the question of whether Keller has been able to move the debate beyond the evangelism of co-workers, the answer is "not much." This chapter has argued that his response aligns closely with existing types of evangelism and ethics. In Keller's case, the purpose of the ethics is essentially to evangelize, which leaves him very close to the position he is criticizing. Simply put, Keller has not gone far enough.

Keller's small step was not the result of a lack of effort or intent. He has ultimately been restricted by our own *a priori* assumptions. Keller is too entrenched in modernity to provide a sufficient critique. It has permeated his theology, thereby limiting its power.

By characterizing Keller's response as a Cartesian conversion, some awareness of individualism is evident; however, the response offered retains the autonomous self at the center of the equation. This core pillar of modernity remains unchallenged.

In engaging with some of Keller's sources, it has been argued that there is insufficient critical engagement with capitalism. This aligns with faith-and-work peers like Volf, who refer to the current state of capitalism as a crisis. Other examples from the writings of Bellah et al., Ferry, and Smith have also been cited. The criticism in Keller is reserved almost entirely for the individual's response to the system, rather than for the system itself. Keller does not share Gunton's appetite for understanding causation. Ironically, Keller writes, "None of us are as detached from our culture or clan as many of us like to think."[105] Regrettably, we must conclude the same of Keller.

Keller's project is grounded in a weak theology. The excessive emphasis on idolatry is one symptom of a narrow and underdeveloped theological perspective. His strong Reformed roots have bequeathed to him a transactional soteriology that primarily engages with ethics and evangelism. While Keller's theology leads him to believe he is protecting the flock, we cannot accuse him of failing to lay down his life for the sheep; rather, he simply does not recognize the other wolves. This review of Keller concludes the preparatory discussions, allowing chapter 6 to outline a response to the preceding chapters.

---

105. Keller, *Romans 1–7*, 128.

6

Theology and Identity in a Market Economy

INTRODUCTION: THE ROLE OF IDENTITY IN REFRAMING FAITH AND WORK THEOLOGY

THE PURPOSE OF THIS chapter is to synthesize the preceding arguments and formulate a constructive response to the research question. At the core of the issue has been the relationship between identity and the market economy. Although this pairing is uncommon in theological writings, work has become the primary source of identity for those employed in the market economy. Given this reality, the writer anticipated that contemporary theology addressing faith and work would struggle to alleviate the "intolerable dichotomy" faced by many Christians.[1] The initial hypothesis suggested that the theological response to faith and work was weakened by a lack of critical engagement and an inadequate connection between identity and the doctrine of God. Another angle to consider is whether Trinitarian theology has anything to contribute to one of the most challenging areas of public theology.

A constructive response will be carefully drawn from the findings of the previous chapters. The critique has revealed significant complexity, far beyond what the existing theology of faith and work is prepared

---

1. Bonhoeffer, *Cost of Discipleship*, 31.

to acknowledge. This complexity is better understood when dividing the research into its two respective streams: faith and work theology, and the theology of identity. While the stream of faith and work theology aligned consistently with the original hypothesis, the connections with identity were stronger than anticipated. Not only was there an ethical dominance, but the disappointing engagement of this ethics with broader social structures further affirmed the strength of the individualist paradigm.

Gunton was the leading dialogue partner in the theology of identity. As a representative of Trinitarian theology, his discussion faced some *a priori* discounting due to low adoption rates. The promise of Trinitarian theology has seemingly failed to deliver. Extracting constructs from Gunton is a challenging yet important task. The key to understanding the value of Gunton's project lies in separating his critique from his construction. This chapter will acknowledge that this concept of separation presents challenges, particularly in engaging with Augustine, who serves as the hinge between Gunton's critical and constructive theology. For this reason, the proposal does not advocate for embracing Gunton's critique while discarding his construction. Rather, the aim is to elevate his critique and temper his construction. Analogously, Gunton takes his readers on a journey that departs from classical theology and embraces a new paradigm centered on *perichoresis* and "open transcendentals." It is possible to journey with Gunton without arriving at his chosen destination—or any destination, for that matter.

The proposal suggests that there is something quite closed about Gunton's open transcendentals. They carry an element of circularity, displaying possible traces of the "tyranny" they seek to overturn. Gunton's application sometimes feels inconsistent, shifting from referring to open transcendentals as "springboards"[2] to discussing the radical ontology that thinkers like Thompson find excessively extreme. True openness lies in the recognition that theology cannot genuinely claim any destination. Unlike the Reformation, the contribution of this study cannot be reduced to a mantra of *sola fides* or *sola scriptura*. As society grapples with the forces of mature capitalism and the 4IR, theology has significant transforming to undertake. This complexity is beyond the scope of any one theologian or particular field. There must be a "no" to Trinitarian theology assuming the role of conductor, but this does not necessitate a relegation to second fiddle.

---

2. Gunton, *One*, 153.

This book argues that identity and the market economy are broad and dynamic fields at the epicenter of the human sciences. Increasingly, we have seen these fields converge, yet they are often addressed separately. The unique contribution of this book is a study of this convergence, highlighting a crisis that demands attention. Not just any crisis, but one that recognizes the market economy as the most powerful force in shaping contemporary identity. To explore this, the research has initiated a broad and unique inquiry across these two large and complex streams, bringing them together to formulate a proposal. In the first stream, there has been an engagement with the complexities of Gunton's theology of identity, particularly his call to the crisis of identity and his significant biographical perspective on individualism. In the second stream, a critical review of faith and work theology is presented, with an emphasis on the theology of Tim Keller. The conclusion of the chapter will examine the post-critique contributions found in Gunton's Trinitarian perspectives.

The reader will be navigated through this argument following the key themes described below:

- Faith and work theology is not equipped to respond to the challenges to identity.
- Gunton's contribution as a theologian of crisis.
- Beyond "grace to the individual": Trinitarian theology's contribution is not just playing second fiddle!

THE INADEQUACY OF FAITH AND WORK THEOLOGY IN ADDRESSING IDENTITY CHALLENGES

Too Few Contributors!

The first critique belongs to the absent. Here is a field within public theology that is arguably one of the most prominent and complex, deserving the attention of the best that theology has to offer. For those living within a market economy, it has become the single biggest shaper of identity; in many cases, the two have become synonymous. We define ourselves by what we produce.[3] Of all the subjects in the public sphere for theolo-

---

3. A reminder that the relation between identity and production can also be indirect. As Bellah et al. point out, if it is not the production that defines us, it is the

gians to engage with, surely this is among the most important. Like the peaks of Everest or K2, the topics of the market economy and identity tower above the rest. They lie at the very center of understanding the shape of our lives on this planet. The mountain analogy extends beyond a dominant presence to accessibility. Like those majestic mountains, they are there for all to see, but hard to scale. The subject is both broad and complex, presenting many challenges to those who study it.

Yet, for all the complexity and risks of the Himalayan summits, they still draw crowds. The base camp population extends well beyond professional climbers to include sports enthusiasts, celebrities, and even postal workers fulfilling a lifelong dream. It is reasonable to expect that the fields of identity and market economy would similarly attract theologians, resulting in significant contributions. Unfortunately, this is not the case. We see a similar lament in the research of Miller,[4] Volf,[5] and Van Duzer.[6] The findings of this book echo those of current contributors. Even Gunton is among those for whom faith and work were not a primary focus. It was noted earlier that despite his critique of modernity, there was very little economic or technological engagement in Gunton's work; his engagement was primarily epistemological. The consequence of the orientations of Gunton and others is that the field of Faith and Work has been left significantly under-resourced.

The causes of this under-resourcing are directly linked to the findings of this book. The argument in chapter 3 posits that limited contributions to Faith and Work are a consequence of Taylor's "blindness" rather than apathy. As Smith reminded us in chapter 1, theology does not recognize the threat.[7] In contrast to the Barmen Declaration, faith and work are not attracting contemporary figures like Barth and Bonhoeffer. Here, we find the connection that enables Gunton to serve as a valuable conversation partner in articulating a theology of faith and work. Gunton was

---

independence that we see production as providing. "Americans tend to think of the ultimate goals of a good life as matter of personal choice. The means to achieve individual choice, they tend to think, depend on economic progress" (Bellah et al., *Habits of the Heart*, 22).

4. Miller, *God at Work*.
5. Volf, *Work in the Spirit*.
6. Van Duzer, *Why Business Matters*.
7. "Christians fail to articulate strategies of resistance because they fail to see a threat. Because they fail to see these cultural institutions and practices as formative—fail to see them as liturgies rather than just neutral, benign 'things we do'—they also fail to recognize what's at stake in them" (Smith, *Desiring the Kingdom*, 126).

a theologian of crisis, perceiving threats that others did not. The following sections will argue that despite his failings, Gunton's theology offers a meaningful contribution to faith and work. Following the wisdom of Erasmus, Gunton is our one-eyed man!

The Ethical Bias

The engagement with the theology of faith and work began in chapter 4, mapping the landscape through the works of leading scholars. Here, Miller's work proved to be a valuable foundation. His book *God Is at Work* provided a comprehensive overview of the movement's history, complemented by Miller's analysis of its theological types. Among the other scholars reviewed, Van Duzer, Volf, Higginson, and Keller were selected for more detailed analysis. The first three were discussed in chapter 4, while Tim Keller was the focus of chapter 5. Keller was analyzed in a representative capacity, with the other scholars included to add both texture and validation to the summation of a Reformed engagement with faith and work.

Miller has been cited above for introducing the concept of paradigm shifts within the Faith and Work movement. These shifts are unsurprising, given that work itself is a young and dynamic field already experiencing its 4IR and enduring several economic cycles. The current Faith and Work era began in the mid-1980s, spurred by a growing desire among Christian workers to integrate faith and work. Numerous factors contribute to this desire. The nature of work is changing, which in turn is impacting our relationship with it. With increased mobility, work has become the key constant for some, serving as their primary community as they advance in their careers. Additionally, growing individualism has increasingly framed work as a lifestyle choice.

Integration of faith and work, according to Miller, can be classified into four types or genres, which were covered in chapter 4. This classification serves as a valuable tool for validating the hypothesis of ethical and missiological bias. Quantitatively, establishing the ethical and missiological bias was relatively straightforward. While the chapter acknowledged a stronger-than-anticipated vocational bias, the ethical perspective remained dominant. However, the simplicity of Miller's model presents some limitations, particularly its rigidity in treating the types as separate entities rather than acknowledging a more fluid relationship between them.

The hypothesis presented in chapter 4 suggested that this ethical bias was filling a void created by a poorly developed theology of identity. This position aligns closely with Miller's own view that the popularity of ethics lies in its neutrality. Essentially, Miller characterizes ethics as the lowest common denominator. What is missing from this analysis is the connection between the rise of individualism and the ethical bias. The argument posits that the primacy of ethics is not simply due to its neutrality, as Miller suggests, but rather a by-product of Descartes's "radical twist," a term popularized by Taylor. Chapter 3 recounts Taylor's[8] perspective: "Yet, within this continuity is a discontinuity, a 'radical twist' that leads to Descartes's shift of inwardness to place the moral source within us." With this twist, we see Augustine's inwardness followed by a shift of gravity toward the individual and their reason. The argument here is that the dominant Christian response of ethics is largely driven by the maturation of this "radical twist."

Van Duzer would object to this view of Cartesian influence; yet in his concluding chapters, he states, "Christians in business need to train themselves through constant practices to discern right from wrong."[9] Keller's position is significantly more extreme, to the point that chapter 5 labels his model as one of Cartesian conversion. Driving this conclusion is Keller's cognitive path away from idolatry. The individual is directed to go inward, examining their motives to meet an "urgent need for those with a powerful compass."[10] This is nothing more than an extension of the ideal of self-determination.

There are instances of a vocational model that are simply extensions of ethics. The point is that not all ethical types label themselves as such; however, the dominant underlying presence of ethical influence is discernible. Miller's own writing provides an example of this. He notes that the trigger for the Faith and Work movement is a desire to integrate and avoid compartmentalization. Miller takes this movement at face value, not evaluating its impact or exploring the underlying drivers. Arguably, this movement represents integration for the individual rather than for the church as a whole. Consequently, the integration of faith and work becomes reduced to an issue of personal fulfillment. This may help explain why the writings are muted on broader macro concerns like class, race, and gender distinctions within the workplace. This raises questions about

8. Taylor, *Sources of the Self*, 143.
9. Van Duzer, *Why Business Matters*, 189.
10. Keller and Alsdorf, *Every Good Endeavor*, 231.

the quality of integration that the movement provided. Without macro engagement, is there any less compartmentalization than what initially prompted its advent? The answer here is no. What has happened is that compartmentalization has merely been escalated to a different level.

The dominance of ethics can also be linked to the emphasis on the subject of teaching, which clearly manifests an underlying cognitive bias. This reveals a diagnosis of ignorance rather than the "curious blindness" of an embedded paradigm. The assumption behind this perspective is that the journey to correct understanding is linear, with teaching seen as a popular remedy. However, this is a simplistic view. In reality, paradigm shifts are much more complex.

Individualism's Narrowing of the Ethical Bias

The most significant contribution of chapter 4 arguably stems from the omissions within the Faith and Work movement. While there were consistent critical views offered regarding the market economy, these perspectives were often muted, dated, or limited to the micro market.

Volf was the most outspoken on a macro level. His insightful book, *Work in the Spirit*, seeks to apply a strong social structural critique. Considering its authorship in the mid-1980s, its criticism was quite progressive. Volf was unafraid to reference terms like "alienation" and "crisis" and openly engage with Marxist ideas. His writing also validated the contributions and criticisms of Bellah et al. and Rosa. Additionally, his unique pneumatological position distinguishes him from his peers, demonstrating an openness to mediation. However, the disappointment lies in the fact that his critique of monetary systems feels dated and is primarily directed at the late industrial age.

Keller's role in the study was to provide an opportunity for deeper engagement with an influential theologian. By delving further, Keller aimed to showcase the connection between his theology and its implications for the relationship between faith and work. The focus of an entire chapter allowed for broader engagement with additional works by the same author, specifically concentrating on the doctrine of God and its related link to identity.

Chapter 5 primarily focused on *Endeavor* and looked to related works for validation. An initial reading of Keller creates the impression of a sage—a widely read author with insights into both realms. It was Keller who introduced Robert Bellah et al. and Luc Ferry. The chapter also lists Nietzsche, Thiselton, and MacIntyre as other key thought leaders in the field. Such a bibliography establishes the expectation of someone well-equipped to bridge the two realities of "faith" and "work." From Keller's work comes arguably the most resonant quotation: "All Christians live in cultures and work in vocational fields that operate by powerful master narratives that are sharply different from the gospel's account of things."[11] This quotation could easily serve as the opening sentence of this project's conclusion. Unlike some of his peers, Keller did not point to the clergy or the institution; he argued that integration is an ecclesial responsibility. All of these factors positioned Keller favorably for a more critical engagement.

Unfortunately, upon closer examination, the initial perceptions dissipate, revealing a narrow and poorly equipped theology. Keller emerged as the representative of faith and work most closely aligned with contemporary culture. So much so that "assimilated" feels like a more appropriate descriptor than "associated." He faced significant criticism in the analysis, to the extent that the title of chapter 5 labels his theology the "Cartesian conversion." Keller has conflated identity with ethics, reducing it to the outcome of a cognitive response.

Yet, for all his failings, the engagement with Keller proved valuable for this study. His Cartesian emphasis and inconsistent handling of concepts were significant in that they illuminated what to examine in others. Chapter 5 observes how Keller lacks Gunton's long reach of causation and engages with Keller's misreading of Ferry, demonstrating that Keller has very little awareness of influences beyond the cognitive—a theme strongly supported by James K. Smith, who Kelly oddly relegated to a footnote.[12]

The conclusion is that Keller is disappointingly wrong: individualism is not idolatry! His peers in the Work and Faith movement are better able to recognize the distinction between identity and ethics, choosing to elevate ethics as the primary genre to help integrate faith and work. They, too, are wrong. Through this elevation of ethics, theology introduces a reinforcing circularity to the principles at the heart of modern individualism. This is a provocative yet important principle behind this proposal.

---

11. Keller and Alsdorf, *Every Good Endeavor*, 183.
12. Keller and Alsdorf, *Every Good Endeavor*, 286.

Individualism's "Cloak of Tyranny"[13]

Gunton's critical account of the modern paradigm paves the way for exploring the impossibility of ethics. By "impossibility," reference is made to the inherent contradiction of individualism: the tyranny that promises autonomy but delivers heteronomy. In Gunton's case, this contradiction is seen in the imbalance of the one over the many. This discontent reflects broader critiques of the market, where contemporary voices highlight the improbabilities—if not impossibilities—embedded in Faith and Work literature.

Van Duzer exemplifies a faith and work integration model where Christians can find balance. "In the Garden, work was situated in a rhythm of activity and rest, work and leisure."[14] While this notion is appealing, Rosa's concept of dynamic stabilization and Markovits's analysis of workforce polarization reveal how unattainable such goals are for many. Similarly, Higginson's advocacy for moderation and prudence over arrogance places responsibility on individuals who are often powerless against the overwhelming forces of the market. The gravitational pull of most concerns toward micro ethics ultimately leads to a failure of faith and work theology to recognize the social structural forces that make a cognitive exit impossible.

In this context, expertise beyond theology becomes essential. Rosa's analysis demonstrates how markets maintain stability only through continuous growth, imposing ever-increasing demands on workers. Markovits,[15] examining the effects of technological change, observes a polarization in the workforce, dividing people into two categories: the "useless" and the "used up." He poignantly remarks, "It is impossible to get rich off human capital except by exploiting yourself and impoverishing your inner life. . . . Meritocracy allows no route to domination besides through the destruction of the authentic self."[16] Markovits is correct: there are some things that are impossible in the market economy.[17]

---

13. A reference to Gunton's descriptor of individualism. It's "creed" of autonomy being a "pretext for the suppression of the authentic human quest for truth" (Gunton, *One*, 123).

14. Van Duzer, *Why Business Matters*, 71.

15. Markovits, *Meritocracy Trap*, 269.

16. Markovits, *Meritocracy Trap*, 285.

17. "To recover leisure [read balance] a person must altogether abandon superordinate work, and the income and status constituted by such work, and exit the elite. Moreover the immense cost of elite education means that this choice will cascade down

Zuboff and Frischmann discuss the 4IR and the emerging phenomenon of behavioral surplus. Previously, global economics saw the World Bank using economic surplus to drive development agendas in less developed countries. Now, large corporations use behavioral surplus to influence consumer agendas. Here, we observe Bellah et al. warning of the unsustainability of individualism.[18]

These perspectives lead to the conclusion that the autobiographical claims of individualism are at odds with reality. These claims define the modern ideal as emerging from the emancipation of a theistic foundationalism. They argue that the layers of determination have been stripped away to reveal humanity in its natural state. The assumption is that such a hard-won victory would foster diversity and increase equality. However, this has not been the case. Through the use of extended cognition and the mining of behavioral surplus, we witness pre-cognitive manipulation that resembles a relative of 1940s fascist heteronomy.

There is a clear gap between Faith and Work literature and certain contemporary authors. The size of this gap suggests that, at best, the perspective of faith and work theology is inadequate. At worst, faith and work literature may be complicit in perpetuating the issue. The term "crisis" is reluctantly used, but it is warranted by the reality portrayed here.[19] Bosch normalizes its use as a necessity for theology. We read his iconic words:

> That there were so many centuries of crisis-free existence for the church was therefore an abnormality. Now, at long last, we are "back to normal" . . . and we know it! And if the atmosphere of crisislessness still lingers on in many parts of the West, this is simply the result of a dangerous delusion. Let us also know that to encounter crisis is to encounter the possibility of truly being the church.[20]

Gunton is a theologian of crisis, raising the alarm where he sees a threat.

---

through the generations. A superordinate who rejects self-exploitation brings his whole world crashing down—on his children" (Markovits, *Meritocracy Trap*, 189).

18. Bellah et al., *Habits of the Heart*, 143.

19. In this study, we see it used by Volf in *Work and the Spirit*, but few others were prepared to take this step.

20. Bosch, *Transforming Mission*, 3.

GUNTON'S CONTRIBUTION AS A THEOLOGIAN OF CRISIS

From a review of the ethical bias within faith and work theology, we now shift our focus to Gunton's theology of crisis. Gunton's critique of individualism echoes similar concerns, situating them within his broader narrative. This narrative argues that the modern emphasis on the self as the center of reality has theological origins, tracing back to Augustine, whom Gunton identifies as the progenitor of individualism. This represents Gunton's reversal: the very aspect that contemporary paradigms seek to abandon is actually shaping their trajectory. Contemporary modern paradigms assert that they have liberated identity from its metaphysical entrapments. However, what has actually occurred is a mere exchange of old presuppositions for new ones. Gunton laments that this shift in presuppositions has affected both society and the church, as evidenced by the latter's self-conception as "an institution mediating grace to the individual."[21] Under the influence of individualism, grace is treated as a commodity or attribute that belongs to the individual, who then chooses a church community based on personal criteria.

Individualism, by its very name, signifies the belief that the individual precedes society.[22] Chapter 5 has illustrated how this permeation of individualism has been validated in Keller's work and is also evident among some of his peers. One enters the church as an individual, and from this standpoint, relationships become something one engages in. In summary, Gunton clarifies how individualism, as an *a priori* doctrine, narrows the focus of theology. His concern lies in the lineage of individualism from Descartes back to Augustine.

The impact of individualism extends far beyond an ethical bias, permeating all aspects of theology. Even the doctrine of *perichoresis* is not immune, often reframed within an individualistic worldview. Rather than prompting a fundamental rethinking of ontology, *perichoresis* is frequently reduced to an ethical imperative—valued for fostering relationships and enabling diversity. This interpretation elevates relationality within the ethical hierarchy without challenging the underlying framework.

---

21. Gunton, *Promise*, 51.

22. Bellah et al. is a central text for Keller and provides a clear summary of individualism that supports this point. "The essence of the Lockean position is an almost ontological individualism. The individual is prior to society, which comes into existence only through the voluntary contract of individuals trying to maximise their own self-interest" (Bellah et al., *Habits of the Heart*, 143).

The pervasive influence of individualism also narrows theology's public engagement, constraining its ability to address macro-level social structures. When broader contexts are considered, the identified problems are frequently distilled into individual responses, reflecting the limited scope recognized by this theological paradigm.

This is where we need to appreciate Gunton's call to crisis. He highlights the importance of identity in a context dominated by ethics. Speaking to a different generation in another context, Gunton's message resonates with the challenges facing theology today, despite its limitations. Regarding criticisms of Gunton's broad brush or selective reading, he excels when it comes to the long reach across the centuries. From his vantage point, he possesses a vision of theology and philosophy that few others share. Unlike many, he engages with the challenges of contemporary culture while consistently keeping atonement at the center of his vision. The crisis that Gunton has identified is the concept of individualism, which dominates the modernist paradigm and has contaminated theology. This is a crisis because it breeds circularity and blindness.

It is a crisis that Gunton not only identifies but also seeks to address. The argument here is that his solution or construction carries significantly less weight than his diagnosis. These two aspects of Gunton need to be separated. This argument was introduced in chapter 3, where Green and McNall were content to defend Augustine one theological concept at a time, yet were intent on treating Gunton as a holistic entity. Nausner improves on Green and McNall by showing appreciation for Gunton's "passionate aspiration to heal the wounds of an egocentric, individualistic, alienating modern culture through an ontology of communion."[23] However, Nausner goes on to reject Gunton's constructive project as a failure.[24] This response echoes Gunton's handling of Augustine. Gunton's condemnation of Augustine was poorly executed, and the same can be said for Nausner's handling of Gunton. The argument being made here is that Gunton's critique must not be conflated with his construction. Each aspect has its own integrity.

The critique of Gunton calls for a more careful navigation of his construction. His call to crisis is best framed within a recap of his journey from his work against foundationalism to a deeper discovery of the Trinity.

---

23. Nausner, "Failure of a Laudable Project," 403.
24. Nausner, "Failure of a Laudable Project," 420.

From Foundationalism to Dualism to Augustine

Too much is made of Gunton's opposition to Augustine. While it is a central theme in his critique of contemporary worldviews, it was never the foundation of his theology. At its core, Gunton's theological project aims to uphold the doctrine of revelation and the primacy of the incarnation, rejecting any reliance on a priori concepts. This foundational concern can be traced back to his doctoral thesis, published as *Becoming and Being* in 1978. In this early work, Gunton critiques Barth while pointing to medieval Augustinianism as a possible influence. From there, his increasing focus on Augustine culminates in *The Promise of Trinitarian Theology*, *The One, the Three, and the Many*, and *The Triune Creator*. However, in Gunton's later works, this focus seems to diminish.

The debate surrounding Gunton's critique is often clouded by his tendency to polarize scholars. Augustine is a prime example, but Gunton's approach extends to others, such as Irenaeus, the Cappadocians, and Coleridge, who are treated more favorably and spared some of the necessary critique. This selective treatment weakens his overall argument. While Gunton's handling of Augustine, as discussed, was less rigorous than it could have been, this shortcoming does not negate the value of his broader critique.

Before Augustine, Gunton expresses his appreciation of Barthian epistemology. A doctrine of revelation places the incarnation at the epicenter of our knowledge of God. "Only a concept of relationality based from the outset in God's economic involvement in the world of the many will be adequate."[25] It is this starting point that brings Gunton up against the dualism of Augustine. While dualism is not Gunton's only complaint, it is the cornerstone of his dispute. For Gunton, this dualism represents a challenge to his deep conviction of preserving the integrity of God incarnate, a conviction that is bound to draw one back to the formative debates at the beginning of the fifth century. There can be no hidden deity behind the incarnation.

Some, like Jenson, argue that Gunton has taken the preservation of integrity too far. Jenson addresses this in his chapter in *The Theology of Colin Gunton*, demonstrating that Gunton has chosen to follow Irenaeus. "A key part of Irenaeus' fidelity to the economy is that he never speaks of the eternal Son as other than that Son who is the man Jesus."[26] Jenson en-

---

25. Gunton, *One*, 140–41.
26. Jenson, *Decision Tree*, 14.

couraged Gunton to adopt the concept of *Logos asarkos* as an alternative, but Gunton remained steadfast. "But Gunton is unwilling to do that, for the sake of the 'historical newness marked by Jesus' birth to Mary'; if the Logos is not somehow other after the birth than he was before, then what was the point of the birth?"[27] Additionally, Gunton's relentless pursuit of certainty may have led him to overextend the application of *perichoresis*, a point that will be explored further in the upcoming discussion. For now, the focus is on Gunton and dualism.

Recapping the Formulation of a Crisis

The formulation of Gunton's crisis was the subject of chapter 3. Fundamental to his argument is the notion that individualism has theological ancestry. This argument can be reviewed in two ways. The first involves the separation into two movements: the shift into the Enlightenment (particularly with Descartes), followed by the movement from the Enlightenment to the present. The second involves an examination of Gunton's development and the corresponding critiques. Chapter 3 opted for the latter approach, and this structure will be echoed here.

Gunton's critique of Augustine and the resulting implications for the development of individualism can be summarized through three key complaints.

- **Complaint 1:** The platonic influence of the intellectual being superior to the material.
- **Complaint 2:** The separating between the immanent and economic Trinity, both through the use of *substantia,* that effectively introduces a stress on an underlying reality within the being of God, and through the mediation of angels that distances God from revelation in Jesus.
- **Complaint 3:** The elevation of the unity of God above the particularity of the three persons.

Gunton's development in this critique is further explored through his works, culminating in a shift reflected in *Enlightenment and Alienation.* In this text, Gunton draws connections between Augustine, Locke, Coleridge, and Descartes, offering a critical reflection on Augustine's

---

27. Jenson, *Decision Tree,* 14.

emphasis on sight as "the model for all perception." He argues that this focus alienates humanity from the world, creating what he describes as a "despotism of the eye," where reliance on sight fosters dependence on a partial and incomplete representation of truth.[28]

Actuality of Atonement adds more depth to the critique of Augustine, which Gunton paraphrases as a "theology of satisfaction." In this work, Gunton establishes another important connection between Augustine and the individualism of Western theology. The focus on the individual is evident in the emphasis on the health of the soul. "The theology of satisfaction tends to concentrate on the legal and moral rather than the cosmic aspects of the divine-human relationship. In that respect, it is a characteristically Western development, bounded on one side by Augustine's preoccupation with the health of the soul and on the other by Luther's preoccupation with justification."[29] This observation underscores the dominance of ethics, which remains a significant issue within faith and work theology.

The next encounter with Augustine in a published book is *The Promise of Trinitarian Theology*, which contains all the core components of Gunton's critique of Augustine. His chapter on Augustine is aptly titled "Augustine, the Trinity, and the Theological Crisis of the West." Here, we find a reference to "crisis" combined with the constructive notion of "promise." Gunton's growing appreciation of Irenaeus and the Cappadocians, influenced by Zizioulas, appears to have shaped this shift in his perspective. His chapter remains relevant even without direct reference to Augustine, as the core focus is on the Trinity and the theological crisis of the West. Notably, although Gunton does not explicitly acknowledge it, Augustine's influence extends far beyond the individual, evolving into a significantly larger and more impactful legacy.

There is further development in *The One, the Three, and the Many*, where we encounter a more pronounced contrast between Augustine and Irenaeus. Also significant is the positioning of Augustine as a predecessor to Descartes. He writes, "We tend to see the thing as constituted by its externality or external relations, the person as internally constituted, largely, I suspect, because we believe that we know ourselves not by observing our relatedness with the other but by some kind of introspection, as a powerful tradition from Plato, through Augustine, Descartes, Kant

---

28. Gunton, *Enlightenment and Alienation*, 36–37.
29. Gunton, *Actuality of the Atonement*, 95.

to Freud."[30] Here we see the inference of Taylor's "radical twist" of Augustine's inwardness, placing the individual at the center of the universe.[31]

Recapping Supporters and Critics

The importance of chapter 3 lies in arguing that Gunton's position has supporters and can withstand its critics. It utilized Taylor, a significant source for Gunton, and engaged in detail with two doctoral publications that examined Gunton's critique of Augustine. All contributors agreed on Augustine's significant influence, though their disagreements varied. Neither McNall nor Green dismissed Gunton outright; instead, they challenged his delivery and emphasis.

Taylor's theory of causation introduces a more moderated perspective, using terms like "nudge" or "push" to describe influence. Unlike Gunton, Taylor's critique focuses primarily on Augustine's inwardness, which he identifies as a precursor to the Cartesian "radical twist." However, Taylor situates Augustine within a broader exploration of causation, attributing greater significance to more recent influences, particularly the Reformation and Puritanism. This broader context highlights Gunton's narrow focus on Augustine, which, while not directly opposed to Taylor's position, makes Gunton's critique appear unbalanced.

Green's contribution serves as a useful correction to Gunton's reading of Augustine, emphasizing the importance of Augustine's context. Gunton would have found much more to lament if the Arian heresy had gained more traction than Augustine. However, Green falls short in his insufficient understanding of Gunton's wider project; his method is not suitable for his subject. Additionally, Green undermines his arguments through inconsistency. He aims to elevate Augustine from foe to friend, yet at the same time wishes to dismiss Gunton's entire assessment of Augustine while arguing that "the criticisms do not ultimately undermine the theology of Colin Gunton."[32] This stance is unrealistic and leaves the reader confused. Finally, and most significantly, Green pays little regard to the possibility of causation. He believes he has extinguished the fire, but here he is mistaken. Despite his supposed "misreading" by Gunton, is there

---

30. Gunton, *One*, 202–3.
31. Taylor, *Sources of the Self*.
32. Green, *Colin Gunton*, 201.

a possibility that Augustine's inwardness had unforeseen consequences? This question appears to have been omitted from Green's agenda.

McNall's approach is clearer than Green's. He exonerates Augustine while scolding Gunton, allowing Gunton to retain his broader complaint against Augustine's legacy. McNall achieves this exoneration through reduction and deferment. The treatment of dualism serves as an important example. McNall writes, "Thus, while Augustine's resulting dualism was of course 'limited,' it is not sufficient to conclude that this does away with Gunton's charge. On the contrary, for Gunton it was precisely the limited nature of Augustine's dualism that allowed it to be passed on to future generations."[33] In summary, McNall argues that Augustine's dualism is less extensive than Gunton alleges, but this dualism nonetheless developed under Augustine's legacy. This, of course, is precisely how causation works. Taylor is much better at capturing this flow than Gunton, but that does not make Gunton incorrect. As with Green, the conclusion is that McNall also misses the opportunity to engage in dialogue with Gunton's broader project.

Concluding Gunton's Crisis

The obvious question for the reader is why we need Gunton's version of the crisis. Given his myopia regarding Augustine and his underplaying of the Reformation, would theology not be better served by more moderate views? Taylor is a good example of a scholar whose perspective on frameworks exhibits far less of the Newtonian rigidity found in Gunton. Could his view not replace Gunton's?

The answer is no. In Gunton, we find a unique blend of a biography of individualism paralleled with an ongoing advocacy for a departure from classical theology. It is only by holding these elements together that the theological crisis becomes apparent. What this encapsulates is a level of circularity in which theology attempts to solve problems using the very presuppositions that caused them in the first place. Gunton is distinct from others in his vision of what is at stake. While there is no denying that Gunton's broad strokes have led to poor handling of figures like Augustine, his project was ambitious. It is doubtful that he could have maintained these strands had his approach been more attentive to detail. The chapter will later argue that the future development of this approach

---

33. McNall, *Free Corrector*, 125.

is beyond the capability of a single scholar and would be better served by a far more collaborative interdisciplinary effort.

The conclusion of this section revisits a statement made in chapter 3, which argued that, even if Gunton was only partially correct, his perspective presents the most critical challenge to the theology of faith and work. Despite its imperfections, Gunton's position carries sufficient conviction to confront contemporary faith and work theology, particularly its varying degrees of blindness to issues of synchronicity. This is not to dismiss the current Faith and Work literature outright. Instead, it calls for the treatment of a condition that, like a tumor, threatens the health of the individual. The message to the Faith and Work movement is that the theological focus on the individual is not the divine liberation of the Reformation but rather a corruption of Enlightenment reasoning and its aftermath. The crisis presented by Gunton persists.

BEYOND GRACE TO THE INDIVIDUAL: TRINITARIAN THEOLOGY'S ROLE IN A BROADER SYMPHONY

As noted earlier, the second sub-question emerged as the most significant and was addressed in the preceding section. However, two additional sub-questions remain unanswered. These pertain specifically to Gunton's constructive theology and his use of *perichoresis* as a means of transitioning from Barth's *analogia entis* to an *analogia relationis*. Recognizing the potential to overextend these discussions, I also explored what aspects of Gunton's theology remain applicable and how they might be practically applied to equip Christians navigating the market economy.

Open Transcendentals and Overreaching

Gunton, like Augustine, was a theologian of crisis. Both faced challenges to Christian doctrine that threatened the integrity of the Christian faith. For Gunton, Augustine's inward journey was precisely the wrong place to seek certainty. Ironically, traces of Augustine's quest for certainty can be found not only in Gunton's own work but also in Keller's theology, in this study, and in the call for self-determination at the heart of individualism. A crisis calls for clarity or some form of resolution, and perhaps this is what led Gunton down the wrong path. Was it his search for closure that drove him to rely too heavily on Coleridge's open transcendentals?

The similarity between Gunton and Keller warrants further discussion. For Keller, everything was viewed through the lens of idolatry in a way that was exceedingly obvious to the uninitiated. Keller recognized the problem of his congregation trying to integrate faith and work—and idolatry was the solution he liberally applied. Behind this myopic application lies an attempt to uphold Luther's reform. In Gunton, we see a reflection of this behavior. More than most, Gunton has a clear understanding of the conflicts and contradictions within the culture of modernity. Yet, to this diverse problem, he has consistently applied a model of *analogia relationis*. This leads to one of the hardest critiques of all: Nausner's observation that there is something of a Cartesian thread to Gunton's response.[34]

Nausner makes a valid point. If the problem is as pervasive as Gunton portrays, then the vast majority of theology is conducted from within that worldview, rather than from a privileged vantage point outside it. Is applying an analogous model really that different from a cognitive exit?

Gunton's constructive model has been critiqued for relying too heavily on Coleridge and the concept of open transcendentals. While it is clear that theology cannot exist without analogy, Gunton's quest for an analogous model that could serve as a filter through which to interpret all theology is overly ambitious. His use of the term "springboard," though directly attributed to him, appears inconsistent with the central themes of his work, which generally emphasize a more prescriptive approach to applying his theological model.[35]

The argument of this book is that Gunton has effectively supported the departure from classical theology. However, his project has been less

---

34. Armstrong has written extensively on fundamentalism in religion. From her insights, we might agree that modernity brings enough anxiety of its own. Adding to this the complexity and mysticism of a relational conception of identity pushes the boundaries further. In relation to the Trinity, Armstrong (*Battle for God*, 69) points out, "The difficulty that many Western Christians today experience with Trinitarian theology shows that they share Newton's bias in favour of reason. Newton's position was entirely understandable." There is a popularity in simplicity and in victory. However, a conceptually challenging view of a partially realized eschatology is a hard sell.

35. "It is important that when these transcendental concepts are used as a springboard for further thought, note should be taken of their extreme generality. They are, as in Coleridge's characterization of the most important ideas, both unfathomable and infinitely suggestive. They introduce a relational dynamic, but also bring with them all the problems associated with analogy" (Gunton, *One*, 153).

convincing in guiding us to a new destination. If Gunton's sole aim was to deliver theology to this new destination, then the conclusion must align with Nausner's view that Gunton's project was a failure. Nevertheless, Nausner's sympathy with Green and McNall's perspectives risks limiting the assessment of Gunton's contributions, particularly his application of analogy, to just one aspect of his theology. The evaluation of Gunton must be broader than what Nausner allows. To achieve this, a clear stance on analogy is needed.

In this debate, Vosloo's account offers a more conservative stance. He writes, "With regard to trinitarian theology, the temptation is real to speculate about analogies between God's inner trinitarian life and our vision for personhood, the church, and society. While such attempts are rhetorically powerful, they are theologically suspect."[36] These cautionary comments gain more depth when read alongside a preceding statement by Vosloo, where he argues with Peters that the Trinity is a "second-order symbol, and that we must be careful to use the symbol to serve as an ethical ideal or divine model for human society."[37] The caution around using the Trinity as an ethical model is valid, but categorizing it as a second-order symbol clearly contrasts with the Trinitarian primacy seen in Barth, Rahner, and now Gunton. An example is the *ordo salutis*, which serves as the epicenter of doctrine. How do we articulate atonement without understanding the movement between Father, Son, and Holy Spirit found on the cross? How does theology articulate atonement as something beyond transactional?

Analogy in theology has led to significant misinterpretation and abuse, yet theology cannot function without it. It becomes abusive when the analogous use of the word "father" is employed to justify patriarchy. It is dangerous when the masculinity of Jesus is used to exclude women from ordained leadership. *Perichoresis* has also suffered at the hands of such interpretations, yet it needs to be retained as a valuable contributor to theology.

Many agree with Gunton's critique of modernism and recognize that the predominant theological response in the West is inadequate. This study offers substantial evidence to support that conclusion. Gunton has effectively identified the crisis and demonstrated the inability of Western theology, in its current form, to address it. The era of classical theology

---

36. Vosloo, "Identity, Otherness and the Triune God," 83.

37. Vosloo, "Identity, Otherness and the Triune God," 79.

has passed. What remains to be determined is which aspects of Gunton's work retain value, particularly in light of concerns about his radical ontology and reliance on open transcendentals.

This proposal calls for a renewed focus on the concept of mediation within theology as a constructive path forward.

Moderating Particularity and Repositioning Mediation

Undergirding Gunton's radical ontology is an emphasis on relationality, particularity, and mediation. Chapter 2 concluded that *perichoresis* enables a concept of personhood that is not contractual and has no room for the market's *ordo salutis* of meritocracy. Correctly understood, *perichoresis* drives an ecclesiology that centers on belonging rather than behaving.

Of relationality, particularity, and mediation, it is particularity that has arguably enjoyed the most prominence through the popularity of Trinitarian theology. Among the perichoretic attributes, it most easily translates into contemporary culture as a validator of diversity. It may also exemplify how the doctrine is sometimes shoehorned into the paradigm of individualism.

This is where Gunton's appeal to mediation comes to the fore, seen through his consistent reference to Irenaeus's analogy of the "two hands" of God. *Perichoresis* demands that particularity undergoes mediation for currency, a challenge that has yet to be fully appreciated. Mediation has a notorious past, and its abuse is the chief fuel behind the ascent of individualism. A return to mediation as a theological contributor must be approached with care.

The fear is that mediation can and will let you down. Augustine sensed this, and his resolution was the journey inward. The Reformation echoes this with its mantras of *sola fide* and *sola scriptura*. Yet what Gunton argues is that grace is not served in individual portions. Much as mediation is messy, we are stuck with it.

There is some irony in this appreciation of Gunton's contribution. Gunton preferred cleaner lines to messy theology. This preference is evident in his polarization of Augustine and Irenaeus, which he assessed with a binary tool that allowed for only a one or a zero. Only in his handling of Barth do we see a healthier balance between appreciation and criticism. In this sense, Gunton was playing two tunes. On the one hand, the notes were clear and simple, while on the other, the chords were fast and disjointed. In doing this, Gunton helped us move beyond Barth to a theology that allows for the exploration of relationality, participation, and particularity.

Although autonomy has relegated mediation to an inferior status, it has not vanished entirely; it remains at the center of our existence. Mediation retains its relevance in the acts of parenthood and partnership. Signs of autonomy running its course are also evident. Cracks are beginning to show as writers pull back the curtain to reveal heteronomy lurking beneath. They are lifting the veil to present autonomy as a medium for mediating heteronomy.

Rosa speaks to a dignity that must be safeguarded by the collective; it cannot be left for the individual to earn. Other contemporary thinkers, such as Brené Brown, engage with mediation through concepts like vulnerability, while Lancioni and others emphasize trust as a crucial commodity in organizations. These participatory terms, steeped in mediation, extend us beyond the limitations of a purely cognitive orientation.

Chapter 4 argued that salvation, in Reformed terms, has a transactional bias intertwined with a Cartesian shadow, often manifest in ethics. The result is bland: a soteriology with a weak eschatology that provides little opposition to the mediation encountered in contemporary "social imaginaries."

The path forward is unclear, but what is clear is that a new path is necessary. Early attempts at Trinitarian theology have been weakened by an eagerness to find alternative analogies; yet, this does not disqualify the valuable contributions they bring to the table. A fit-for-purpose solution does not exist. *Perichoresis* is not the axis of a new theological solution; however, it does have a role to play in rebuilding a theology of identity.

CONCLUSION: A CASE FOR MEDIATION

The purpose of this chapter was to synthesize the preceding arguments and formulate a constructive response to the research question. The chapter contends that contemporary theology is micro-dominant, centered on personal ethics and individual mission. Our *ordo salutis* remains heavily reliant on transactional analogies. When viewed through Gunton's concept of "crisis," this micro-focus can be traced to the foundational assumptions of classical theology. These foundations are not only relevant to theological discourse but also echo in the development of individualism, which often defines itself in opposition to them. This crisis, therefore, extends beyond the church, influencing all who operate within this paradigm.

In agreement with Gunton, the argument is that contemporary theology is not sufficiently equipped to address the important matter of identity. Gunton's often-quoted observation holds true: the church is "conceived essentially as an institution mediating grace to the individual rather than as the community formed on the analogy of the Trinity's interpersonal relationships."[38]

The call to re-evaluate the theology of faith and work is not as presumptuous as it sounds. In a contemporary environment that has witnessed significant shifts in recent years, it is the failure to adapt that is the more presumptuous stance. Take cryptocurrencies as an example of such a paradigm shift. They have achieved the previously inconceivable task of stripping away expensive and time-consuming aspects of exchange control, completely disempowering the monetary policy of the most powerful governments in the world. Similarly, the COVID-19 pandemic drove a dramatic shift in perceptions of office work and business travel. Remote work, once considered a fad or a niche option for those without office space, became the norm for many of the world's largest firms, with employees working from home for extended periods.

The Faith and Work movement requires another shift to address these contemporary realities. This includes two essential components. The first involves adopting a more critical stance toward current paradigms. While this may appear to contradict the "constructive" ethos of integrating faith and work, such a view is misguided. The concern that adopting a critical outlook might reinforce the dualism the Faith and Work movement seeks to dismantle is overly simplistic. Rosa's *Resonance* provides a compelling counterpoint, demonstrating that remodeling critical theory into a constructive force does not create contradiction but enhances engagement. The second recommended component is a greater openness to the contributions of Trinitarian theology, particularly concerning the role of mediation.

---

38. Gunton, *Promise*, 51. The reference to the "individualization" of redemption is a recurring theme in Gunton. In *The Triune Creator* he draws on Feuerbach's critical observation of Christianity (Gunton, *Triune Creator*, 162): "Nature, the world, has no value, no interest, for Christians. The Christian thinks only of himself and the salvation of his soul" (Feuerbach, *Essence of Christianity*, 287). Again, in the same volume, Gunton (*Triune Creator*, 171) states: "Redemption means the completion of the whole project of creation, not the saving of a few souls from hell."

7

Concluding Reflections, Lessons, and Future Directions

INTRODUCTION: A CALL FOR THEOLOGICAL RENEWAL

REFORMED THEOLOGY, IN ITS current state, has struggled to address the profound impact of the market economy on human identity. Theologians engaging this intersection often fall short of offering a sufficiently critical response, leaving significant gaps in the discourse. Faith and work theology, shaped by the pervasive influences of individualism and market forces, risks eroding the distinctiveness of Christian identity. This challenge is compounded by an over-reliance on the genres of ethics and mission, which fail to address the deeper theological crises at play.

To counter these shortcomings, a revision of faith and work theology is imperative, beginning with the reprioritization of identity as a central focus. While Colin Gunton's theology might appear distant from direct engagement with economic systems, his trenchant critique of individualism and his application of Trinitarian theology offer valuable insights. These contributions hold potential to inspire a more robust theological response to the challenges posed by the market economy.

This chapter aims to synthesize the findings of this study and directly address the central research questions that guided the investigation.

CONCLUDING REFLECTIONS, LESSONS, AND FUTURE DIRECTIONS 273

Beyond merely revisiting these questions, it seeks to articulate the broader significance of the conclusions reached, offering reflections on their implications for the discipline of theology. Research, as much a process of discovery as resolution, often raises new questions even as it answers others. This chapter embraces that dynamic, proposing areas for future inquiry that build on the core themes explored here and extend into related fields.

This final chapter serves, in part, as a delivery note—an assurance that the promises made in the introduction and throughout the research have been fulfilled. While it draws on earlier arguments, particularly those developed in chapter 6, the focus here is not on reiteration but on offering a reflective commentary on the research process. By examining key decisions, unexpected findings, and their implications, the chapter provides a deeper understanding of the journey undertaken.

As outlined in chapter 1, this study was structured around two main avenues of inquiry. The first explored contemporary identity through the lens of Colin Gunton's Trinitarian theology. The second examined the application of theology within the market economy, as reflected in the Faith and Work literature exemplified by Timothy Keller. The merging of these two channels revealed that contemporary faith and work theology is inadequately equipped to address the complexities of Christian identity in the market economy. This inadequacy stems, in large part, from unexamined presuppositions that require critical reassessment or outright rejection.

Gunton's radical ontology and his interpretation of *perichoresis*, while not a comprehensive solution, contribute significantly to this reassessment. Ironically, Gunton's constructive proposals sometimes mirror the very problems he critiques. Nevertheless, his incisive critique of Western paradigms offers an indispensable framework for rethinking theological priorities. As David Ford reminds us, Christianity "needs continually to be rethought," and Gunton's insights should play a more central role in this process.

The chapter concludes by emphasizing the importance of these findings, both in their substance and originality. Gunton's critique of causality and his identification of a theological crisis offer profound implications for reimagining faith and work theology. Even if Gunton's conclusions are not entirely definitive, his insights demand engagement and underscore the urgency of addressing the theological and cultural forces shaping identity today. The final section transitions to propose potential areas for further research, building on the foundational work of this study.

FUTURE DIRECTIONS FOR INQUIRY

Drawing from the insights of this study, several key areas emerge as opportunities for deeper exploration. Gunton's role as a theologian of crisis calls for further examination, particularly in the practical implications of his constructive theology. How might alternative theological frameworks, such as an *ordo salutis* grounded in worship, vulnerability, and trust, be lived out in the context of a market-driven economy?

Gunton's omission of Rahner, a central figure in Trinitarian theology, presents another avenue for investigation. Despite shared critiques of classical theology, Gunton's Protestant commitments may have limited his engagement with Rahner's sacramental insights. Exploring these parallels could illuminate new connections between Trinitarian mediation, pneumatology, and the sacraments, offering richer intersections between systematic and practical theology.

The influence of Zizioulas and Coleridge on Gunton's development of *analogia relationis* warrants a closer look, particularly whether there is evidence of a softening in his radical ontology later in life. Similarly, Volf's pneumatology, while foundational to faith and work theology, invites comparison with Pannenberg's perspectives. Such studies could deepen understanding of the Spirit's role in these theological frameworks and their implications for modern identity.

Timothy Keller's work, though influential, reveals theological gaps when examined alongside figures like Luther. A comparative study could investigate how concepts of grace differ between these thinkers and what this means for Keller's approach to faith and work theology. Gunton's critique of Augustine, while thorough, leaves minimal engagement with the Reformers. This omission raises questions about their role in shaping modern individualism—a theme that Taylor connects directly to the Reformation. Revisiting this relationship could enrich debates on causation within theology and identity.

Gunton's limited focus on ecclesiology also invites further exploration. How do contemporary expressions of leadership and authority within ecclesial and organizational contexts intersect with faith and work?

Additionally, Karen Armstrong's observations on the Trinity provoke reflection on whether Trinitarian theology's complexity has hindered broader engagement, particularly among those influenced by modern rationalist biases.

The conclusion of this study highlights the importance of mediation—embodied in worship, vulnerability, and trust—in reforming faith and work theology. This theme merits a dedicated study, probing its transformative potential for Christian practice in transactional environments. Finally, as individualism's ideal of autonomy faces both entrenchment and challenge, a future-focused exploration of theology and sociology could yield profound insights. How might growing recognition of emotion as a formative force shape theological engagement over the next decade?

These areas for further inquiry offer a fertile ground for advancing the conversation on faith, work, and identity in a rapidly changing world.

REFLECTIONS ON THE JOURNEY OF INTEGRATION

This book set out to weave together two distinct yet interconnected streams—faith and work theology and Gunton's theology of identity. This ambitious integration revealed the profound opportunities and challenges inherent in bringing these two fields into dialogue. By addressing the dominance of an ethical paradigm in faith and work literature and the relational ontology of Gunton's theology, the study highlights both the possibilities for richer theological engagement and the critical gaps that remain.

The decision to structure the book with dedicated chapters for each stream, followed by a synthesis of findings, proved instrumental in maintaining a balance between breadth and depth. This approach allowed for foundational exploration and specialization, providing a framework to address critical issues with clarity and focus. Through this structure, the book contextualized Gunton's theology within his broader intellectual formation and presented a detailed critique of his engagement with Augustine. This reframing shifted the focus toward Gunton's contributions to understanding individualism, liberating his ideas from being overly tied to the Augustinian debate.

The faith and work stream similarly benefited from contextualization. Key figures like Keller were positioned within the broader Faith and Work movement, whose diversity was explored through the contributions of various scholars. While this movement often reflects an ethical focus, it also provided fertile ground for examining how theological resources are applied—or, in some cases, underutilized—in addressing modern identity and market forces.

REVISITING THE CORE THEMES

This section reflects on the key questions that guided the study, linking them to the insights and findings emerged. Beginning with foundational inquiries and culminating in the overarching question, the discussion unfolds in reverse order to highlight how each builds upon the other. Along the way, the exploration of these questions has revealed underlying presuppositions, offering opportunities for reflection and reframing. These moments of reconsideration, while at times challenging, underscore the dynamic nature of theological inquiry and the learning that has shaped this journey.

Tracking *Perichoresis*

One of the central inquiries of this book concerns the relational ontological resources found in Gunton's use of *perichoresis* and their implications for identity as created in the image of God. This exploration also examines how these insights align with or diverge from the Reformed tradition and where Gunton's interpretations may overreach. While this question appears multifaceted, its unifying focus lies in understanding *perichoresis* as a concept critical to reshaping theological priorities.

Perichoresis: *A Repositioned Perspective*

Gunton's use of *perichoresis* reflects a bold attempt to address key gaps in faith and work theology, particularly the need for a relational ontology that challenges individualistic paradigms. Over the course of this study, however, the initial assumptions regarding the application of *perichoresis* were refined. Gunton's theological contributions emerged in two distinct movements: his critique of individualism's historical development and his constructive advocacy for perichoresis as a means of reorienting theological emphasis.

While Gunton's critique of classical theology is persuasive, his constructive efforts to apply *perichoresis*, framed through the lens of open transcendentals, have faced criticism for overreach. Nonetheless, the enduring value of *perichoresis* lies in its potential to transition theological discourse from an *analogia entis* (analogy of being) to an *analogia relationis* (analogy of relationship). Despite challenges in gaining widespread acceptance, this book defends *perichoresis* as a vital resource for theological renewal.

The Role of Analogy and Perichoresis

Analogy, as a tool in theology, is both indispensable and fraught with potential for misuse. Just as the concept of "father" has been used to justify patriarchy or the masculinity of Jesus to exclude women from leadership, *perichoresis* has been similarly misinterpreted. Yet, *perichoresis* must remain central to theology for its ability to foster relationality, particularity, and mediation.

Gunton's emphasis on mediation, as seen in his frequent reference to Irenaeus's analogy of the "two hands" of God, underscores the interconnectedness required for theological coherence. Properly understood, mediation challenges individualism's dominance and invites an ecclesiology centered on belonging over behavior—a marked departure from much of faith and work theology. This reframing of mediation, particularly in the context of worship and vulnerability, holds the potential to address the individualism entrenched in modern theological paradigms.

Evaluating the Reformed Tradition

The exploration of *perichoresis* extends naturally to its validation within the Reformed tradition. The findings reveal that the dominance of ethical and evangelistic concerns in faith and work theology stems not solely from a neglect of the Trinity but from the pervasive influence of individualism. While Keller and others within this tradition reference the Trinity, these references are often secondary to frameworks rooted in idolatry and transactional atonement.

This individualistic paradigm, shaped by Augustinian satisfaction theory and reflecting what Taylor describes as the "Cartesian shadow," has narrowed the theological imagination. It is not the absence of ontological resources that limits these frameworks but rather the lens through which they are interpreted and applied.

Concluding Thoughts on Perichoresis

Gunton's exploration of *perichoresis* offers both promise and challenges. While his critique of individualism provides a compelling foundation for rethinking relational ontology, his constructive proposals require further refinement to reach their full potential. By situating *perichoresis* within broader theological and ecclesial contexts, this book highlights its significance as a tool for addressing the limitations of faith and work theology and invites ongoing dialogue about its application in modern theological discourse.

Gunton's Biography of Individualism

The exploration of radical individualism and its connection to Christian traditions emerged as one of the most significant themes of this book. What began as a supporting inquiry for the discussion on *perichoresis* evolved into a deeper engagement with Gunton's critique of individualism and its broader implications for contemporary theology. Framed through the provocative lens of a question—"What is the link between Augustine and Adidas?"—this section investigates the extent to which Christian traditions have contributed to the individualism so pervasive in today's global market economy.

Gunton's Reversal: Unmasking Individualism

Gunton's theology presents a striking reversal of contemporary paradigms. While modern thought often claims to free identity from metaphysical entrapments, Gunton argues that such liberation merely replaces old presuppositions with new ones. His critique centers on the role of Christian theology, particularly the influence of Augustine, in shaping the foundations of individualism.

Yet, the findings of this study suggest that too much weight may have been placed on Gunton's opposition to Augustine. While more nuanced approaches to Augustine are possible, Gunton did not fully explore them. Instead, his theology remains anchored in a desire to preserve the primacy of revelation and the incarnation, deliberately avoiding reliance on *a priori* concepts. This focus shifts the conversation from a critique of Augustine to a broader interrogation of how theology has contributed to the rise of individualism.

Causation and Critique: Balancing Perspectives

The question of causation in theology is inherently ambitious, and Gunton's approach, while compelling, often leans toward polarization and broad generalizations. This study sought to temper these tendencies by incorporating Charles Taylor's moderating influence, as well as critiques from scholars like Green and McNall. These voices provide a more measured perspective, preserving the urgency of Gunton's critique while refining its application.

This balanced approach highlights the relevance of Gunton's critique for contemporary faith and work theology. Despite its imperfections, his work offers a valuable framework for addressing the blind spots of this tradition, particularly its limited engagement with synchronicity and structural forces. Individualism's dominance, as Gunton notes, often reduces complex theological challenges to individual moral responses—a tendency that restricts theology's ability to address public and social structures effectively.

Gunton's Enduring Contribution

Gunton's insights into the historical development of theology, particularly his critique of dualism and its impact on ontology and the *ordo salutis*, remain indispensable. While alternative sources could address the question of individualism without reference to Gunton, they lack the depth and breadth of his analysis. By unmasking the theological roots of modern individualism, Gunton provides a lens through which to critique contemporary faith and work theology and its often uncritical acceptance of individualistic paradigms.

Rethinking Faith and Work Through Gunton

This exploration demonstrates the necessity of reevaluating the assumptions underpinning contemporary theological discourse. Gunton's critique challenges faith and work theology to move beyond its ethical and individualistic focus, encouraging a more comprehensive engagement with the communal and structural dimensions of identity. In doing so, it calls for a deeper, more holistic theological response to the complexities of identity formation within the global market economy.

The Trinity and the Roots of Individualism in Faith and Work

The question of how Keller's theology reflects Gunton's critique of Reformed theology—particularly its focus on mediating grace to the individual—brings into sharp relief the intersections of Trinitarian theology, individualism, and faith and work. While initially framed to examine causation, this inquiry evolved to highlight the pervasive influence of individualism as an independent force. Rather than a direct link between an inadequate theology of the Trinity and individualism, the findings point to the broader dynamics shaping theological discourse and practice in the modern era.

Reframing the Question: Individualism as a Force

Gunton's phrase, "mediating grace to the individual," served as a recurring touchstone throughout this exploration. However, the research revealed that this framing overly simplifies the issue. The dominance of individualism within faith and work theology is not solely the result of a deficient Trinitarian framework but reflects a more complex interplay of historical, philosophical, and theological forces.

The ethical focus prevalent in faith and work literature underscores this complexity. As chapter 4 argued, the emphasis on ethics fills a void left by an underdeveloped theology of identity. While Miller identifies ethics as a neutral, unifying framework, this study builds on Taylor's concept of Descartes's "radical twist," which shifted the moral source inward, reinforcing the primacy of individual reasoning. This inward turn has deeply influenced Christian theology, where the centrality of ethics often aligns with the maturation of individualism.

Keller's Collapse of Identity into Ethics

Keller's theology offers a case study in how modernity's individualistic underpinnings shape Faith and Work discourse. His reduction of identity to ethics—a pattern described in this study as the "Cartesian conversion"—demonstrates the limitations of his framework. By labeling individualism as idolatry, Keller acknowledges the issue but fails to address its depth. His critique remains too deeply embedded in the modern worldview to effectively disentangle from the dynamics he seeks to challenge. As Keller himself admits, "None of us are as detached from our culture or clan as many of us like to think."[1] This observation aptly applies to his own work, where his entrenchment in modern individualism constrains his theological reach.

Keller's peers in the Faith and Work movement show a better grasp of the distinction between identity and ethics, yet they also elevate ethics as the primary framework for integration. This perpetuates a circularity that aligns with modern individualism, undermining their critique of it.

The Trinity and Keller's Doctrine of Grace

A critical aspect of this inquiry was to determine whether Keller's emphasis on ethics stems from his doctrine of the Trinity. The findings suggest the opposite: Keller's Trinitarian theology is shaped by his adherence to individualism, not the other way around. This inversion results in an obscured understanding of grace, where the relational and communal dimensions of the Trinity are subordinated to the ethics-driven framework of modern individualism.

Rethinking Theology for Faith and Work

The exploration of Keller's theology reveals the broader challenge facing faith and work theology: its entanglement with the cultural dynamics it critiques. By framing identity through the lens of ethics and

---

1. Keller, *Romans 1–7*, 128.

individualism, it reinforces the very paradigms it seeks to transcend. This study invites a reexamination of how Trinitarian theology can serve as a corrective, emphasizing relational and communal dimensions over transactional and individualistic interpretations.

Toward a Critical and Constructive Theology of Faith and Work

This question addressed how Gunton's use of *perichoresis*, with its profound implications for human identity, might reshape the priorities of faith and work theology to better equip Christians for a deeper engagement with the market economy. While Keller's theology is initially referenced in the question, the findings indicate that his framework requires a complete reimagining. The focus, therefore, shifts to how Gunton's Trinitarian theology can provide both a critical lens and constructive tools for navigating the complexities of identity and vocation in modern economic systems.

Critique and Construction: A Necessary Tandem

One of the central insights of this study is that critique and construction cannot function in isolation. While Gunton's critique of classical theology is incisive, his constructive proposals, particularly through the application of *perichoresis*, remain less persuasive. The necessity of a theological shift is evident, and *perichoresis* contributes significantly to reorienting priorities within faith and work theology. However, this reorientation must resist the temptation to use analogy to construct rigid models. As Vosloo[2] cautions, the Trinity must remain dynamic, a relational reality rather than a static framework.

Relationality, Particularity, and Mediation

Gunton's theological vision, as articulated through *perichoresis*, emphasizes relationality, particularity, and mediation. These three elements form the foundation for a new paradigm capable of addressing the limitations of current faith and work theology. Among them, mediation emerges as

---

2. Vosloo, "Identity, Otherness, and the Triune God."

CONCLUDING REFLECTIONS, LESSONS, AND FUTURE DIRECTIONS 283

pivotal. Drawing on Irenaeus's analogy of the "two hands" of God, Gunton offers a framework that integrates relationality and particularity into a coherent theological vision.

Mediation, as understood through Gunton, challenges the transactional norms of the market economy. It repositions identity not as an individual achievement but as a relational and communal reality, rooted in the dynamic interplay of the Trinity. This shift has profound implications for how Christians engage with the market economy, emphasizing belonging and interdependence over competition and self-reliance.

Reimagining Priorities for Faith and Work

The implications of this theological shift are transformative. Faith and work theology, often constrained by ethical and individualistic frameworks, can find new depth by embracing the relational ontology proposed by Gunton. This involves not only critiquing the individualism inherent in market-driven identities but also constructing a vision that prioritizes worship, vulnerability, and trust as central practices.

By integrating Gunton's Trinitarian insights, faith and work theology can move beyond surface-level engagement with the market economy to address its deeper structural and relational dimensions. This reimagined framework equips Christians to navigate the complexities of their vocations with a renewed sense of purpose and relational identity.

CONCLUSION: REIMAGINING FAITH, IDENTITY, AND THE MARKET ECONOMY

This book has explored the intricate interplay between identity, theology, and the market economy, guided by the foundational question of how Gunton's link between identity and the doctrine of God might enrich Reformed theology's engagement with the complexities of modern life. At its core, this inquiry has sought to address the pervasive influence of individualism on Christian identity and to propose theological pathways that move beyond the limitations of existing frameworks.

Human identity remains one of the most contested and formative aspects of contemporary life, deeply shaped by the forces of the market economy. The enduring question of "Who defines identity?" lies at the heart of this discussion. The prevailing narrative of individual autonomy has long dominated, reinforced by cultural, economic, and theological currents. Gunton's work challenges this trajectory, offering a compelling critique of individualism as a product not of emancipation but of theological descent.

While the Faith and Work movement has sought to address the intersection of theology and work, its resources often fall short, leaving Christians with frameworks that inadvertently reinforce the very individualism they aim to critique. This theological blind spot stems, in part, from an inadequate connection between human identity and the doctrine of God, as well as an over-reliance on transactional views of atonement and ethics-driven paradigms.

Gunton's contributions, particularly his emphasis on relational ontology and mediation, offer a redemptive path forward. By reframing identity through the lens of *perichoresis* and the Trinity, Gunton provides a theological vision rooted in belonging, vulnerability, and trust. These elements challenge the transactional dynamics of the market economy, calling Christians to embrace a relational understanding of identity that transcends individualism.

However, Gunton's theology is not without its challenges. His pursuit of certainty sometimes led to overreach, and his constructive proposals, while innovative, occasionally risked simplifying the complexities they sought to address. Yet, his willingness to confront the crisis of individualism head-on, coupled with his efforts to redirect theology away from classical roots, underscores his enduring significance as a theologian of dissent.

In advocating for a shift in theological priorities, this book emphasizes the need for identity to take precedence over ethics and evangelism in faith and work theology. Addressing the pervasive influence of the market economy is a task that extends beyond any single scholar or tradition. It demands a collective, interdisciplinary effort, with Trinitarian theology playing a central role in reshaping the conversation.

Among Gunton's many insights, the theme of mediation emerges as particularly critical, finding practical expression in worship, vulnerability, and trust. These practices offer a way forward for faith and work theology, equipping the broader Christian community to engage more deeply with the challenges and opportunities of identity formation in a market-driven world. This work calls on every Christian leader to recognize that the formation of identity is not an ancillary concern but a foundational task for the church in the twenty-first century.

Bibliography

Agang, Sunday. "Work." In *African Public Theology*, edited by Sunday Agang et al., 81–95. Carlisle, UK: Langham, 2020.
Alford, Helen, and Michael Naughton. *Managing as If Faith Mattered: Christian Social Principles in the Modern Organisation*. South Bend: University of Notre Dame Press, 2001.
Alsdorf, Katherine Leary. "Katherine Leary Alsdorf's profile page." LinkedIn. Last Modified October 29, 2021. https://www.linkedin.com/in/katherine-leary-alsdorf-39216459.
Amazon.com. "Amazon Best Sellers: Christian Business & Professional Growth." Accessed April 23, 2019. https://www.amazon.com/Best-Sellers-Books-Christian-Business-Professional-Growth/zgbs/books/297488.
Anizor, Uche. *Trinity and Humanity: An Introduction to the Theology of Colin Gunton*. Milton Keynes: Paternoster, 2016.
Armstrong, Karen. *The Battle for God: Fundamentalism in Judaism, Christianity and Islam*. London: HarperCollins, 2000.
Ayres, Lewis. *Augustine and the Trinity*. Cambridge: Cambridge University, 2010.
―――. "Foreword." In *Colin Gunton and the Failure of Augustine: The Theology of Colin Gunton in Light of Augustine*, edited by Bradley G. Green, xi–xii. Lutterworth, 2012.
Barth, Karl. *Church Dogmatics 1/1*. Translated by Geoffrey W. Bromiley and Thomas F. Torrance. London: T&T Clark, 1975.
Bellah, Robert N., et al. *Habits of the Heart: Individualism and Commitment in American Life*. Berkeley: University of California Press, 1985.
Bidwell, Keith. "Losing the Dance: Is the 'Divine Dance' a Good Explanation for the Trinity?" In *Engaging with Keller: Thinking Through the Theology of an Influential Evangelical*, edited by Iain D. Campbell and William M. Schweitzer, 73–97. Darlington, UK: EP, 2013.
Blanchard, Ken, and Phil Hodges. *Lead Like Jesus*. Nashville: HarperCollins, 2005.
Blanchard, Ken, and Spencer Johnson. *The One Minute Manager*. New York: William Morrow & Col, 1982.
Bonhoeffer, Dietrich. *The Cost of Discipleship*. London: SCM, 1937.
Bosch, David J. *Transforming Mission: Paradigm Shifts in Theology of Mission*. Maryknoll, NY: Orbis, 1991.

Bourne, Richard, and Ian Adkins. *A New Introduction to Theology: Embodiment, Experience and Encounter.* London: T&T Clark, 2020.
Brown, David. *The Divine Trinity.* London: Duckworth, 1985.
Bultman, Rudolf. *New Testament and Mythology.* Philadelphia: Fortress, 1984
Campbell, Iain D. "Keller on 'Rebranding' the Doctrine of Sin." In *Engaging with Keller: Thinking Through the Theology of an Influential Evangelical*, edited by Iain D. Campbell and William M. Schweitzer, 26–48. Darlington, UK: EP, 2013.
Center for Faith and Work. "About: Who We Are." https://faithandwork.com.
Covey, Stephen R. *The Seven Habits of Highly Effective People.* 25th Anniversary Edition. New York: Simon and Schuster, 2013.
Crawford, Matthew B. *Shop Craft as Soulcraft: An Inquiry into the Value of Work.* New York: Penguin, 2009.
Cunningham, David S. *These Three Are One: The Practice of Trinitarian Theology.* Oxford: Blackwell, 1998.
Eldred, Ken. *God Is at Work.* Ventura, CA: Regal, 2005.
Fergusson, David A., and Paul T. Nimmo. "Introduction." In *The Cambridge Companion to Reformed Theology*, edited by David A. Fergusson and Paul T. Nimmo, 1–10. Cambridge: Cambridge University Press, 2016.
Ferry, Luc. *A Brief History of Thought: A Philosophical Guide to Living.* New York: Harper Collins, 2011.
Feuerbach, Ludwig. *The Essence of Christianity.* Translated by George Eliot. New Hork: Harper & Brothers, 1957.
Ford, David. *The Modern Theologians.* Oxford: Blackwell, 1997.
Frischmann, Brett, and Evan Selinger. *Re-engineering Humanity.* Cambridge: Cambridge University Press, 2018.
Gay, David H. *A Case of Mistaken Identity: A Critique of Timothy Keller on Regeneration.* Independently Published, 2020.
Gladwell, Malcolm. *Outliers: The Story of Success.* London: Little, Brown, 2008.
———. *The Tipping Point.* London: Little, Brown, 2000.
Goossen, Richard J., and R. Paul Stevens. *Entrepreneurial Leadership: Finding Your Calling, Making a Difference.* Downers Grove, IL: InterVarsity, 2013.
Green, Bradley. *Colin Gunton and the Failure of Augustine: The Theology of Colin Gunton in the Light of Augustine.* Eugene, OR: Pickwick, 2011.
Greenleaf, Robert K. *The Power of Servant Leadership.* San Francisco: Berrett-Koehler, 1998.
Gunton, Colin E. *Act and Being: Towards a Theology of the Divine Attributes.* London: SCM, 2002.
———. *The Actuality of the Atonement: A Study of Metaphor, Rationality, and the Christian Tradition.* London: T&T Clark, 1988.
———. *Becoming and Being: The Doctrine of God in Charles Hartshorne and Karl Barth.* Oxford: Oxford University Press, 1978.
———. *A Brief Theology of Revelation.* London: T&T Clark, 1995.
———. *Christ and Creation.* Carlisle, UK: Paternoster, 1992.
———. *Enlightenment and Alienation: An Essay Towards a Trinitarian Theology.* London: HarperCollins, 1985.
———. *Father, Son and Holy Spirit: Essays Toward a Fully Trinitarian Theology.* London: T&T Clark, 2003.

———. "God, Grace and Freedom." In *God and Freedom*, edited by Colin E. Gunton, 119–34. London: T&T Clark, 1995.
———. *Intellect and Action*. London: T&T Clark, 2000.
———. *The One, the Three and the Many: God, Creation and the Culture of Modernity*. Cambridge: Cambridge University Press, 1993.
———. *The Promise of Trinitarian Theology*. London: T&T Clark, 1991.
———. *Revelation and Reason: Prolegomena to Systematic Theology*. London: T&T Clark, 2008.
———. *The Triune Creator: A Historical and Systematic Study*. Grand Rapids: Eerdmans, 1998.
———. *Yesterday and Today: A Study of Continuities in Christology*. 2nd ed. London: Darton, Longman & Todd, 1983.
Habets, Myk, et al., eds. *The Handbook of Colin Gunton*. London: T&T Clark, 2021.
Hardy, Lee. *The Fabric of This World: Inquiries into Calling, Career Choice, and the Design of Human Work*. Grand Rapids: Eerdmans, 1990.
Hart, D. G. "Looking for Communion in All the Wrong Places: Tim Keller and Presbyterian Ecclesiology." In *Engaging with Keller: Thinking Through the Theology of an Influential Evangelical*, edited by Iain D. Campbell and William M. Schweitzer, 155–75. Darlington, UK: EP, 2013.
Harvey, Lincoln, ed. *The Theology of Colin Gunton*. London: T&T Clark, 2010.
Heron, Alasdair I. C. *A Century of Protestant Theology*. Cambridge: Lutterworth, 1980.
Higginson, Richard. *Faith, Hope and the Global Economy: A Power for Good*. Downers Grove, IL: InterVarsity, 2012.
Holmes, Stephen R. "Gunton and Coleridge." In *The Handbook of Colin Gunton*, edited by Myk Habets et al., 315–26. London: T&T Clark, 2021.
———. "In Memoriam Colin Gunton." Shored Fragments, May 6, 2013.https://web.archive.org/web/20240303054503/http://steverholmes.org.uk/blog/?p=6973.
———. "The Rev Prof Colin Gunton." *The Guardian*, June 3, 2003. https://www.theguardian.com/news/2003/jun/03/guardianobituaries.highereducation.
———."Towards the Analogia Personae et Relationis." In *The Theology of Colin Gunton*, edited by Lincoln Harvey, 32–48. London: T&T Clark, 2010.
Horton, Michael. "Reflections on Gospel Theology." In *Shaped by the Gospel: Doing Balanced, Gospel-Centered Ministry in Your City*, by Timothy Keller, 75–89. Grand Rapids: Zondervan, 2016.
Jenson, Robert W. *A Decision Tree of Colin Gunton's Thinking*. London: T&T Clark, 2010.
Keller, Timothy. *King's Cross: Understanding the Life and Death of the Son of God*. London: Hodder and Stoughton, 2011.
———. *Making Sense of God: An Invitation to the Skeptical*. New York:Viking, 2016.
———. *The Prodigal God: Recovering the Heart of the Christian Faith*. London: Hodder and Stoughton, 2008.
———. *Prayer: Experiencing Awe and Intimacy with God*. London: London: Hodder and Stoughton, 2014.
———. *Romans 1–7 For You*. Purcellville, VA: The Good Book, 2014.
———. *Romans 8–16 For You*. Purcellville, VA: The Good Book, 2014.
———. *Shaped by the Gospel*. Grand Rapids: Zondervan/Redeemer, 2016.
Keller, Timothy, and Katherine L. Alsdorf. *Every Good Endeavor: Connecting Your Work to God's Work*. New York: Riverhead, 2014.

Kotter, John P. *Leading Change*. Cambridge: Harvard Business School, 1996.
Kuhn, Thomas S. *The Structure of Scientific Revolutions*. Chicago: University of Chicago Press, 1962.
Lencioni, Patrick. *The Five Dysfunctions of a Team*. San Francisco: Jossey-Bass, 2002.
Lindsay, D. Michael. *Faith in the Halls of Power: How Evangelicals Joined the American Elite*. Oxford: Oxford University Press, 2007.
Lints, Richard. *The Fabric of Theology: A Prolegomenon to Evangelical Theology*. Grand Rapids: Eerdmans, 1993.
Markovits, Daniel. *The Meritocracy Trap*. London: Allen Lane, 2019.
Maxwell, John C. *The 21 Irrefutable Laws of Leadership*. Nashville: Thomas Nelson, 1998.
McNall, Joshua. *A Free Corrector: Colin Gunton and the Legacy of Augustine*. Minneapolis: Fortress, 2013.
Miller, David W. *God at Work: The History and Promise of the Faith at Work Movement*. Oxford: Oxford University Press, 2007.
Mind Tools. "PEST Analysis: Identifying the 'Big Picture' Opportunities and Threats." https://www.mindtools.com/pages/article/newTMC_09.htm.
Nash, Laura. *Believers in Business: Resolving the Tensions Between Christian Faith, Business Ethics, Competition, and Our Definitions of Success*. Nashville: Thomas Nelson, 1994.
Nausner, Bernhard. "The Failure of a Laudable Project: Gunton, the Trinity and Human Self-Understanding." *Scottish Journal of Theology* 62:4 (2009): 403–20.
Niebuhr, H. R. *Christ and Culture*. New York: Harper, 1951.
Peters, Ted. *God as Trinity: Relationality and Temporality in Divine Life*. Louisville: Westminster John Knox, 1993.
Polanyi, Michael. *Personal Knowledge: Towards a Post-Critical Philosophy*. Chicago: University of Chicago Press, 1962.
Rae, Murray. "Introduction." In *The Handbook of Colin Gunton*, edited by Myk Habets, Adam Picard, and Murray Rae, 1–6. London: T&T Clark, 2021.
Rahner, Karl. *The Trinity*. Translated by Joseph Donceel. London: Burns and Oates, 1970.
"The Rev Professor Colin Gunton." *The Times*, May 19, 2003. https://www.thetimes.co.uk/article/the-rev-professor-colin-gunton-lqvznchx730.
Rieger, Joerg. *No Rising Tide: Theology, Economics, and the Future*. Minneapolis: Fortress, 2009.
Rosa, Hartmut. *Resonance: A Sociology of Our Relationship to the World*. Cambridge: Polity, 2019.
Rosemann, Philip W. *Trinitarian Ontologies After Kant*. Cambridge: Cambridge University Press, 2019.
Schwöbel, Christoph. "The Renaissance of Trinitarian Theology: Reasons, Problems and Tasks." In *Trinitarian Theology Today: Essays on Divine Being and Act*, edited by Christoph Schwöbel, 1–30. London: T&T Clark, 1995.
———. *Trinitarian Theology Today: Essays on Divine Being and Act*. London: T&T Clark, 1995.
Sharma, Robin S. *The Leader Who Had No Title*. New York: Free Press, 2010.
———. *The Monk Who Sold His Ferrari*. London: HarperCollins, 1997.
Smith, James K. A. *Desiring the Kingdom: Worship, Worldview, and Cultural Formation*. Cultural Liturgies 1. Grand Rapids: Baker Academic, 2009. E-book.

———. *How Not to Be Secular: Reading Charles Taylor*. Grand Rapids: Eerdmans, 2014.

Stevens, R. Paul. *Doing God's Business: Meaning and Motivation for the Marketplace*. Grand Rapids: Eerdmans, 2006.

———. *The Other Six Days: Vocation, Work, and Ministry in Biblical Perspective*. Grand Rapids: Eerdmans, 1999.

———. *Work Matters: Lessons from Scripture*. Grand Rapids: Eerdmans, 2021.

Stevens, R. Paul, and Richard J. Goossen. *Entrepreneurial Leadership*. Downers Grove, IL: InterVarsity, 2013.

Taylor, Charles. *Modern Social Imaginaries*. Durham: Duke University Press, 2004.

———. *Sources of the Self: The Making of the Modern Identity*. Cambridge: Cambridge University Press, 1989.

Taylor, William. *Revolutionary Work: What's the Point of the 9 to 5?* Leyland, UK: 10Publishing, 2016.

Thompson, Mark. "Has Colin Gunton's Theological Project Really Failed?" Theological Theology, Dec. 1, 2009. http://markdthompson.blogspot.com/2009/12/has-colin-guntons-theological-project.html.

Torrance, Alan. *Persons in Communion: Trinitarian Description and Human Participation*. London: T&T Clark, 1996.

Torrance, James B. *Worship, Community, and the Triune God of Grace*. Carlisle, UK: Paternoster, 1996.

Van Duzer, Jeff. "Free Markets and the Reign of God: Identifying Potential Conflicts." In *Global Neighbors: Christian Faith and Moral Obligation in Today's Economy*, edited by Douglas A. Hicks and Mark R. Valeri, 109–32. Grand Rapids: Eerdmans, 2008.

———. *Why Business Matters to God (And What Still Needs to Be Fixed)*. Downers Grove, IL: InterVarsity, 2010.

Venter, Rian. "Taking Stock of the Trinitarian Renaissance: What Have We Learned?" *HTS Teologiese Studies/Theological Studies* 75 (2019) a5407. https://doi.org/10.4102/hts.v75i1.5407.

Volf, Miroslav. *Exclusion and Embrace: A Theological Exploration of Identity, Otherness, and Reconciliation*. Nashville: Abingdon, 1996.

———. *Work in the Spirit: Toward a Theology of Work*. Eugene, OR: Wipf & Stock. 1991.

Vosloo, Robert. "Identity, Otherness and the Triune God: Theological Groundwork for a Christian Ethic of Hospitality." *Journal of Theology for Southern Africa* 119 (2004) 69–89.

Webster, John. "Gunton and Barth." In *The Theology of Colin Gunton*, edited by Lincoln Harvey, 17–31. London: T&T Clark, 2010.

Williams, Rowan. *On Augustine*. London: Bloomsbury, 2015.

Wright, N. T. *Surprised by Hope: Rethinking Heaven, the Resurrection, and the Mission of the Church*. London: SPCK, 2007.

Wuthnow, Robert. *After Heaven: Spirituality in America Since the 1950s*. Berkeley: University of California Pres, 1998.

———. *Poor Richard's Principle: Recovering the American Dream Through the Moral Dimensions of Work, Business, and Money*. Princeton: Princeton University Press, 1996.

Yale Law School. "Daniel Markovits." https://law.yale.edu/daniel-markovits.

Zizioulas, John D. *Being as Communion: Studies in Personhood and Church*. St. Vladimir's Seminary, 1997.

———. "The Cappadocian Contribution." In *Trinitarian Theology Today*, edited by Christoph Schwöbel, 44–60. London: T&T Clark, 1995.

Zuboff, Shoshana. *The Age of Surveillance Capitalism: The Fight for a Human Future at the New Frontier of Power*. London: Profile, 2019.

www.ingramcontent.com/pod-product-compliance
Lightning Source LLC
Chambersburg PA
CBHW061431300426
44114CB00014B/1632